Springer Series in Transitional Justice

Series Editor:
Olivera Simic

For further volumes:
http://www.springer.com/series/11233

James Edward Beitler III

Remaking Transitional Justice in the United States

The Rhetorical Authorization of the Greensboro Truth and Reconciliation Commission

 Springer

James Edward Beitler III
Feinstein College of Arts and Sciences
Roger Williams University
Bristol, RI, USA

ISBN 978-1-4614-5294-2   ISBN 978-1-4614-5295-9 (eBook)
DOI 10.1007/978-1-4614-5295-9
Springer New York Heidelberg Dordrecht London

Library of Congress Control Number: 2012944754

Printed on acid-free paper

Springer is part of Springer Science+Business Media (www.springer.com)

For Brita Elizabeth & Sweet Baby James

Preface

In June of 2004, a group of citizens from North Carolina created the Greensboro Truth and Reconciliation Commission (GTRC) to address lingering issues surrounding the November 3, 1979 murders of five members of the Communist Workers Party by members of the Ku Klux Klan and American Nazi Party. From its inception and throughout its operation, one of the central issues facing the Commission was its authorization. While the Commission was often recognized as being the "first of its kind" in the USA, the distinction did not automatically result in widespread public support. Many in the Greensboro community were opposed to the initiative, and the city council voted not to endorse the Commission's work. How, then, did the Commission—how does any grassroots transitional justice initiative—attempt to garner the authority needed to carry out its mandate and bring about lasting change?

Remaking Transitional Justice in the United States offers an answer to this question by exploring the rhetorical activity surrounding the operation of the GTRC—rhetorical activity that was at once local and global. I argue that the development of the field of transitional justice has given rise to a transnational rhetorical tradition that provides those working in the field with rich rhetorical resources. Then I demonstrate, through a series of rhetorical analyses, how Greensboro stakeholders attempted to reaccentuate this rhetorical tradition in their own rhetorical performances to construct authority and bring about justice. My book concludes by reflecting on the development of transitional justice in the United States and by discussing the implications of the project for scholars and practitioners working in the field.

The theme of interdependence is woven throughout my account of the Commission's authorization. It is a theme that, in an increasingly connected world, matters profoundly to all individuals and institutions working for social change, as well as those studying their work. I was reminded of this fact 6 years ago, shortly after attending the GTRC's Report Release Ceremony at the Annie Merner Pfeiffer Chapel at Bennett College in Greensboro. Looking into the chapel's history, I discovered that it had been fitting for the Commission to deliver its findings there: the chapel had already served, several times, as the site for other gatherings devoted to the redress of racial and economic disparities in Greensboro and the USA. The chapel was the location where, in 1937, Bennett College students and professors planned a boycott of Greensboro movie theaters (Ahearn, 2006, p. B1). It was also the site where—on February 11, 1958, nearly 50 years before the commissioners took the stage—Martin Luther King, Jr. delivered a sermon entitled "Room in the Inn" to an auditorium overflowing with Greensboro citizens.[1] The size of the crowd that came to hear King preach in 1958 belies the fact that he did not initially receive a warm reception in Greensboro. As Greensboro historian William Chafe (1980) noted, "Fearful of economic reprisals, A&T College and the black public schools refused to make their auditoriums available for King's speech. Many ministers also held back, unwilling to identify openly with the direct-action tactics associated with King's Montgomery bus boycott" (p. 112). In the end, only Willa Player, the President of Bennett College, offered King a place to speak: "'I told them,' Player recalled, 'that this is a liberal arts college where freedom rings—so Martin Luther King can speak here'" (Chafe, 1980, p. 112). On that occasion, King (1958/2000) preached about whether there had been "any real progress in the area of race relations" (p. 3), advocated for nonviolent protest (p. 22), and claimed, "We've come a long, long way, but we have a long, long way to go" (p. 5).

It was a sermon that turned out to be important for one member of the audience in particular—Ezell Blair, Jr., a high school student at the time, who, 2 years later, would take a seat at the segregated Woolworth's lunch counter in downtown Greensboro with three other black men. That action would, in turn, lead to similar protests across the South. When, some years later, Blair was interviewed by Chafe about his role in initiating the sit-in movement, he talked about some of the influences that led him to take a seat at that lunch counter: one was King's 1958 speech, about which Blair remarked, "[H]is words were such that the vibrations that came over the microphone, over the loud speaker….It was so strong, I could feel my heart palpitating, it brought tears to my eyes" (as cited in Carson, 1992, p. 38). Another influence, Blair said, was Langston Hughes's poem "The Negro Speaks of Rivers," introduced to him by his eleventh-grade English teacher (Chafe, 1980, p. 112). The poem's speaker connected African-American identity, in part, to Africa: "I bathed in the Euphrates when dawns were young/I built my hut near the Congo and it lulled me to sleep/I looked upon the Nile and raised the pyramids above it" (Hughes, 1994, p. 23).

When King spoke at Bennett in the February of 1958, he, too, had been thinking about Africa. Roughly 1 year before his address in Greensboro, King had traveled to Ghana to join in that country's independence celebration (Carson, 1992, p. 8). While he was there, he met with anticolonial activist Michael Scott to discuss the ongoing civil rights initiatives both in the USA and in Africa (Carson, 1992, p. 8). King is said to have "expressed admiration for the bus boycott then taking place in Johannesburg, South Africa, and remarked that there was 'no basic difference

---

[1] Elsewhere the speech is referred to as "A Realistic Look at Race Relations" (Carson, 1992, p. 94). No recording or transcript of this speech was thought to exist until 1999, when the audio recording of the speech was rediscovered in the archives at Bennett College. Bennett College later made a transcript of the speech available in *The Bennett College Social Justice Lecture Series* (King, 1958/2000).

between colonialism and racial segregation…at bottom both segregation in America and colonialism in Africa were based on the same thing—white supremacy and contempt for life'" (as cited in Carson, 1992, pp. 8–9). Later that year, on July 27, 1957, King traveled to New York City to meet with Ambrose Reeves—the Anglican Bishop of Johannesburg, South Africa—to take stock of the twin liberation movements occurring in South Africa and in the USA (Carson, 1992, p. 45). That same year he also joined the National Committee of the American Committee on Africa (ACOA)—an organization that would initiate an anti-apartheid protest on December 10th to condemn the recent arrests of Nelson Mandela, Walter Sisulu, Oliver Tambo, and 153 other South African antiapartheid activists (Carson, 1992, p. 516).[2] The ACOA protest helped contribute to a victory in South Africa: on December 17th, the South African government dropped the charges against 61 of the 156 activists.

Over the next decade, the ACOA was instrumental in establishing economic sanctions against South Africa, and such actions were significant in bringing about South African reforms. Les de Villiers, a South African diplomat to the USA, acknowledged that the ACOA's tactics helped to bring about the end of apartheid rule in South Africa (Korey, 1999, p. 7). Nelson Mandela (1993/2012) made similar claims when he received the Nobel Peace Prize in Oslo, Norway. In his acceptance speech for the award, he referred to all those around the world who helped to end institutionalized apartheid in South Africa, citing, in particular, Martin Luther King, Jr. (de Villiers, 1995, p. 194; Mandela, 1993/2012, para. 4–5, 8–9).

Likewise, South African Archbishop Emeritus Desmond Tutu praised Americans for their support of the antiapartheid cause in South Africa on a number of occasions—one of which was at Guilford College in Greensboro, North Carolina on November 3, 2005, the 26th anniversary of the Greensboro killings. In that speech, entitled "Reconciling Love," Tutu (2005) remarked, "I now speak on behalf of millions of my compatriots when I say, even now, thank you for that remarkable support you gave to help us." Tutu did not mention Martin Luther King, Jr. explicitly in the speech he gave in Greensboro; however, he did repeat something that King had said while he was in Greensboro in 1958. During King's visit to Bennett College, he had been interviewed by the student campus publication *The Bennett Banner*. In the

---

[2]King served as vice-chairperson of the December 10th protest alongside U.S. chairperson Reverend James Pike and international chairperson Eleanor Roosevelt, and he was also instrumental in publicizing it. In a letter dated November 8, 1957, addressed to Chester Bowles, a man actively involved in international relations throughout his lifetime, King and Pike wrote, "We are writing to you in the conviction that the time has come for a world-wide protest against the organized inhumanity of the Government of the Union of South Africa" (as cited in Carson, 1992, p. 313). Bowles responded enthusiastically to the idea of a protest, as did imprisoned South African activist Oliver Tambo, who sent a letter addressed to King, which thanked those involved in sponsoring the event: "We, the oppressed people of South Africa, highly appreciate this step and we now appeal to you to give your full support" (as cited in Carson, 1992, p. 325). Oliver Tambo was not the only person in South Africa who received the American Committee on Africa's message. Two days after the December 10th day of protest, the South African Foreign Minister could be heard on the radio decrying the ACOA as "decidedly pinkish" and characterizing its leader as "a known leftist" (de Villiers, 1995, p. 23).

interview, King repeatedly emphasized the importance of human dignity (Carson, 1992, pp. 364–367). He and the student interviewers also talked about forgiveness:

> [*Interviewer 3:*] Doctor, I have just a few questions. Now you talk about forgiveness and that you must forgive. Do you find that really in your heart you can forgive the men who, say, killed Emmett Till or castrated this innocent man? And don't you find it really hard […]
>
>   [*King:*] [*interrupting*] Well, if you really love on the basis of Christian concepts, forgiveness is very difficult. *It isn't easy* [emphasis added]. And when it becomes so easy it really isn't forgiveness. There is pain and agony. (Carson, 1992, p. 366)

Nearly 50 years later, in the same U.S. city, Desmond Tutu (2005) spoke the same words to a community that had, in the interim, seen the integration of public businesses and schools and had struggled to address the November 3, 1979 murders. "Forgiveness," Tutu said, "is not cheap. *It isn't easy* [emphasis added]. It cost God the death of God's son."

As these examples highlight, in their work for justice and equality, both King and Tutu made use of transnational networks in bringing about social change. Interdependence was, moreover, a central theme of both of their messages. In an oft-quoted passage from "Letter from Birmingham Jail," King wrote, "Injustice anywhere is a threat to justice everywhere. We are caught in an inescapable network of mutuality tied in a single garment of destiny" (King, 1963/2004, p. 693). Similarly, Tutu grounded his arguments against apartheid in the South African concept of *ubuntu*. "We are," he asserted in *No Future Without Forgiveness*, "bound up in a delicate network of interdependence because, as we say in our African idiom, a person is a person through other persons" (2004, p. 35). Willa Player, Martin Luther King, Jr., Ezell Blair, Jr., Langston Hughes, Michael Scott, Ambrose Reeves, Nelson Mandela, Desmond Tutu: these people—and many others, known and forgotten—have formed an extensive and complex transnational network, a web of interdependence, of individuals working for social change. However, the individuals listed (and not listed) here are not all there is to the network. The narrative above also attests to the fact that the network is stitched together through rhetorical activity: Player *defended* King's right to speak, King *advocated* nonviolence, Blair *was moved to act* by King's words, the ACOA *condemned* the South African government's actions against Mandela and others, and Tutu—speaking in Greensboro—*echoed* King's remarks and *praised* the international community for their support.

Which brings us to the subject of the present work. When Tutu spoke in Greensboro, he did not simply praise the international community for their support. He also lent his support to the GTRC:

> It is…a very great privilege to come to this city, which is the very first in the USA to have set up a Truth and Reconciliation Commission, embodying—wonderfully—the theme of this series of lectures—reconciling love. And the world salutes Greensboro. And I wonder whether we shouldn't ourselves here want to recognize all of those wonderful people associated with this extraordinary initiative. Maybe we should give them a small clap. Don't you think? (Tutu, 2005)

My book aims to bring rhetorical activity of this sort into relief, focusing, in particular, on the discursive connections between those working in the field of transitional justice and the Greensboro Truth and Reconciliation Commission. These connec-

tions were instrumental in empowering the GTRC in its work—work that culminated in the Annie Merner Pfeiffer Chapel on May 25, 2006, when the seven
commissioners presented their *Final Report* to the Greensboro community. On that
occasion, commissioner Pat Clark summarized the Commission's main findings:

> We found that the offense of November 3, 1979 [was] woven through with issues of race
> and class. Our report discusses underlying issues including racial and economic justice,
> white supremacy, and the failure of the police and justice system to provide equal protection
> to all residents. (Seel, 2006)

Following Clark's comments, the Annie Merner Pfeiffer Chapel erupted in applause.
While such applause was undoubtedly intended to recognize the diligence of the
commissioners and the significance of their findings, it also attested to the
Commission's authority, which was constructed, in no small part, by drawing upon
the rich rhetorical resources of the field of transitional justice.

References

Ahearn, L. (2006, May 28). Bellwether city: A book for the train ride home. *News & Record*, p. B1.
Carson, C. (Ed.). (1992). *The papers of Martin Luther King, Jr.* (Vol. 4). Berkeley, CA: University
    of California Press.
Chafe, W. H. (1980). *Civilities and civil rights: Greensboro, North Carolina, and the black struggle
    for freedom*. New York, NY: Oxford University Press.
de Villiers, L. (1995). *In sight of surrender: The U.S. sanctions campaign against South Africa,
    1946–1993*. Westport, CT: Praeger.
Hughes, L. (1994). The Negro speaks of rivers. In A. Rampersad & D. Roessel (Eds.), *The col-
    lected poems of Langston Hughes* (1st ed., p. 23). New York, NY: Knopf.
King, M. L., Jr. (2000). Room in the inn. In L. E. Williams (Ed.), *The Bennett College social justice
    lecture series* (Vol. 2, pp. 1–23). Greensboro, NC: Bennett College. (Speech originally delivered
    in 1958).
King, M. L., Jr. (2004). Letter from Birmingham jail. In D. McQuade & R. Atwan (Eds.), *The
    writer's presence: A pool of readings* (pp. 692–707). Boston, MA: Bedford/St. Martin's.
    (Original work published 1963).
Korey, W. (1999). Human rights NGOs: The power of persuasion. *Ethics & International Affairs,
    13*, 151–174. doi:10.1111/j.1747-7093.1999.tb00333.x.
Mandela, N. (2012). Nobel lecture [Transcript]. Retrieved from http://www.nobelprize.org/nobel_
    prizes/peace/laureates/1993/mandela-lecture.html (Speech originally delivered in 1993).
Seel, L. (Producer). (2006). *Greensboro Truth and Reconciliation Commission report release cer-
    emony* [DVD]. Greensboro, NC. (Obtained from Laura Seel.)
Tutu, D. (1999). *No future without forgiveness*. New York, NY: Doubleday.
Tutu, D. (2005). Reconciling love: a millennium mandate. *2005–2006 Bryan series lectures on
    spirit and spirituality* [videocassette]. Greensboro, NC: Hege Library, Guilford College.

Acknowledgements

Writing is a social practice, and I am deeply appreciative of the many individuals and communities who helped make this book possible. Thank you first to the exceptional community of scholars in the Joint Program in English and Education at the University of Michigan, where much of this project was conceived and written. Thank you especially to Anne Ruggles Gere, Anne Curzan, Alisse Portnoy, Lesley Rex, and Mary Schleppegrell for your constructive feedback on my dissertation. Thank you, too, to Katherine Mack, Susan Jarratt, and the other members of the "Free Speech and the Production of Truth" workshop group for your comments at the Rhetoric Society of America's 2011 Summer Institute. I also benefited from conversations at the 7th Biennial Symposium of the Association for Rhetoric and Communication in South Africa, organized by Erik Doxtader and Philippe-Joseph Salazar. At Roger Williams University, the Foundation to Promote Scholarship and Teaching awarded me release time to complete this project, and my colleagues at RWU have been wonderfully supportive of my work. I am particularly grateful to the members of the Department of Writing Studies, Rhetoric, and Composition for providing encouragement from the first moment I arrived on campus. I am also appreciative to all those associated with the Greensboro Truth and Reconciliation Commission, especially Executive Director Jill Williams and commissioner Barbara Walker. Thank you for going out of your way to answer my questions about the GTRC. I am also grateful to Olivera Simic, the series editor—as well as Dubravka Zarkov and the other members of the series review board, the manuscript reviewers, and Welmoed Spahr and Morgan Ryan at Springer. Finally, thank you to all of the members of my family. My parents, Jim and Melissa, have been incredibly supportive of my work. And my wife, Brita, has been a constant source of encouragement, love and joy. I love you, and I dedicate this book to you and to our son, James.

Contents

Abbreviations

ACOA	American Committee on Africa
AFF	Andrus Family Fund
AFL-CIO	American Federation of Labor and Congress of Industrial Organizations
ANC	African National Congress
AZAPO	Azanian Peoples' Organization
CAMCWP	Committee to Avenge the Murder of the Communist Workers Party 5
CPUSA	United States Communist Party
CWP	Communist Workers Party
DTRC	Metropolitan Detroit Truth and Reconciliation Commission on Racial Inequality
FBI	Federal Bureau of Investigation
GTRC	Greensboro Truth and Reconciliation Commission
GTCRP	Greensboro Truth and Community Reconciliation Project
ICTJ	International Center for Transitional Justice
IFP	Inkatha Freedom Party
KKK	Ku Klux Klan
LTRC	Liberian Truth and Reconciliation Commission Diaspora Project
METRC	Maine Tribal-State Child Welfare Truth and Reconciliation Commission
MRDI	Michigan Roundtable for Diversity and Inclusion
MTP	Mississippi Truth Project
NAACP	National Association for the Advancement of Colored People
NCAC	North Carolina Advisory Committee to the US Commission on Civil Rights
NCCJ	National Conference for Community and Justice
NGO	Non-governmental Organization
NTLA	National Transitional Legislative Assembly
PPEHRC	Poor People's Economic Human Rights Campaign
SATRC	South African Truth and Reconciliation Commission
SCLC	Southern Christian Leadership Conference
TRC	Truth and Reconciliation Commission

Chapter 1
The Problem of Power: Authorizing a Truth and Reconciliation Commission in Greensboro, North Carolina

Abstract This chapter introduces the socio-political context and events of November 3, 1979 as well as the context and events leading up to the formation of the Greensboro Truth and Reconciliation Commission (GTRC). Drawing upon various accounts of Greensboro's history, it highlights, in particular, city officials' responses to both November 3, 1979 and the formation of the GTRC 25 years later. In doing so, it demonstrates that a central issue facing the GTRC was how to establish the authority to act efficaciously. This account leads into a discussion of the book's theoretical framework—which involves using the concepts "rhetorical tradition," "rhetorical performance," and "reaccentuation" to explore the interplay between specific instances of language use and patterns of language use in the field of transitional justice. With this framework in place, the chapter introduces the book's central arguments and concludes with a brief overview of each of the book's chapters.

J.E. Beitler III, *Remaking Transitional Justice in the United States*,
Springer Series in Transitional Justice, DOI 10.1007/978-1-4614-5295-9_1,
© Springer Science+Business Media New York 2013

"I am cognizant of the interrelatedness of all communities and states. I cannot sit idly by in Atlanta and not be concerned about what happens in Birmingham. Injustice anywhere is a threat to justice everywhere. We are caught in an inescapable network of mutuality tied in a single garment of destiny."

Martin Luther King, Jr. (King 1963/2004, p. 693)

Introduction

On the morning of November 3, 1979, members of the Communist Workers Party (CWP) gathered in Greensboro, North Carolina to demonstrate against the Ku Klux Klan (KKK) and to petition for the labor rights of factory workers. The event, which was to include a parade and rally, was part of the CWP's campaign to combat racism in the city and improve working conditions in the local textile factories. However, the prevailing attitudes of Greensboro citizens had made the CWP's past work difficult. Many distrusted the group on account of its ideological orientation, and—though Greensboro had served as the birthplace of the sit-in movement nearly 20 years earlier—racial inequalities persisted in the city, especially in relation to education, employment, housing, and access to health care. In the months leading up to the third of November, there had been a recent surge in Klan activity connected to a proposed screening of *Birth of a Nation*, and the CWP's plans to form labor unions in the textile factories had been met with resistance from whites unwilling to collaborate with blacks. The parade and rally was the CWP's latest attempt to bring about change in the city.[1]

---

[1] The story of the CWP's development is a complex one. The United States Communist Party's (CPUSA's) interest in North Carolina as a site of resistance had begun nearly 60 years earlier. CPUSA members from northern cities had grown increasingly interested in the South as a site for resisting social, political, and economic inequalities in 1919; nevertheless, throughout much of the twenties, they did not intervene directly, focusing their activities on fact finding about southern injustices (Taylor, 2009, pp. 6–13). Historian Gregory Taylor (2009) recounted how the decision of the CPUSA to intervene in the South—and, in particular, in North Carolina—was tied to Paul Crouch, a native North Carolinian who had been discharged from the military and imprisoned at Alcatraz for supposedly claiming to want to overthrow the government (p. 13). As he grew in the ranks of the CPUSA, Crouch advocated for Party intervention in his home state (p. 18). In 1928, the Party decided to organize in Charlotte, and they began unionizing efforts in 1929 (pp. 19–20). The North Carolina Communist Party was active for three decades; however, as Taylor showed, the Party began to disintegrate in the 1950s as a result of McCarthyism, several tactical missteps by its leaders, "assaults by former members and FBI informants," and arrests of its members (pp. 186, 206). According to FBI records, there was only one person listed on the membership roles by 1960 (p. 206). "By 1960," Taylor wrote, "the North Carolina Communist Party was dead" (p. 186).

Nevertheless, in the early- to mid-seventies, there was a resurgence of interest in Communism from groups that had developed as an indirect result of the CPUSA's activity but that wanted to distance themselves from the CPUSA. Elizabeth Wheaton (1987) recounted the development of these groups in her book *Codename Greenkil*:

Adults and children gathered at the parade starting point, singing songs and carrying placards. But before the parade could begin, members of the KKK and American Nazi Party arrived at the scene in a slow-moving caravan of vehicles. A fight ensued, and shots were fired. Eighty-eight seconds later, five members of the CWP were dead, and ten others were wounded. Despite the fact that the CWP's leaders had requested police protection for the parade and rally, there were no policemen at the scene. There were, however, reporters covering the rally, and several cameramen captured much of attack on film. Yet despite this video evidence of the killings, the KKK and American Nazi Party members who had fired on the demonstrators were acquitted in both a state murder trial and a federal criminal trial. All-white juries decided both verdicts.

To attain the first acquittal, the defense pleaded that the killings were a case of self-defense: they pointed to the fact that both parties had guns and noted that CWP members precipitated the violence by beating on the cars. The second trial turned on whether or not the Klan members and Nazis had violated the civil rights of the protestors because of their race, their religion, and/or their participation in an integrated activity. Jurors said no: they believed "that the exchange of gunfire was equal and that the prosecution's evidence of racial motivation rather than anti-communism was unconvincing" (Greensboro Truth and Reconciliation Commission [GTRC], 2006, p. 289).

In 1985, a federal civil trial took place. In that trial, members of KKK, the American Nazi Party, and the Greensboro Police Department were found jointly liable for the wrongful death of one of the five victims, and the city of Greensboro paid the $385,000 settlement on behalf of these three groups. Viewing the relatively small settlement as proof of systemic injustice, many surviving members of the CWP continued to seek some form of redress by pleading their case to the Greensboro public, but many Greensboro citizens had long distanced themselves from anyone associated with the events of November 3, 1979. Greensboro Mayor Jim Melvin, for example, claimed that the KKK and Nazi members who carried out the killings

---

A number of ultra-left sects studied the science [of Marxist revolution] intensely, convinced that the old Communist Party-U.S.A. had sold out to the capitalist system. The CP-USA had been around since the 1920s, and what had it accomplished? It had made some headway in union organizing in its early years, but had been steadily backsliding into oblivion since then. It was time to launch a new communist party, a party that went beyond Marxism to incorporate the more recent teachings of Lenin and Mao…By 1974 a host of preparty communist groups was active. The October League, which grew out of the Georgia Communist League, was predominantly white and based in the South. The Revolutionary Workers League was all black, with strongholds in the South, the Northeast, and the West Coast. In New York, the Puerto Rican Revolutionary Organization and the Asian Study Group became the Workers Viewpoint Organization. (pp. 20–21)

In 1975, a small group from Durham—Jim Waller, Paul Bermanzohn, and Sally Avery—formed the Communist Workers Committee. According to Wheaton, "[T]hey would soon join forces with the black revolutionaries in Greensboro, Nelson Johnson and Sandi and Mark Smith, to organize textile workers at Cone Mills" (p. 34). These individuals united under the banner of the Workers Viewpoint Organization, which changed its name in October of 1979 to the Communist Workers Party (p. 21).

were not members of the Greensboro community—"nor were they welcome"—and that the CWP "actively sought the confrontation" by engaging in "'dare-you-to-step-across-the-line' maneuvers" (North Carolina Advisory Committee [NCAC], 1981, p. 5). Critical of media coverage that "drew conclusions that race relations in Greensboro were poor and that discord and ill will abounded," Melvin described Greensboro as "a quiet community that allows everyone to have full rights and to express them openly and freely on all subjects" (NCAC, p. 5). Such viewpoints were consistent with what Greensboro historian William Chafe (1980) described as "a culture of white progressivism" that pervaded the city (p. 6). In his book *Civility and Civil Rights*, Chafe (1980) maintained that Greensboro had long suffered from what he called a "progressive mystique": Greensboro's progressives believed that public disagreement of any kind was destructive of a "genteel and civilized way of life," and these beliefs, along with the accompanying calls for consensus and moderation, functioned as a means of preserving the status quo (p. 7).[2] Given the socio-political context of the time, it is perhaps not surprising that the survivors' calls for justice were unanswered.[3]

As of 2004, several aspects of Greensboro's socio-political context had not changed substantially from the late seventies and early eighties. William Chafe still held that the progressive mystique operated in powerful ways in the city (GTRC, 2006, p. 38), and many racial inequalities still existed, particularly in relation to income. City administrators' views about November 3, 1979 had not changed much either. Like his predecessor Jim Melvin, Mayor Keith Holliday attempted to distance the people of Greensboro from the events of November 3, 1979, which he described as "a confrontation between *two extremist groups* [emphasis added] where over ninety percent of the participants were from *outside of Greensboro* [emphasis added]" (Truth and reconciliation: Listen for yourself, 2005). Nevertheless, a call by a group of concerned Greensboro citizens for a public inquiry into the events of November 3, 1979 began to gain traction among some members of the community. Several factors allowed the case to reappear. Two of the former members of the CWP had recently

---

[2] According to William Chafe (1980), in a 1949 study of southern politics conducted by V.O. Key, Greensboro had been celebrated for its "progressive outlook…especially [in] industrial development, education, and race relations" (p. 2). But this evaluation, Chafe argued, was incorrect: throughout the first half of the twentieth century, there were widespread racial inequities in the city. In 1957, three years after *Brown v. Board of Education* declared school segregation unconstitutional, desegregation in Greensboro was a mere pretense. At that time, six blacks were admitted to all-white schools; however, "the action was taken," Chafe noted, "not to promote integration, but—as the school board leader later recalled—to 'hold an umbrella' over the rest of the state and preserve segregation" (p. 159). In 1961, the rate of desegregation in North Carolina was 0.026% (p. 159).

[3] Taylor (2009) has argued that the "murders and the failed court cases marked the end of the CWP and the end of active efforts on the part of various Communist groups in North Carolina" (p. 212). While Taylor may be correct that the activity of Communist groups diminished after the November 3, 1979 murders and court cases, the survivors of the CWP remained active in the public sphere long after the event. Over the next two decades, they would continue to tell their story—in a variety of venues—with mixed success. Along the way, some of the survivors changed some of their views about Communism. Others took on professional roles, as academics and medical doctors. In rhetorical terms, they began to affiliate themselves with other rhetorical traditions besides those of Communism. It would be through these avenues that their story would gain its widest hearing.

published books about the event (Waller, 2002; Bermanzohn, 2003), and artists and documentarians were beginning to explore the events of November 3, 1979 in ways that were more sympathetic to the survivors' perspectives.[4]

Outside of Greensboro, the formation of the International Center for Transitional Justice (ICTJ)—co-founded by Alex Boraine, Priscilla Hayner, and Paul van Zyl— also provided the group of concerned Greensboro citizens with a means of moving forward with their inquiry into the events of November 3, 1979. Mechanisms of transitional justice—such as trials, tribunals, truth commissions, lustration, reparations, and amnesty—had been employed throughout the world with the aim of "address[ing] legacies of past human rights abuses, mass atrocity, or other forms of severe social trauma, including genocide or civil war, in order to build a more demo-cratic, just, or peaceful future" (Bickford, 2005, p. 1045). While these mechanisms had primarily been used at the national level in countries in the southern hemisphere to address large-scale violence, members of the ICTJ believed that a truth commis-sion might help the people of Greensboro attain a kind of justice. Such justice would not be primarily retributive; rather, it would involve communal restoration through truth-telling and perhaps even reconciliation. While a grassroots truth commission in Greensboro could not award reparations or amnesty, with enough support it might be able to compel public testimony and bring about a version of justice. (Writing about other truth commissions, Teresa Godwin Phelps (2004) has given one expla-nation of what such justice entails in her book *Shattered Voices: Language, Violence, and the Work of Truth Commissions.* For Phelps (2004), the justice offered by truth commissions counterbalances the suppression of language that often accompanies torture and other forms of physical violence. Such justice, Phelps has claimed, "is dynamic and ongoing, not perfect of course, but a visible manifestation of an ethical and political commitment that honors truth, individual worth, dignity, and equality" (pp. 40, 72).) A Greensboro truth commission might give the survivors a forum to have their perspectives heard and publicly acknowledged.

With assistance from the ICTJ, the group of Greensboro citizens formed the first truth commission of its kind in the United States: the Greensboro Truth and Reconciliation Commission. The GTRC was comprised of seven commissioners, and it worked for 2 years—gathering evidence, holding community forums and three public hearings, and writing a report. At the end of this process, the GTRC held a Report Release Ceremony to present its findings to the community.

---

[4] One example was Emily Mann's play *Greensboro: A Requiem,* which premiered on February 6, 1996 at the McCarter Theater in Princeton, NJ and was later performed in Greensboro by the University of North Carolina at Greensboro Theater Department as part of the twentieth anniversary commemoration of November 3, 1979. Composed of the primary sources surrounding the killings, the play was both a eulogy for the murder victims and a commentary on contemporary race relations (Mann, 1997). Several documentaries were also produced about November 3, including "88 Seconds in Greensboro," produced by the Public Broadcasting Service's Frontline Series (Cran, Tepper, & Cran, 1983); "Lawbreakers: The Greensboro Massacre," an episode of The History Channel's *Lawbreaker* series (Morowitz & Brummel, 2000); and "Greensboro's Child," which framed the event in light of the life story of Kwame Cannon, who, as a boy, attended the CWP rally with his mother and later received two life-sentences for burglary, a judgment which many in the community thought to be racially motivated and excessive given the nature of Cannon's crimes (Coon, 2002).

From the Commission's inception and throughout its operation, one of the primary challenges faced by the commissioners and their supporters was establishing the GTRC's authority in the community. Many past truth commissions had been granted at least some state-sponsored authority to carry out their respective mandates, but the GTRC was a grassroots initiative that did not even have the full support of city officials: in April of 2005, in a motion that some saw as further proof of Greensboro's racial divide, the city council voted 6–3—along racial lines—not to endorse the work of the Commission (Truth and reconciliation: Listen for yourself, 2005). Without city- or state-sponsored support, how and on what grounds did the Commission attempt to establish the authority necessary to accomplish its mandate and bring about justice?

Synopsis

Remaking Transitional Justice in the United States explores rhetorical attempts to authorize the GTRC. The book demonstrates that the development of the field of transitional justice has given rise to a transnational rhetorical tradition that provides those working in the field with series of "enabling constraints"—discursive patterns that create opportunities for subsequent action, even as they limit that action in particular ways.[5] The book then shows how Greensboro stakeholders attempted to reaccentuate—to invoke and transform—facets of this rhetorical tradition in their rhetorical performances to construct authority and bring about justice. More than a mere study of the influences that shaped the rhetoric surrounding the operation of the GTRC, this book aims to understand, in rhetorician James Jasinski's (1997) terms, how rhetorical traditions "'actually function' in the field of textual action" (p. 216). Complexities emerge as I trace how the facets of the rhetorical tradition offered by transitional justice were performed to meet the contingent demands of the Greensboro context.

Taken together, the arguments presented in the pages that follow are important for a number of reasons. Perhaps most importantly, they offer insights into the development of transitional justice in the United States and in other liberal democracies. There are many communities throughout the world that are haunted by violence and are defined by relationships of hatred and prejudice, distrust and fear. Given the pervasiveness of these communities, there is an ongoing need to better understand how mechanisms of transitional justice like truth commissions are implemented and how these institutions come to have the authority to bring about change and redress injustices. As one of only a few community-based truth commissions in the world and—as the Commission's supporters marketed it—"the first of its kind" in the United States, the GTRC offers a productive site for these inquiries (Greensboro Truth and Community Reconciliation Project [GTCRP], 2004).

---

[5] The phrase "enabling constraints" comes from Judith Butler (1997, p. 16).

The purpose of this chapter is to clarify the key terms of these claims and to lay the historical, methodological, and theoretical groundwork for the study. I begin by providing additional background about the events of November 3, 1979. Because the events surrounding that day are highly contested, and because my object of analysis in this project is not the happenings of November 3, 1979 but the GTRC's responses to those happenings, I provide background about the events by way of a survey of past accounts of the events by others. The survey of these accounts brings into relief what is contested regarding the events of November 3, 1979. Following this survey, I describe how the GTRC came to be in more detail and elaborate on one of the central challenges facing the Commission as it constructed its own account of November 3, 1979—its need to establish authority. I then define authority and artic-ulate what is at stake in studying how it is constructed. Next I describe—and provide detailed rationale for—the project's methodology (a type of rhetorical criticism navigating between close reading and critical rhetoric) and make explicit the theo-retical commitments associated with this approach. Defining constructs like rhetori-cal tradition, rhetorical performance, and *ethos* clarifies how rhetors construct authority in general and sets the stage for the demonstration, throughout this book, of how the advocates of the GTRC constructed authority in their particular context. The chapter concludes with a more extensive overview of each of the subsequent chapters of this book.

A Contest of Narratives

Many accounts of the events of November 3, 1979, as well as explanations of its causes and descriptions of its repercussions, have appeared over the past three decades. From November 4, 1979 to November 1985 alone, Greensboro's two newspapers—*The Greensboro Daily News* and *The Daily Record*—ran over 400 articles about November 3, 1979 and its aftermath (GTRC, 2006, p. 510). In addi-tion, accounts have also appeared in political pamphlets, memoirs, books, plays, and documentaries. With these many accounts have come a variety of viewpoints about what happened on November 3, 1979 and who is to blame (Wheaton, 1987, p. 4). In what follows, I look briefly at a few of the accounts that proliferated in 1979 and in the early 1980s. Doing so brings into relief the impetus for the formation of the GTRC, which I then describe in detail.

Within weeks after November 3, 1979, CWP survivors formed the Committee to Avenge the Murder of the Communist Workers Party (CAMCWP), and the group published a newsprint poster, which read: "AVENGE the MURDER of the CWP 5! TURN the COUNTRY UPSIDE DOWN TO BEAT BACK the NEW WAVE of KKK, NAZI and FBI ATTACKS!" (1979). The CAMCWP viewed the killings as an act of political assassination by the government, and CWP survivors Paul and Sally Bermanzohn reinforced and developed this perspective in a book published the following year: *The True Story of the Greensboro Massacre: Why the government conspired with the Klan and Nazis to murder the Communist Workers Party 5 in*

Greensboro on November 3, 1979. An account by eyewitnesses (1980). Bermanzohn and Bermanzohn (1980) described the November 3, 1979 killers as government "sharpshooters" and their actions on November 3 as a "military maneuver" (p. 19). Thus, in the immediate aftermath of the killings, one of the issues to emerge was whether or not November 3, 1979 was part of a capitalist government's conspiracy against the CWP and its communist ideology. Consistent with this account, the CWP also claimed that the killings pointed to class-based inequities.

Members of the Black Liberation Movement looked at the event differently. In 1980, they published the pamphlet "The Greensboro Massacre: Critical Lessons for the 1980's" (Cabral). Although the authors of the pamphlet agreed that the events of November 3, 1979 involved "collusion" between the state and the Klan and Nazis, they were adamant that the conspiracy was not, as the CWP claimed, simply against the CWP:

> By launching the attack they did on November 3rd, [Klan members] were able to deal a real blow not only to their immediate targets [the CWP] but to the Black masses and their struggle. By invading the Black community and openly killing people the Klan raised the threat of open terror against the Black struggle in a sharper way than had been done in years. At the same time by launching the attack against an isolated band of pre-dominantly white leftists, they created conditions that would make it particularly difficult [for groups like the Black Liberation Movement] to build the kind of militant mass response that would give the Black community confidence that the terrorist threat could be effectively countered. They also greatly inspired their basic racist constituency; and by combining racism with anti-communism, they created conditions for building the broadest possible base of support among white people for their action. (Cabral, 1980, para. 43)

For members of the Black Liberation Movement, then, the events of November 3, 1979 were perceived as deeply racist, albeit in complex ways. It is also worth noting that the Black Liberation Movement's charges of racism were directed, at least in part, at city officials.[6]

For their part, most city officials (as well as many members of the Greensboro community) rejected the notion that November 3, 1979 was about questions of race. According to the pamphlet, Mayor of Greensboro Jim Melvin reportedly claimed that "the murders in no way reflected the nature of race relations in the city" (Cabral, 1980, para. 53).

By November 1980, one year after the killings, the debate over whether or not November 3, 1979 was related to questions of race and racism was widespread throughout the Greensboro community—a fact attested to in a report published by the NCAC to the United States Commission on Civil Rights. The report, entitled

---

[6] The writers of the pamphlet continued, "In responding to the obvious questions around the absence of police protection [for the CWP marchers], the Mayor and Police Chief promised a full investigation. Meanwhile, they pushed a Black police Lieutenant out front, claiming he had been in charge that day and could answer [the media's] questions….By pushing the Black cop out front, the power structure obviously hoped to frustrate the developing protest by saying 'If you want someone to attack, you have to attack this Black cop first'" (Cabral, 1980, para. 53).

"Black/White Perceptions: Race Relations in Greensboro," was "initiated by the NCAC as a result of conflicting assessments of the causes of the confrontation in Greensboro on November 3rd, 1979, during which 5 persons were slain at an anti-klan rally" (NCAC, 1981, p. ii). A compilation of a series of oral interviews by city leaders, business people, citizens working in education and in the media, and members of the religious community, the report provided a summary of the many different perspectives circulating in Greensboro at the beginning of the 1980s about the events of November 3, 1979.

One of the Greensboro citizens interviewed was John Ellison, Jr., the Executive Vice President of the Ellison Company. According to the report, "Mr. Ellison told the Committee that in his view the November 3, 1979 tragedy was not an outgrowth of the climate of race relations in the city, but that the incident was primarily 'an isolated conflict between two extremist groups,' neither with widespread following or support in either the black or white community" (NCAC, 1981, p. 12). Another interviewee, Grand Dragon of the North Carolina Chapter of the KKK Virgil Griffin, also dismissed notions that November 3, 1979 was primarily about race. He protested the "characterization of the November 3, 1979 demonstration as 'a civil rights march,'" claiming, instead, that "the Communist Party was assembling for a 'Death to the Klan' rally and 'to advocate violence to overthrow our government'" (NCAC, 1981, p. 10). CWP spokesperson Nelson Johnson—one of the survivors of November 3, 1979—claimed that, by enlisting the KKK and Nazis on November 3, 1979, the government purposefully manufactured racial tensions in order to mask other problems; according to the report, Johnson claimed that "the Nazis and Klan were being used [by the state apparatus] as 'shock troops of capitalism' for the purpose of turning one race against the other thereby diverting the focus of attention from the real source of people's political and economic problems" (NCAC, 1981, p. 9). Other interviewees saw November 3, 1979 as connected much more directly to race. For example, Ed Whitfield, the co-chairman of Concerned Citizens Against the Klan, reportedly "expressed the view of his organization that the November 3 incident and the flurry of activities and kinds of investigations conducted in its wake were very much a reflection of the 'real' character of race relations in the Greensboro area" (NCAC, 1981, p. 9). Fred Taylor, the Director of the Southern Christian Leadership Conference (SCLC) noted that "the entire Nation has had a renewed interest in race relations since the November 3rd 'massacre' in Greensboro" (NCAC, 1981, p. 17). And John Erwin, Vice President of the Greensboro Chapter of the National Association for the Advancement of Colored People (NAACP), told the Commission that November 3, 1979 "did not cause race relations to regress, but helped bring facts to light" regarding discrimination against minorities and the poor (NCAC, 1981, p. 12).

Continuing this catalogue of interpretations of the events of November 3, 1979 would fill several volumes. However, despite the fact that this survey is necessarily partial, it reveals a crucial point: there have been many interpretations of what happened on November 3, 1979, and almost all of them have been contested. Journalist Elizabeth Wheaton, who reported on the Greensboro killings for the Institute for

Southern Studies in 1981 and later published a book about the event, commented on this fact:

> The full story of the Greensboro killings may never be revealed, not because there is a lack of information but because there are a multiplicity of perspectives from which we can view the available facts. It is as though we were looking through a kaleidoscope and the events fell into one pattern when viewed through the CWP's perspective, another through that of the Klan and Nazis, and yet another through that of the police and federal agents. Each pattern has its own logic, but when they are superimposed, the image becomes a jumble of contradictions and conflict. (1987, p. 4)

This observation rang as true in 1999 as when Wheaton first made it, and the lack of agreement about what happened on November 3, 1979 was one of the main reasons that members of the Greensboro community decided to form a truth commission.

In 1999, on the 20th anniversary of the killings, individuals in Greensboro commemorated the deaths of the victims (GTRC, 2006, p. 427). During these events, victims' families and other members of the community discussed ways in which they might address the divisions in the community. This discussion led members of the group to contact the Andrus Family Fund (AFF), a philanthropic organization committed to collaborating "with those working to create safer environments" and contributing "to the body of knowledge and experience about what is necessary to create effective change…by focusing on Transition—that critical juncture in time and process—that, if properly attended to, affects positive change" (AFF, n.d.). The AFF put the group in contact with the ICTJ, which recommended forming a truth commission (Bermanzohn, 2003, p. 370).

Based on the suggestions of the ICTJ, the individuals eventually formed an independent coalition—the Greensboro Truth and Community Reconciliation Project (GTCRP)—with the expressed purpose of forming a truth commission. In the spring of 2002, with the support of both the ICTJ and the AFF, the Project formed a National Advisory Committee and a Local Task Force in order to develop a process for selecting commissioners and describe what the commissioners' duties would be. Almost a year later, in mid-February of 2003, the National Advisory Committee and the Local Task Force revealed the selection process for commissioners and approved the "Mandate for the Greensboro Truth and Reconciliation Commission," a document detailing the purposes of the yet-to-be-established GTRC: to promote "healing and reconciliation of the community" through truth-seeking and dissemination of information; to "clarify the confusion" surrounding the events of November 3; to acknowledge "feelings of loss, guilt, shame, anger, and fear"; and to "facilitate changes in social consciousness" (GTCRP, 2003, p. 1). The seven commissioners were selected about 1 year later, and, in mid-June of 2004, they were sworn in at a public ceremony at the Historic Depot in downtown Greensboro. From June 2004 to May 2006, the GTRC worked to complete its mandate, attempting to examine "the context, causes, sequence and consequence of the events of November 3, 1979" (GTCRP, 2003, p. 1).[7]

---

[7] In their book *Learning from Greensboro: Truth and Reconciliation in the United States,* Magarrell and Wesley (2008) have described logistical aspects of the formation of the GTRC in greater detail. *Remaking Transitional Justice in the United States* focuses primarily on the rhetorical features of the Commission's formation and authorization.

What emerged from the Commission's inquiry was another narrative about November 3, 1979. The Commission's report described the "malicious intent" of the KKK and Nazis who arrived at the CWP rally, the "inflammatory" language of both the CWP and the KKK, the "intentionality [of the Greensboro police] to fail to provide adequate protection" at the rally, and the attempts by the Greensboro police and the city managers to "deliberately [mislead] the public regarding what happened on Nov. 3, 1979" (GTRC, 2006, pp. 370–376). The commissioners situated these findings within the context of larger claims about racial and class-based inequities in Greensboro, commenting, for example, on the "injustice in the justice system"—a system that "tends to be disproportionately imperfect against people of color and poor people" (GTRC, 2006, p. 377). In drawing conclusions about the role of race and class in precipitating the events of November 3, 1979, commissioners believed they had established a foundation upon which a measure of justice might be achieved. But what was to ensure that the GTRC's narrative would be understood by the people of Greensboro as worth taking seriously and not simply as another viewpoint, an addition to the long list of contested narratives circulating in the community?

Authorizing Transitional Justice in Greensboro

From the Commission's inception, establishing authority was a fundamental task of both the members of the Project and the commissioners themselves. A memo—sent to members of the Project by Lisa Magarrell, a senior associate for the ICTJ and consultant to both the Project and the Commission—confirms that the question of authority was given explicit consideration by the Commission's architects. In the memo, Magarrell (2002) prompted the Project to consider from where the Commission would derive its authority (p. 2). To do so, she described two types of truth commissions: those that had been "granted quasi-juridical power" and those that had relied "on voluntary participation and collaboration" (p. 2) The former, she noted, had derived their authority from legal sources, allowing them "to compel appearances, testimony, [and] access to documents and information"; the latter had relied on alternative forms of authority, of which she listed three: public opinion, moral authority, and persuasion. "What power," she concluded, "does the Commission need and where will it come from?" (p. 2).

Largely out of necessity, the Project established the Commission according to the second of the two models presented by Magarrell. Several previous truth commissions had had the support of their governments and, thus, had been granted at least some state-sponsored authority to carry out their respective mandates. The South African Truth and Reconciliation Commission (SATRC) was one example of a truth commission that had been granted considerable state-sponsored authority: through an act passed by the South African Parliament in 1995, the SATRC was given the authority to "grant individualized amnesty, search premises and seize evidence, subpoena witnesses, and run a sophisticated witness-protection program" (Hayner, 2001, p. 41). Unlike the SATRC, the GTRC lacked such powers: its mandate stated,

"The Commission will have no authority either to pursue criminal or civil claims or to grant immunity from such claims" (GTCRP, 2003, p. 2).[8]

Since the Commission lacked such powers and did not have an endorsement from the city, members of the Project and the commissioners themselves had to construct authority in other ways.[9] How did they do it? The pragmatic answer to this question is that they canvassed for support in the Greensboro community. The Commission's architects circulated a petition throughout the community prior to the Commission's installation that asked individuals to pledge their support for the truth and reconciliation process, and they also collected letters of support from prominent individuals within and outside the Greensboro community, several of which were eventually posted on the Commission's website. Another of their important attempts to garner authority for the Commission was the Swearing In and Seating Ceremony, held in 2004, to install the commissioners. Made up of speeches, testimonies, prayers, and song, the ceremony helped to constitute the grounds upon which commissioners would act. Once the Commission itself had been established, commissioners conducted a door-to-door campaign, sponsored a local television program called "TRC Talk," published a weekly newsletter, and set up a blog where community members could ask questions about the Commission and dialogue with commissioners about their work. They also petitioned members of the Greensboro community for written statements about the events of November 3, 1979 and sponsored community-wide forums about reconciliation. The commissioners' most important events in their bids for authority were their three public hearings and Report Release Ceremony.

While this list of canvassing practices provides a sketch of the ways that the Project and the commissioners worked to garner authority for the Commission, it says little about the specific ways they made their case for the Commission to the Greensboro community. For a more thorough answer that highlights the complexities of the Commission's authorization, it is necessary to look closely at these practices and, given that most of these practices are discursive in nature, to analyze what was said and written in these instances. To that end, this book turns to rhetorical studies to provide its theoretical framework. This field is well suited to explore the

---

[8] In *Learning from Greensboro,* Magarrell and Wesley (2008) reflected on the importance of the question of authority to the GTRC's operation. They wrote, for example, about the need to drum up public support for the process and the difficulties of engaging people, noting, "With no subpoena power or ability to offer immunity from legal action to entice people to come forward, one of the big questions was, 'If we build it, will people come?'" (Magarrell & Wesley, 2008, pp. 53–54). Moreover, in the Foreword to Magarrell and Wesley's book, former SATRC member Bongani Finca noted that an important aspect of the GTRC's operation had to do with the "question of legitimacy" (pp. viii-ix). Magarrell and Wesley also cited Sofia Macher, a former member of the Peruvian Truth and Reconciliation Commission, who, after visiting Greensboro in April of 2005, wrote, "The fact that the Greensboro TRC does not have official status means that the legitimacy of its work depends solely on the community itself, and this is no easy task" (p. 99).

[9] Leman-Langlois and Shearing (2003) considered a similar question in their inquiry into the South African Truth and Reconciliation Commission: "Our focus," they wrote, "is on this process of authorization [of the "truth" offered by the South African TRC] and its purposes and consequences" (p. 223).

book's central questions, in part, because of rhetoric's traditional associations with persuasion—which has been one of the primary ways that unofficial truth commissions (as well as official truth commissions) have garnered authority for themselves. But the profit of turning to rhetorical studies goes beyond rhetoric's emphasis on persuasion. The discipline allows one to attend both to discourse, language-in-use, and to discursive formations, structures of language that shape and are shaped by language-in-use. These foci allow one to analyze how language provides both opportunities and constraints for its users, and to explore the complexities of human agency in relation to language.

Theoretical Framework

To introduce this project's theoretical framework, it is productive to highlight two different approaches to rhetorical criticism: close reading and critical rhetoric.[10] Sketching these two approaches brings into relief a debate over methodology in the field of rhetorical studies, in which the definition of rhetoric is contested, as is the nature of the object of critical analysis, the role of human agency in rhetorical production, and the perceived relationship between theory and method (Gaonkar, 1990, p. 290). The discussion sets the stage for my own approach to reading the texts surrounding the operation of the GTRC—an approach that takes both approaches into account.

   Proponents of each approach typically have had different aims. Those who have practiced critical rhetoric have aimed to create possibilities for emancipation by exposing the ways in which power circulates in and through discourse and marginalizes individuals and groups (Jasinski, 2001, p. 117, 122). To accomplish this aim, they have investigated the traces of what Michel Foucault referred to as discursive formations—i.e., those structures of language "that produce knowledge claims that the system of power finds useful"—to expose their logic (Wolin, 1999, p. 184). One of the primary aims of those practicing close reading has been to understand how discourse, be it oral or written language-in-use, persuades and/or acts in the world (Leff, 2000, p. 554). They have accomplished this aim by scrutinizing the grammatical moves and word choices; the clause, sentence, and paragraph structures; the patterns of style and argument; and the figures of speech and thought that unfold within the discourse (Jasinski, 2001, p. 93).[11]

---

[10] Dilip Gaonkar (1990) highlighted these two approaches in the *Western Journal of Speech Communication*'s special issue on rhetorical criticism.

[11] Gaonkar (1990) productively described close reading as "neither an engaging paraphrase of what is 'said' nor a laborious cataloguing (troponomy) of formal features. The positive stress on the interpretative act suggests that 'close reading' is actually a mode of critical writing that aspires to reconstitute the text. And such reconstitution is attempted and sometimes achieved through an interpretative act of making explicit 'the rhetorical dynamics implicit within' the text. Thus, textual criticism is a species of grounded interpretation" (p. 312).

Proponents of each approach have held different views about their objects of study, that is, about the nature of the "text" to be analyzed. For practitioners of close reading, the text has been described as a "field of action," with identifiable boundaries, where aesthetic form and representational content intersect; whereas, for practitioners of critical rhetoric, texts have been conceptualized as the "fragments" or "residues" of discursive formations (Jasinski, 2001, pp. 571–573). Put another way, the former have conceptualized texts as "constructed products" to be unpacked, while the latter have conceptualized texts as "constitutive processes" to be uncovered or reconstructed (Gaonkar, 1990, pp. 290–291). These differences with regard to the nature of the text point to a larger difference between the two approaches regarding the definition of rhetoric itself: rhetoric has been conceptualized either an "intentional art" or an "extensional power" (Leff, 1992, p. 225). This difference is not insignificant, especially with regard to questions about human agency. Practitioners of close reading have usually ascribed agency to humans: humans, they have argued, are able to use language strategically to respond to situational exigencies and accomplish particular purposes. Proponents of critical rhetoric have called human agency into question: individuals are constituted as subjects in and through discursive formations, which shape their identities and so-called actions.

Finally, proponents of the two approaches have differed on the starting point for critical inquiry. Critical rhetoric, like much of postmodern critical practice, has assumed the impossibility of an atheoretical stance. The critic should, therefore, explicitly articulate the theoretical presuppositions informing his or her inquiry. Close reading, at least in its earliest conceptions, did not take as its starting point a theoretical orientation. For example, in his early descriptions of close reading, rhetorician Michael Leff, a forerunner of the practice, expressed skepticism about the possibility that one could "apprehend (or redescribe) rhetorical phenomena exclusively in the meta-language of theory" (Gaonkar, 1990, p. 311). Leff (2000) claimed that theory building should not precede the analysis of the rhetorical text; that is, close reading begins not with abstract rhetorical theory but "with a severely empirical orientation" (p. 547). Leff's claim that the critic's first orientation should be empirical did not mean that he eschewed theory entirely: since close reading "necessarily entails principles or categories 'not native to the original,' it requires an exercise of judgment at some level of abstraction, and it eventuates in something we might call *theoretical understanding of the particular case*" (p. 547). In other words, theory in Leff's schema was not discarded but relocated and redefined: it was rendered contingent upon the specificity of the rhetorical text under consideration—a kind of "generalization within cases" (p. 551). Close reading, as its advocates have conceptualized it, eventuates in a double boon: it "not only leads to a richer understanding of the particular text but also contributes to, in Gaonkar's terms, 'the thickening of [theoretical] concepts through grounded critical readings'" (Jasinski, 2001, p. 94)

Instead of affirming the validity of one approach and denying the validity of the other, I maintain that both close reading and critical rhetoric have merit, depending on what one wants to bring into relief. Thus, rather than frame such approaches as antithetical, they are presented here as complementary, insofar as they allow one to analyze how language provides both opportunities and constraints for its users, and to explore the complexities of human agency in relation to language. In the chapters that follow, there is an attempt to take both approaches into account.

The value of taking the close reading approach into account is tied, in part, to the need among scholars studying transitional justice for more studies that consider the discourse, or language-in-use, surrounding truth commissions. This need stems from the fact that there have been a limited number of scholars who have taken a language-oriented approach to the study of truth commissions, and, among those who have, most have focused on the philosophical and/or theoretical issues sur-rounding truth commissions to the neglect of interpreting actual texts.[12] Teresa Godwin Phelps (2004) spoke to this point in her book *Shattered Voices*: "[T]here is," she wrote, "much that *Shattered Voices* does *not* do: it does not take on the many-headed hydra question of what 'truth' is in truth reports....Nor does it inves-tigate actual victim responses to truth reports. Although I know and have talked to some victims, I purposely left this book theoretical. Empirical work is a welcome next step" (pp. 179–180).

The value of close reading for those studying transitional justice is also tied to the approach's dual functions. It offers a means by which one can better understand particular mechanisms of transitional justice, while simultaneously helping to develop more robust accounts of theoretical concepts as they get worked out in practice. My general aims in each chapter of this book, therefore, are twofold: I hope to contribute to the current understanding of the GTRC and to the "the thick-ening of concepts [of transitional justice] through grounded critical readings" (Gaonkar, 1989, p. 270).

Having highlighted the benefits of close reading, I want to acknowledge two problems with the approach, as least as I have articulated it here. First, I take issue with the possibility, expressed by Leff in his early conceptions of close reading, that an empirical orientation can precede a theoretical one.[13] In this regard, I agree with proponents of critical rhetoric who have maintained that all critics approach their inquiries with particular biases and that these should be stated as explicitly as pos-sible. Second, a close reading runs the risk of producing a formalistic and overly aesthetic account that fails to consider the ways that larger social forces have shaped (and, for that matter, have been shaped by) the discourse it explores.[14] This problem stems from conceptualizing rhetoric as intentional art as opposed to an extensional power. Rhetorical criticism is, I believe, better served by acknowledging that both rhetoric-as-intentional-art and rhetoric-as-extensional-power have some validity, and that text-as-constructed-product and text-as-constitutive-process should not be

---

[12] For examples of language-oriented studies of truth commissions that take a more theoretical approach, see Phelps (2004) and Doxtader (2001, 2003, 2004, 2007, 2009).

[13] In subsequent work, Leff (1992) acknowledged this point, admitting that his approach "does not simply promote a direct encounter with rhetorical texts, but that it involves something very like a theory of rhetorical reading" (p. 223).

[14] Leff himself (1992) noted this problem as well. He wrote, "[T]he project is incomplete on its own terms, since it does not accommodate issues of power and social circumstance that decisively influence the focal object of study" (p. 226).

conceptualized as contested ways of defining the text but rather as two different—mutually constitutive—phenomena.[15]

Remaking Transitional Justice in the United States embraces both approaches by adapting a theoretical framework developed by communication scholar John Murphy. Murphy (1997) acknowledged that rhetoric is both an intentional art and an extensional power.[16] His framework, moreover, not only allows the critic to negotiate these tensions but also offers a means of conceptualizing how authority is derived rhetorically—a central aim of this book.

Murphy (1997) used alternative terms to describe discursive formations and discourse: he referred to the former as rhetorical traditions and the latter as rhetorical performances. Drawing upon the work of Thomas Farrell, Murphy defined rhetorical traditions as "common patterns of language use" that are "'marked by characteristic figurative and argumentative devices,' and shaped by dialogic interactions in which actors share, repeat, critique, revise and satirize the tradition itself" (p. 72). Such patterns of language use exist solely as "linguistic potentialities" and are only "manifested" in and through the performances (p. 72). Rhetorical performances are constructed products (and fields of action); however, they are implicated in the constitutive processes of rhetorical traditions.

Rhetorical traditions provide individuals with a set of "enabling constraints" for their performances (Butler, 1997, p. 16; Murphy, 1997, p. 85). On the one hand, Murphy noted that rhetorical traditions "imply (when accepted) certain notions of preferable behavior" and "organize the 'social knowledge' of communities" (p. 72). In other words, rhetorical traditions are in some sense constitutive of individuals' identities and actions. On the other hand, Murphy emphasized that these patterns of language use do not simply constrain but also enable individuals to act:

> Even the most constraining of traditions…partake of the multiple languages (heteroglossia) and voices (polyphony) of the social world (Bakhtin, 1981, pp. 259–422). Rhetorical traditions exist in history; they shape and share the ambiguities of historical experience and communal life. As a result, there are layered and dissonant voices within and between traditions. Traditions 'speak' to each other and to pressing problems of the day. No one tradition can finalize the world or itself. (pp. 72–73)

---

[15] This approach has some precedent. According to Leff (1992), many scholars have attempted to negotiate or to merge "the two opposing orientations" (pp. 225–226).

[16] As Leff revised his thinking about close reading, he also developed a framework with which to negotiate these tensions (1997). He argued that rhetorical production and interpretation are not distinct practices: rhetorical production is always only made possible by interpretation of prior texts—an "intertextual network," which "constitutes a tradition" (Leff, 1997, p. 93). This insight implies that the practice of close reading involves tracing how texts under investigation make use of the resources of intertextual networks to make meaning (Leff, 1997; Jasinski, 2001, p. 95). One strategy that Leff (1992) advocated for bringing into relief the ways in which texts draw upon intertextual networks is to focus on controversy—or "oppositional discourse" (p. 229). For yet another strategy, see Leff and Sachs (1990) on the concept of iconicity as an interpretative strategy. By looking at controversies as embodied in texts, critics are able to expose "the issues of power and situated interest that inform their whole development" (pp. 229–230). This approach "pushes" close readers beyond texts-as-constructed-products as they identify the intertextual networks that rhetors make use of to produce their texts (Leff, 1992, p. 228; Jasinski, 2001, p. 95).

Because rhetorical traditions draw on many languages and contain many voices, they never totally constrain or discipline individuals, who are able to perform rhetorical traditions in new configurations to meet the demands of new contexts. Rhetorical traditions provide individuals with resources for invention, where invention is understood to be the "reaccentuation" of the resources of rhetorical traditions "into coherent artistic representations of community life in contingent circumstances" (Murphy, 1997, pp. 71, 74–75).

Reaccentuation—the central theoretical term of my study—involves invoking, in a rhetorical performance, any of the characteristic figurative and argumentative devices that comprise one or more rhetorical traditions and adapting (or even transforming) these devices through selection, arrangement, emphasis, evaluation, etc., in order to bring them to bear on current circumstances (Murphy, 1997, pp. 74–75). When rhetors reaccentuate the elements of a rhetorical tradition or of multiple rhetorical traditions, they put their own "'imprint' on prior discourse" without totally erasing the prior discourse, calling forth and making use of facets of the tradition "to accomplish different purposes from those for which the materials were originally intended" (Erickson, 2004, p. 166; Murphy, 1997, p. 74).[17] The concept of reaccentuation affirms the possibility of human agency, seeing the rhetor as a kind of *bricoleur*, an agent "who acts by making do or improvising with the limited materials that are available in a particular situation. The rhetor is a language 'tinkerer' pasting together bits of linguistic material and persuasive strategy"—taken from rhetorical traditions—"to meet the demands of the occasion" (Jasinski, 2001, p. 329).[18]

Thus Murphy's framework, unlike many postmodern critical approaches, does not attempt to completely do away with the notion of the author. Nor does it attempt to do away with author's etymological cousin—authority. In fact, Murphy's framework provides a means of conceptualizing how authority is derived rhetorically. Authority, Murphy (1997) claimed, "derives from the reaccentuation of rhetorical traditions in a performative display of practical reason," and, drawing again upon Farrell (1993), he added that "[s]uch a view sees authority 'as a variation of *ethos*,' in which actors reaccentuate, that is, adapt, modify, and position in the 'open-ended present'...the wisdom of the past" (p. 75).[19] While I agree with Murphy that authority stems from reaccentuating rhetorical traditions, I find his emphasis on

---

[17] My definition of "reaccentuation" includes three components: there is an *action* (elements of a rhetorical tradition are invoked in performance), which involves *innovation* (the elements are adapted or transformed), in order to accomplish a *contextually defined purpose*.

[18] For more on the figure of the *bricoleur*, see Erickson (2004, pp. 165–167). Another resource for exploring the figure of the *bricoleur* is Michel de Certeau's (1998) *The Practice of Everyday Life*, which grounded human action in "making do" and "making use" (pp. 29–42).

[19] Murphy's (1997) explanation of how rhetors derive authority was consistent with the term's etymology (p. 76). Authority comes from the Latin *auctōritas*—a word that, as Lynn Clarke (2005) has noted, "embodied a respect for 'tradition,' an interest in preserving...the 'sacred founding' of the Roman body politic" (p. 2). But *auctōritas* did not simply involve passively respecting and preserving tradition; the term was also closely related to the verb *augere* (meaning "to augment") and often entailed notions of "producing, production, [and] invention" and "deliberate judgment" as well (Arendt, 1993, pp. 121–122; Clarke, 2005, p. 2).

performances of practical reason—or *phronesis*—to be limiting. Reaccentuating rhetorical traditions in a performative display of practical reason is indeed one way for a rhetor to establish authority rhetorically, but there are many other types of performances that also may establish authority. Rhetors may, for instance, establish authority when they reaccentuate rhetorical traditions in their performances to establish moral character (*arête*) or goodwill (*eunoia*). For Aristotle, moral character and goodwill were, along with practical reason, the three components of *ethos,* and, while my understanding of *ethos* differs from the threefold schema of Aristotle, I would like to suggest that one productive way to broaden Murphy's claims about authority is to move beyond considerations of performances of practical reason to performances of *ethos* more generally (Aristotle, trans. 1991, pp. 37–38, 120).[20] Building on Murphy's explanation, then, I maintain that authority may be derived rhetorically as rhetors reaccentuate rhetorical traditions in performances of *ethos.*

As a number of scholars have pointed out, *ethos*—which is often described in terms of Aristotle's threefold schema or simply as the character of the rhetor—may be productively defined in terms of one's "positionality" in discourse (Jarratt & Reynolds, 1994, p. 47; see also Halloran, 1982; Reynolds, 1993; Hyde, 2004).[21] Such a definition is based, in part, on the term's usage in ancient Greece: *ethos* was frequently used in reference to a familiar or oft-frequented *place* (Hyde, 2004, p. xiii; Halloran, 1982, p. 60; Reynolds, 1993, p. 328). The term can be conceptualized, therefore, in terms of one's discursive position or "standpoint," which includes the rhetor's stance as well as the place from which the rhetor stands (Jarratt & Reynolds, 1994, p. 53; Reynolds, 1993, p. 326). Consistent with these contemporary reflections on *ethos,* I define the term as the rhetor's subject position as it is constructed in and through his or her (and occasionally others') rhetorical performances. Describing *ethos* in terms of subject positions highlights the ways in which it is both a product of larger social and political forces (i.e., rhetors *are positioned* by the constitutive processes of rhetorical traditions) as well as an active response to the contingent circumstances of a given rhetorical situation (i.e., rhetors *position themselves* in their rhetorical performances) (Murphy, 1997, p. 74).[22] It is by constructing such positions, by "placing" themselves in the midst of larger traditions and in the midst of their particular contexts, that rhetors establish and reinforce the

---

[20] Warranting this move is the fact that many scholars working in the field of rhetorical studies have seen a close relationship between authority and *ethos,* although they have articulated this relationship in many different ways (Farrell, 1993; Halloran, 1982; Reynolds, 1993). Halloran (1982) equated the two terms: "In its simplest form, *ethos* is what we might call the argument from authority" (p. 60). Farrell (1993) expressed the relation between *ethos* and authority differently from Halloran, calling authority a "variation of ethos" (p. 290). Nedra Reynolds (1993) highlighted the "potential of ethos…to examine how writers establish authority and enact responsibility from positions not traditionally considered authoritative" (p. 326).

[21] I have noted similar connections between *ethos* and positionality in analyzing Desmond Tutu's "Foreword" to the *Truth and Reconciliation Commission of South Africa Final Report* (Beitler, 2012, pp. 4–6).

[22] Such an approach has affinities with positioning theory (Davies & Harré, 2001; Harré & Slocum, 2003).

warrants, grounds, and justifications for their actions and claims, that is, their authority.

Central Arguments

The Rhetorical Tradition of Transitional Justice

One of the central arguments of this book, which lays the groundwork for understanding efforts to authorize the GTRC, is that the field of transitional justice has given rise to a transnational rhetorical tradition that provides those working in the field with a series of "enabling constraints." To make this case, Chap. 2 examines scholarship on the SATRC that takes a rhetorical approach, either implicitly or explicitly. This discussion provides the necessary background for the rhetorical analyses in subsequent chapters, which explore how the elements of the tradition discussed in Chap. 2 are reaccentuated by the GTRC to meet the contingent demands of their context. More than a traditional review of the literature, Chap. 2 marshals past scholarship to demonstrate how the discourse surrounding truth commissions consists of patterned ways of using language.

Reaccentuating the Rhetorical Tradition in Greensboro

As a rapidly growing body of scholarship has recognized, discourse produced in one context often travels to other contexts. Kay Shaffer and Sidonie Smith (2004) have examined how testimony—such as that produced during the public hearings of the SATRC—was consumed or deployed by others in different contexts to accomplish a variety of different ends. Katherine Mack (2012) has explored how *topoi*— i.e., places of argument—that emerged during the operation of the SATRC circulated elsewhere (pp. 9–11). Of this circulation, Mack has written, "The transnational circulation of people and ideas across cultural and geographic contexts has created new situations in which persuasion can occur. Rhetoric *happens* when rhetors take up arguments and tropes from this global flow to effect change or achieve identification in a particular location or situation" (2012, p. 1).[23] Rhetorical traditions, in other words, may have transnational scope, and the second primary argument of

---

[23] Mack's manuscript (2012) serves as a wonderful complement to *Remaking Transitional Justice in the United States*. She, too, has taken a rhetorical approach to the study of truth commissions, describing the *topoi* of the SATRC and exploring how such *topoi* travel beyond their initial contexts. Whereas Mack's project primarily addresses rhetorical scholars to make the case that TRCs are rhetorical and are a generative site for exploring transnational rhetorical activity, my project addresses those working in the field of transitional justice and argues that the field has given rise to a transnational rhetorical tradition, which transitional justice stakeholders—such as the GTRC commissioners—can reaccentuate to establish their authority and bring about change.

Remaking Transitional Justice in the United States involves showing—through rhetorical analyses of the GTRC's founding documents, ceremonies, public hearings, and correspondence with the ICTJ—how Greensboro stakeholders reaccentuated elements of the rhetorical tradition of transitional justice in an attempt to construct authority and accomplish their mandate.

Chapter 3 explores the reaccentuation of *ubuntu* at the GTRC's Swearing In and Seating Ceremony and in subsequent publications distributed throughout the Commission's operation. *Ubuntu*—a South African concept that describes human identity in terms of one's interconnectedness with others—was an important part of the discursive architecture of the SATRC,[24] and SATRC Chairperson Desmond Tutu (1999a, 1999b, 2005; see also Battle, 1997) frequently deployed the term. In Greensboro, in the absence of city or state support for the Commission, *ubuntu* was invoked in order to build solidarity between the Greensboro and South African initiatives and to call attention to the GTRC's standing in global civil society—thereby helping establish the GTRC's authority.

Chapter 4 analyzes the discourse at the GTRC's public hearings to demonstrate how the commissioners reaccentuated the organizational rhetoric of past truth commissions in order to position the Commission as representative of the Greensboro community at large. In this chapter, special consideration is given to the commissioners' rhetorical efforts to call attention to the Commission's unity-in-diversity as a means of modeling reconciliation and interaction for the people of the city. Chapter 5 analyzes features of the GTRC's 529-page *Final Report*, revealing how the commissioners attempted to lay claim to the title "Truth and Reconciliation Commission's" through rhetorical acts of redefinition and, in doing so, responded to their naysayers. More specifically, the commissioners collapsed Louis Bickford's distinction between "official" and "unofficial" truth commissions and maneuvered around Pricilla Hayner's widely accepted definition of truth commission—in order to critique prevalent views about the progress of race relations in Greensboro.

Having demonstrated in Chaps. 3–5 how the GTRC used the rhetorical mechanisms of transitional justice in an attempt to establish its authority, Chap. 6 looks more broadly at the development of the field of transitional justice in the United States. It surveys several US-based initiatives—the Mississippi Truth Project (MTP), the Maine Tribal-State Child Welfare Truth and Reconciliation Commission (METRC), the Metropolitan Detroit Truth and Reconciliation Commission on Racial Inequality (DTRC), the Liberian Truth and Reconciliation Commission Diaspora Project (LTRC), and two short-term truth commissions that addressed

---

[24] In 1993, before the SATRC was established, the authors of the postamble to South Africa's interim Constitution used the term to describe what the country's transition from an apartheid regime to a democracy needed to look like. "There is a need," they wrote in their historic postamble, "for understanding but not for vengeance, a need for reparation but not for retaliation, a need for *ubuntu* but not victimization" (as cited in Tutu, 1999b, p. 45). It was this threefold call for understanding, reparation, and *ubuntu* that prompted the South African Parliament (1995) to pass "The Promotion of National Unity and Reconciliation Act," the legislative act responsible for establishing the SATRC.

issues of poverty—to explore how the rhetorical tradition of transitional justice is being reaccentuated elsewhere in the country. Through this examination, Chap. 6 considers the place of transitional justice in liberal democracies. The chapter concludes by discussing the ramifications of this book's central arguments for scholars and practitioners working in the field of transitional justice.

Reconceptualizing Transitional Justice

In their book *Learning from Greensboro: Truth and Reconciliation in the United States*, Lisa Magarrell and Joya Wesley (2008) have provided a detailed account of the formation and operation of the GTRC, as well as valuable reflections on many elements of the TRC process in Greensboro. In their words, the purpose of their book was "to chronicle the moving and illuminating effort of the initiating Project and the GTRC it created, to peel back layers of lies and half-truths covering up this ugly piece of Greensboro's past" (p. xii). To do so, they focused on "the story of the truth-seeking process, the politics and people involved, and the ongoing work in the community to put the report to meaningful use" (p. xiii). While Magarrell and Wesley's *Learning from Greensboro* has offered a wealth of observations and insights on the GTRC and "its utility as an inspiration to further truth-seeking efforts in the United States," their book does not frame the Commission's work—or the field of transitional justice—in rhetorical terms.[25] By adopting a rhetorical perspective, my book provides new insights about the work of the GTRC and the field of transitional justice.

Conceptualizing the field of transitional justice in rhetorical terms is not a widespread practice, as an overview of the scholarship of the field suggests (Bassiouni, 2002; Hayner, 2001; Kritz, 1995; McAdams, 1997). Studies of the practices of transitional justice have tended to fall into one of two categories: predominately descriptive accounts (with some normative elements) or predominantly normative accounts (with some descriptive elements).[26] Predominantly descriptive accounts have typically

---

[25] For example, in describing the approach taken by truth commissions, Magarrell and Wesley (2008) stated, "Methodologically, truth commissions involve an amalgam of history, sociology, law, psychology, plain common sense, and whatever else is needed…" (p. 39). While these disciplines are certainly crucial to the approach that truth commissions take, it is also the case that the activities of truth commissions are, for the most part, discursive in nature. To give a second example, when writing about the mandate for the GTRC, Magarrell and Wesley (2008) noted, "The mandates of other truth commissions provided some guidance to people in Greensboro tasked with producing a draft for discussion. From there, drafters went to work on deciding the level of detail in setting out the Commission's tasks…" (p. 52). Here Magarrell and Wesley mentioned the influence of past commissions on the Greensboro process, but they did not elaborate on the specific discursive features of past truth commissions' mandates that were adapted to create the GTRC's mandate. My book suggests that we need to pay greater attention to the rhetorical moves at work in truth commission approaches and processes.

catalogued the practices of transitional justice, as well as their origins and effects. They have often done so by focusing on one or more case studies, an approach lending itself to comparative analysis and frequently resulting in a kind of typology of transitional justice practices.[27] Predominantly normative accounts have gone one step further: they have developed a set of criteria to evaluate past transitional justice practices and to guide the actions both of countries undergoing transformations toward democracy and of the international community's response to those countries.[28]

The majority of these studies, whether normative or descriptive, have explained transitional justice in terms of the institutional models it offers, or they have tended to focus on ways to adapt mechanisms of transitional justice—such as amnesty, reparations, truth-telling, etc.—to new contexts.[29] While these tendencies have not been unproductive, they have given short shrift to some of the other models that the field offers—namely, the patterned ways of using language, the figurative and argumentative devices, that accompany these institutions.[30] This book, therefore, is relevant to scholars and practitioners of transitional justice insofar as it brings into relief mechanisms of transitional justice that have been frequently overlooked: rhetorical mechanisms.

---

[26] This distinction is, of course, somewhat artificial: *all* descriptive accounts involve choices about what to describe and what not to describe and are, therefore, normative. It is worth noting that, regarding the scholarship on truth commissions in particular, Leman-Langlois and Shearing (2003) distinguished between "three broad types": normative or jurisprudential analysis, 'therapeutic' evaluations, and descriptive accounts (p. 223). Most therapeutic evaluations, however, tend to double as normative accounts.

[27] For predominately descriptive accounts of transitional justice, see Elster (2004); Minow (1998); and Doxtader and Villa-Vicencio (2003). Regarding truth commissions in particular, Hayner's (2001) *Unspeakable Truths* remains one of the most comprehensive descriptive accounts to date. Hayner (2001) described the purposes for truth commissions, surveyed 21 commissions, and considered some of the key issues surrounding truth commissions as they have arisen in various cases.

[28] Aukerman (2002), Crocker (1998, 1999), and Zalaquett (1995) have all attempted to develop normative frameworks of transitional justice. Regarding TRCs in particular, Garkawe (2003) and van Zyl (1999) have expressed cautious optimism about using the TRC model as a means of dealing with other human rights abuses, while Landsman (1996) has expressed greater skepticism about doing so. For additional examples of normative accounts, see Amstutz's (2004) call for political forgiveness as a strategy of transitional justice; Daye's (2004) development of a model of political forgiveness based on the transition in South Africa; and Posner and Vermeule's (2004) assertion that recent scholarship mistakenly treats transitional justice as distinct from ordinary justice and lawmaking as it occurs in democracies.

[29] There has been, moreover, a tendency to focus on transitional justice initiatives as separate from one another. While initiatives have often been compared and contrasted with one another, the interconnections between initiatives have been explored less often.

[30] That said, some studies have taken a sustained look at the rhetorical performances constituting and underlying the large-scale practices of transitional justice (Doxtader, 2001, 2003, 2004, 2007, 2009; Mack, 2012; Phelps, 2004; Salazar, 2002; Shaffer & Smith, 2004; Teitel, 2002). Though these language-oriented studies have not explicitly referred to the "rhetorical tradition" of the field of transitional justice, they have provided the grounds for one of this project's central arguments— namely, that there are rhetorical traditions circulating within the field of transitional justice. Chapter 2 explores these studies, and others, in greater detail.

Attending to the rhetorical tradition of transitional justice is especially important for the study of truth commissions in the United States context and other liberal democracies. As Philpott (2006, pp. 11–44) has noted, the goals of political reconciliation offered by national truth commissions have often been seen as incompatible with the values of liberalism. To the extent that the two are incompatible, it is unlikely that the United States' national or state governments will issue a call for a truth commission in the near future: most truth commissions will probably develop along lines similar to that of the GTRC—as grassroots initiatives that draw heavily on the rhetorical resources of past commissions and the transnational networking made possible by an emergent global civil society.

From Greensboro to South Africa

During one of my visits to Greensboro, on the morning before I attended the GTRC's Report Release Ceremony, I decided to explore the city's historic downtown area. Walking north on Elm Street, the city's main thoroughfare, I saw a number of traces of civil rights initiatives. One marker of this history, located at the corner of Martin Luther King, Jr. Drive and Elm Street, was a statue—a bronze-colored bust of King. Beneath the bust was a plaque, with the following inscription:

> Dr. Martin Luther King, Jr., planned to speak at Trinity AME Zion Church in Greensboro (A few blocks from here) on April 4, 1968. He canceled his visit to Greensboro to remain in Memphis where he was assassinated on that day.

Further north from King's statue, I saw the Woolworth's storefront. With its gold-plated lettering set against a stark red background, Woolworth's stood out on the strip. The store was being renovated as a museum, a tribute to the site where four black college students from North Carolina A&T University refused to move from their seats at a Greensboro lunch counter over 50 years ago. Even further north on Elm Street was another marker—this one, much less visible. It was the unassuming office building where the GTRC had rented office space during their operation. From King to Woolworth's to the Commission: it would be possible to develop this northbound journey on Elm Street into a narrative about the development of civil rights in Greensboro and frame the story as the means of authorization for the GTRC to carry out its mandate. But such an account would be incomplete. In order to understand the Commission's authorization, it is also necessary to look to a rhetorical tradition that has heretofore been most prominent *outside* of the United States— the rhetorical tradition of transitional justice.

References

Amstutz, M. R. (2004). *The healing of nations: The promise and limits of political forgiveness.* Lanham, MD: Rowman & Littlefield.

Andrus Family Fund. (n.d.). Mission statement. Retrieved March 1, 2012, from http://www.affund. org/docs/Mission_Statement.html.

Arendt, H. (1993). *Between past and future: Eight exercises in political thought.* New York, NY: Penguin.

Aristotle. (1991). *On rhetoric: A theory of civic discourse.* (G. A. Kennedy, Trans.). New York, NY: Oxford University Press.

Aukerman, M. (2002). Extraordinary evil, ordinary crime: A framework for understanding transitional justice. *Harvard Human Rights Journal, 15,* 39–97. Retrieved March 1, 2012, from http://www.law.harvard.edu/students/orgs/hrj/iss15/aukerman.shtml.

Bakhtin, M. M. (1981). Discourse in the novel. In M. Holquist (Ed.), *The dialogic imagination* (pp. 259–422). (C. Emerson and M. Holquist, Trans.). Austin, TX: University of Texas Press.

Bassiouni, M. C. (Ed.). (2002). *Post-conflict justice.* Ardsley, NY: Transnational.

Battle, M. (1997). *Reconciliation: The ubuntu theology of Desmond Tutu.* Cleveland, OH: Pilgrim.

Beitler, J. (2012). Making more of the middle ground: Desmond Tutu and the *ethos* of the South African Truth and Reconciliation Commission. *Relevant Rhetoric, 3,* 1–21. Retrieved June 1, 2012, from http://relevantrhetoric.com/wp-content/uploads/making-more-of-the-middle-ground.pdf.

Bermanzohn, S. A. (2003). *Through survivors' eyes: From the sixties to the Greensboro massacre.* Nashville, TN: Vanderbilt University Press.

Bermanzohn, P. C., & Bermanzohn, S. A. (1980). *The true story of the Greensboro massacre: Why the government conspired with the Klan and Nazis to murder the Communist Workers Party 5 in Greensboro on November 3, 1979. An account by eyewitnesses.* New York, NY: Câesar Cauce.

Bickford, L. (2005). Transitional justice. In D. Shelton (Ed.), *Encyclopedia of genocide and crimes against humanity* (Vol. 3, pp. 1045–1047). Detroit, MI: Macmillan Reference.

Butler, J. P. (1997). *Excitable speech: A politics of the performative.* New York, NY: Routledge.

Cabral/Robeson Collective & Greensboro Collective. (1980). The Greensboro massacre: Critical lessons for the 1980's: Part I: The massacre and aftermath [Pamphlet]. In P. Saba, (Ed.) *Encyclopedia of anti-revisionism on-line.* Retrieved March 1, 2012, from http://www.marxists. org/history/erol/ncm-5/greensboro/part1.htm.

Chafe, W. H. (1980). *Civilities and civil rights: Greensboro, North Carolina, and the black struggle for freedom.* New York, NY: Oxford University Press.

Clarke, L. (2005). Contesting definitional authority in the collective. *Quarterly Journal of Speech, 91*(1), 1–36. doi:10.1080/00335630500157490.

Committee to Avenge the Murder of the Communist Workers Party (Workers Viewpoint) 5. (1979). AVENGE the MURDER of the CWP 5! [Newsprint Poster]. J. A. Armfield Papers (Item#: 9.69:1226), Greensboro Historical Museum, Greensboro, NC. Retrieved March 1, 2012, from http://library.uncg.edu/dp/crg/item.aspx?i=1226#complete.

Coon, A. (Producer). (2002). *Greensboro's child* [Video file]. Retrieved October 7, 2007, from http://www.greensboroschild.com.

Cran, W., Tepper, S. (Producers), & Cran, W. (Director). (1983, Jan. 24). 88 seconds in Greensboro. In D. Fanning (Executive Producer), *Frontline* [News Documentary]. Boston, MA: Public Broadcasting Service. Retrieved October 10, 2007, from http://www.pbs.org/wgbh/pages/frontline/programs/transcripts/102.html.

Crocker, D. (1998). Transitional justice and international civil society: toward a normative framework. *Constellations, 5*(4), 492–517. doi:10.1111/1467-8675.00110.

Crocker, D. (1999). Reckoning with past wrongs: A normative framework. *Ethics and International Affairs, 13,* 43–64. doi:10.1111/j.1747-7093.1999.tb00326.x.

Davies, B., & Harré, R. (2001). Positioning: The discursive production of selves. In M. Wetherell, S. Taylor, & S. Yates (Eds.), *Discourse theory and practice: A reader* (pp. 261–271). London: Sage.

Daye, R. (2004). *Political forgiveness: Lessons from South Africa*. Maryknoll, NY: Orbis Books.

de Certeau, M. (1998). *The practice of everyday life*. Minneapolis, MN: University of Minnesota Press.

Doxtader, E. (2001). Making rhetorical history in a time of transition: The occasion, constitution, and representation of South African reconciliation. *Rhetoric & Public Affairs, 4*(2), 223–260. doi:10.1353/rap. 2001.0023.

Doxtader, E. (2003). Reconciliation—a rhetorical concept/ion. *Quarterly Journal of Speech, 89*(4), 267–292. doi:10.1080/0033563032000160954.

Doxtader, E. (2004). The potential of reconciliation's beginning: A reply. *Rhetoric & Public Affairs, 7*(3), 378–390. doi:10.1353/rap. 2005.0005.

Doxtader, E. (2007). The faith and struggle of beginning (with) words: On the turn between reconciliation and recognition. *Philosophy and Rhetoric, 40*(1), 119–146. doi:10.1353/par.2007.0011.

Doxtader, E. (2009). *With faith in the works of words: The beginnings of reconciliation in South Africa, 1985–1995*. East Lansing, MI: Michigan State University Press.

Doxtader, E., & Villa-Vicencio, C. (Eds.). (2003). *Through fire with water: The roots of division and the potential for reconciliation in Africa*. Trenton, NJ: Africa World Press.

Elster, J. (2004). *Closing the books: Transitional justice in historical perspective*. New York, NY: Cambridge University Press.

Erickson, F. (2004). *Talk and social theory: Ecologies of speaking and listening in everyday life*. Malden, MA: Polity Press.

Farrell, T. B. (1993). *Norms of rhetorical culture*. New Haven, CT: Yale University Press.

Gaonkar, D. P. (1989). The oratorical text: The enigma of arrival. In M. C. Leff & F. J. Kauffeld (Eds.), *Texts in context: critical dialogues on significant episodes in American political rhetoric* (pp. 255–276). Davis, CA: Hermagoras Press.

Gaonkar, D. P. (1990). Object and method in rhetorical criticism: From Wichelns to Leff and McGee. *Western Journal of Speech Communication, 54*(3), 290–316.

Garkawe, S. B. (2003). The South African Truth and Reconciliation Commission: A suitable model to enhance the role and rights of the victims of gross violations of human rights? *Melborune University Law Review, 27*(2), 334–380. Retrieved abstract March 1, 2012, from http://epubs.scu.edu.au/law_pubs/172/.

Greensboro Truth and Community Reconciliation Project. (2003). Mandate for the Greensboro Truth and Reconciliation Commission. Retrieved October 5, 2007, from http://www.greensborotrc.org/mandate.php.

Greensboro Truth and Community Reconciliation Project. (2004, June 12). Swearing In and Seating Ceremony of the Greensboro Truth and Reconciliation Commission [DVD]. Copy in possession of author.

Greensboro Truth and Reconciliation Commission. (2006). *The Greensboro Truth and Reconciliation Commission final report: An examination of the context, causes, sequence and consequence of the events of November 3, 1979*. Retrieved March 1, 2012, from http://www.greensborotrc.org/.

Halloran, S. M. (1982). Aristotle's concept of ethos, or if not his somebody else's. *Rhetoric Review, 1*(1), 58–63. doi:10.1080/07350198209359037.

Harré, R., & Slocum, N. (2003). Disputes as complex social events: On the uses of positioning theory. *Common Knowledge, 9*(1), 100–118. doi:10.1215/0961754X-9-1-100.

Hayner, P. B. (2001). *Unspeakable truths: Confronting state terror and atrocity*. New York, NY: Routledge.

Hyde, M. J. (2004). *The ethos of rhetoric*. Columbia, SC: University of South Carolina Press.

Jarratt, S., & Reynolds, N. (1994). The splitting image: Contemporary feminisms and the ethics of *ethos*. In J. S. Baumlin & T. F. Baumlin (Eds.), *Ethos: New essays in rhetorical and critical theory* (pp. 37–64). Dallas, TX: Southern Methodist University Press.

Jasinski, J. (1997). Instrumentalism, contextualism, and interpretation in rhetorical criticism. In A. G. Gross & W. M. Keith (Eds.), *Rhetorical hermeneutics: Invention and interpretation in the age of science* (pp. 195–224). Albany, NY: State University of New York Press.

Jasinski, J. (2001). *Sourcebook on rhetoric: Key concepts in contemporary rhetorical studies.* Thousand Oaks, CA: Sage.

King, M. L., Jr. (1963/2004). Letter from Birmingham jail. In D. McQuade & R. Atwan (Eds.), *The writer's presence: A pool of readings* (pp. 692–707). Boston, MA: Bedford/St. Martin's.

Kritz, N. J. (Ed.). (1995). *Transitional justice: How emerging democracies reckon with former regimes.* Washington, DC: United States Institute of Peace Press.

Landsman, S. (1996). Alternative responses to serious human rights abuses: Of prosecution and truth commissions. *Law and Contemporary Problems, 59*(4), 81–92. Retrieved September 19, 2012, from http://jstor.org/stable/1192192.

Leff, M. C. (1992). Things made by words: Reflections on textual criticism. *Quarterly Journal of Speech, 78,* 223–331. doi:10.1080/00335639209383991.

Leff, M. C. (1997). The idea of rhetoric as interpretive practice: A humanist's response to Gaonkar. In A. G. Gross & W. M. Keith (Eds.), *Rhetorical hermeneutics: Invention and interpretation in the age of science* (pp. 89–100). Albany, NY: State University of New York Press.

Leff, M. C. (2000). Textual criticism: The legacy of G. P. Mohrmann. In C. Burgchardt (Ed.), *Readings in rhetorical criticism* (pp. 546–557). State College, PA: Strata.

Leff, M. C., & Sachs, A. (1990). Words the most like things: Iconicity and the rhetorical text. *Western Journal of Speech Communication, 54,* 252–273. doi: 10.1080/10570319009374342.

Leman-Langlois, S., & Shearing, C. D. (2003). Repairing the future: The South African Truth and Reconciliation Commission at work. In G. P. Gilligan & J. Pratt (Eds.), *Crime, truth and justice: Official inquiry, discourse, knowledge* (pp. 222–242). Cullompton, UK: Willan.

Mack, K. (2012). *A generative failure: The public hearings of South Africa's Truth and Reconciliation Commission.* Manuscript in preparation.

Magarrell, L. (2002). *Developing a truth commission mandate and selecting a commission [Memo to Greensboro Massacre Reconciliation Project].* New York, NY: International Center for Transitional Justice Library.

Magarrell, L., & Wesley, J. (2008). *Learning from Greensboro: Truth and reconciliation in the United States.* Philadelphia, PA: University of Pennsylvania Press.

Mann, E. (1997). Greensboro: A requiem. In *Testimonies: Four Plays* (pp. 247–330). New York, NY: Theatre Communications Group.

McAdams, A. J. (Ed.). (1997). *Transitional justice and the rule of law in new democracies.* Notre Dame, IN: University of Notre Dame Press.

Minow, M. (1998). *Between vengeance and forgiveness: Facing history after genocide and mass violence.* Boston, MA: Beacon.

Morowitz, N., & Brummel, B. (Producers). (2000, Oct. 14). Lawbreakers: The Greensboro massacre [Documentary]. New York, NY: A&E Television Networks.

Murphy, J. M. (1997). Inventing authority: Bill Clinton, Martin Luther King, Jr., and the orchestration of rhetorical traditions. *Quarterly Journal of Speech, 83*(1), 71–89. doi: 10.1080/00335639709384172.

North Carolina Advisory Committee to the United States Commission on Civil Rights. (1981). *Black/white perceptions: Race relations in Greensboro: A report.* Washington, DC: United States Commission on Civil Rights. Edward Burrows Papers (Item# 1.5.123), The University of North Carolina at Greensboro, Greensboro, NC. Retrieved March 1, 2012, from http://library.uncg.edu/dp/crg/item.aspx?i=123.

Parliament of the Republic of South Africa. (1995, July 19). *Promotion of national unity and reconciliation act 34 of 1995.* Retrieved March 1, 2012, from http://www.justice.gov.za/legislation/acts/1995-034.pdf.

Phelps, T. G. (2004). *Shattered voices: Language, violence, and the work of truth commissions.* Philadelphia: University of Pennsylvania Press.

Philpott, D. (2006). Beyond politics as usual: Is reconciliation compatible with liberalism? In D. Philpott (Ed.), *The politics of past evil: Religion, reconciliation, and the dilemmas of transitional justice* (pp. 11–44). Notre Dame, IN: University of Notre Dame Press.

Posner, E., & Vermeule, A. (2004). Transitional justice as ordinary justice. *Harvard Law Review, 117*(3), 761–825.

Reynolds, N. (1993). Ethos as location: New sites for understanding discursive authority. *Rhetoric Review, 11*(2), 325–338. doi:10.1080/07350199309389009.

Salazar, P. J. (2002). *An African Athens: Rhetoric and the shaping of democracy in South Africa.* Mahwah, NJ: L. Erlbaum.

Shaffer, K., & Smith, S. (2004). *Human rights and narrated lives: The ethics of recognition.* New York, NY: Palgrave Macmillan.

Taylor, G. S. (2009). *The history of the North Carolina Communist Party.* Columbia, SC: University of South Carolina Press.

Teitel, R. G. (2002). Transitional justice as liberal narrative. In O. Enwezor (Ed.), *Experiments with truth: Transitional justice and the processes of truth and reconciliation: Documenta 11_ Platform 2* (pp. 241–260). Ostfildern-Ruit: Hatje Cantz.

Truth and reconciliation: Listen for yourself. (2005, April 20). *News & Record* [Audio file]. Retrieved April 20, 2008, from http://blog.news-record.com/staff/scoopblog/2005/04/truth_and_recon_1.shtml.

Tutu, D. (1999a). Foreword by chairperson. In *Truth and Reconciliation Commission of South Africa Report* (Vol. 1, pp. 1–23). New York, NY: Grove's Dictionaries.

Tutu, D. (1999b). *No future without forgiveness.* New York, NY: Doubleday.

Tutu, D. (2005). Reconciling love: A millennium mandate. *2005–2006 Bryan series lectures on spirit and spirituality* [videocassette]. Hege Library, Guilford College, Greensboro, NC.

Van Zyl, P. (1999). Dilemmas of transitional justice: The case of South Africa's Truth and Reconciliation Commission. *Journal of International Affairs, 52*(2), 647–667. Retrieved March 1, 2012, from http://0-search.proquest.com.helin.uri.edu/docview/220709979?accountid=25133.

Waller, S. (2002). *Love and revolution: A political memoir.* Lanham, MD: Rowman & Littlefield.

Wheaton, E. (1987). *Codename greenkil: The 1979 Greensboro killings.* Athens, GA: University of Georgia Press.

Wolin, S. (1999). On the theory and practice of power. In N. Coupland, S. Sarangi, & C. Candlin (Eds.), *After Foucault: Humanistic knowledge, post-modern challenges* (pp. 179–201). New Brunswick, NJ: Rutgers University Press.

Zalaquett, J. (1995). Confronting human rights violations committed by former governments: Principles applicable and political constraints. In N. J. Kritz (Ed.), *Transitional justice: How emerging democracies reckon with former regimes* (Vol. 1, pp. 3–31). Washington, DC: United States Institute of Peace Press.

Chapter 2
The Rhetorical Tradition of Transitional Justice

Abstract This chapter surveys prior scholarship about transitional justice, with an emphasis on studies about the South African Truth and Reconciliation Commission. It marshals this research to make the case that the development of the field of transitional justice has given rise to a rhetorical tradition that provides those working in the field with a series of "enabling constraints." It highlights the specific argumentative devices of the rhetorical tradition, such as the ideograph of reconciliation, truth commissions' means of establishing *ethos*, and the genre of the truth commission final report. This discussion provides the necessary background for the rhetorical analyses in subsequent chapters, which explore how the elements of the tradition discussed here were reaccentuated by the members of the Greensboro Truth and Reconciliation Commission to meet the contingent demands of their own context.

J.E. Beitler III, *Remaking Transitional Justice in the United States*,   29
Springer Series in Transitional Justice, DOI 10.1007/978-1-4614-5295-9_2,
© Springer Science+Business Media New York 2013

"Rhetorical traditions consist of common patterns of language use, manifest in performance, and generative of a shared means for making sense of the world."

John M. Murphy (1997, p. 72)

Introduction

The field of transitional justice is an expansive one. Its practices are wide-ranging, as are the research methods used to explore those practices. However, in the scholarly literature, transitional justice has most frequently been talked about in terms of the repertoire of policies and mechanisms available to countries and communities to address past injustices, including amnesty, historical inquiry and truth telling, reparations, lustration, and trials.[1] These mechanisms have often been discussed or evaluated in terms of their ability or lack of ability to bring about democracy as well as other perceived normative goods, including retribution, justice, official acknowledgment, reconciliation, and forgiveness. What many of these policy-oriented and/or mechanism-oriented studies have implicitly acknowledged but have not explicitly explored is the role of language in such practices. For example, when the *International Journal of Transitional Justice* debuted, the editors (Fletcher & van der Merwe, 2007) defined the journal in interdisciplinary terms and highlighted the importance of effective communication (p. 2); however, when describing the journal's disciplinary scope, they did not include disciplines such as communication, linguistics, language studies, and rhetorical studies:

> [W]e [those working in the field of transitional justice] have seen increased interest from political scientists, anthropologists, theologians, philosophers, sociologists, educators, psychologists, epidemiologists, forensic anthropologists and conflict resolution/peacebuilding scholars in examining the complexities of justice and social reconstruction….The theoretical papers [in this journal] come from scholars in anthropology, law, political science, education, geography, and sociology. (pp. 2–3)

Despite this omission, an increasing number of scholars have recognized the value of language-oriented studies for both critics and practitioners working in the field (Doxtader, 2001, 2003, 2004, 2007, 2009; Mack, 2012; Phelps, 2004; Salazar, 2002; Shaffer & Smith, 2004; Teitel, 2002). What much of this language-oriented research has implied, and the present chapter attempts to demonstrate, is that the field of transitional justice has given rise to a rhetorical tradition. In other words, in the activities and inquiries that comprise the field of transitional justice, there are "common patterns of language use…marked by characteristic figurative and argumentative devices" (Murphy, 1997, p. 72).[2] These patterns provide those working in the

---

[1] For example, Olsen, Payne, and Reiter (2010) restricted their analysis to "the five main mechanisms most commonly recognized by scholars and practitioners as transitional justice: trials, truth commissions, amnesties, reparations, and lustration" (p. 805).

[2] I define "patterns" as regular or reoccurring forms, sequences, or arrangements of rhetorical features that are found in, and often across, particular rhetorical situations or contexts.

field with a series of "enabling constraints": they both limit action and, simultaneously, make new action possible (Butler, 1997, p. 16; Murphy, 1997, p. 85).

The intent, in demonstrating these points, is not to be exhaustive, which—given the scope and history of the field of transitional justice—is more than any one book could accomplish; rather, it is to provide sufficient evidence to demonstrate the existence of this rhetorical tradition and highlight a few of its features. For the purposes of the current project, then, the focus is on those aspects of the rhetorical tradition associated with truth commissions, with a special emphasis on the patterns surrounding the South African Truth and Reconciliation Commission (SATRC). The SATRC was instituted in 1995 to address "gross violations of human rights" in the country through mechanisms of public truth-telling, individual amnesty, and reparations (SATRC, 1999, p. 48). As the most powerful and well-known truth commission to date (Hayner, 2001, pp. 41–43), the SATRC has arguably had a greater impact on the field of transitional justice than any other truth commission. For that reason, it is a productive site to study to highlight the field's rhetorical tradition.

Rather than focus on the discourse produced by the SATRC itself, this chapter focuses primarily on scholarship about the Commission. While the rhetorical tradition of transitional justice could certainly be explored using primary documents, journalistic accounts, or creative responses to the Commission, much of the scholarship on the SATRC has implicitly—and, on occasion, explicitly—focused on issues of language use. These studies serve as sites where the rhetorical tradition can be productively explored. This chapter, then, employs a review of the scholarly literature about the SATRC to advance one of this book's central arguments: the field of transitional justice has given rise to a rhetorical tradition.

To make this case, it is necessary to show that "patterns of language use" have, in fact, circulated within the field. That is, it is not enough to note specific instances of rhetorical activity. What must be shown is that this rhetorical activity has included repetitions, characteristic features, and specific conventions. This point highlights an important complication when exploring rhetorical traditions: examining a rhetorical tradition directly—as if it was, for example, a distant star that could be viewed with the naked eye—is not possible. Rhetorical traditions themselves are not directly visible; they can only be viewed by looking at specific rhetorical performances, which are traces or instantiations of the tradition. Demonstrating the existence of a rhetorical tradition is, in other words, less like examining a visible star than it is like observing a black hole. Though they cannot be seen directly, black holes can be studied because they exert powerful effects on their galactic environments, influencing the way that light around them behaves. Similarly, rhetorical traditions shape language use, and, by pointing out patterns in specific performances, we can begin to infer what the tradition looks like. This chapter draws upon scholarship about the SATRC to highlight several of these patterns.

A second issue, related to the first, is that rhetorical traditions are not static: even as they shape rhetorical performances, the performances shape the traditions. Tradition and performance are, in other words, mutually constitutive. As features of the traditions are performed, the patterned ways of using language can become reified or can develop into new patterns. Some patterns may emerge as others dwindle from common usage. Because rhetorical traditions can be shaped by their instantiations in rhetorical performances, it is necessary when studying them to take into account the historical and geographical context—when and where the performances occur. While there are likely to be common or interrelated patterns when comparing the rhetorical tradition of transitional justice at different times and places, the tradition—when analyzed at a particular location—is different today than it was in previous decades; and the tradition—when analyzed at a particular time—differs from one context to the next. As such, the tradition can be studied both synchronically and diachronically, and it can be studied in or across various locales. In reading scholarship devoted to the SATRC, this chapter attempts to elucidate features of the rhetorical tradition of transitional justice that emerged in South Africa in the mid- to late-nineties. Subsequent chapters of this book demonstrate how these features were reaccentuated in Greensboro, North Carolina from 1999 to 2006.

In addition, it is important to note that rhetorical traditions shape all aspects of discourse—grammar, word choice, figures of speech, appeals, arguments, genres, etc. Patterns of any one of these aspects of discourse may reinforce or attenuate the rhetorical force of other patterns. In order to gesture toward the scope of the rhetorical tradition of transitional justice and point to the need for subsequent analyses that explore its complexity in more detail, this chapter reveals patterns of language use that occur at three levels: word choice, argument, and genre. More specifically, it focuses on the use of the term "reconciliation" in South Africa, the construction of the SATRC's institutional *ethos,* and the Commission's *Final Report.* My observations in this chapter provide the necessary background for the rhetorical analyses of subsequent chapters, which explore how the elements of the tradition discussed here were reaccentuated by the GTRC to meet the contingent demands of its context.

Reconciliation as Ideograph

Rhetorical traditions contain patterned ways of using words and phrases. One means, therefore, of bringing into relief the rhetorical tradition of transitional justice is to highlight the recurring ways that words are used rhetorically in the field. To that end, this section of the chapter surveys scholarship about the SATRC that, either implicitly or explicitly, has explored the ideograph of reconciliation. I begin by explain what ideographs are and how they function rhetorically.

Not all rhetorical activity is consciously created or evaluated by an audience. One of the ways that texts function rhetorically is to constitute individuals' and groups' identities, often in unconscious ways (Charland, 1987). As many contemporary rhetoricians have acknowledged, it is not possible for an audience to understand a text with complete objectivity or to make unbiased judgments about the persuasiveness of its claims, in part because of our own presuppositions and in part because, as texts unfold, they shape us, calling us to embrace ideologies that are not necessarily articulated explicitly in the text (Charland, 1987). Michael Calvin

McGee (1980) explored one way that this sort of rhetorical activity occurs at the level of words and phrases—through the use of ideographs.

McGee (1980) distinguished between argumentation, which typically involves a rhetor demonstrating the truth of a proposition to an audience able to judge the statement's veracity, and what he called the "rhetoric of control"—"a system of persuasion" used to reinforce the ideologies of the powerful, often through unconscious appeal (p. 6). The latter need not be propositional in nature: some terms or phrases, which McGee referred to as "ideographs" and likened to Chinese characters, "signify and 'contain' a unique ideological commitment" (p. 7). More specifically, McGee defined the ideograph as "an ordinary-language term found in political discourse. It is a high-order abstraction representing collective commitment to a particular but ill-defined normative goal" (p. 15). One of the examples he gave, which holds much significance to those working in the field of transitional justice, is the phrase "rule of law":

> Within the vocabulary of argumentation, the term "rule of law" makes no sense until it is made the subject or predicable of a proposition. If I say "The rule of law is a primary cultural value in the United States"…I have asserted a testable claim that may be criticized with logically coordinated observations. When I say simply "the rule of law," however, my utterance cannot qualify logically as a claim. Yet I am conditioned to believe that [terms like "the rule of law"] have an obvious meaning, a behaviorally directive self evidence. Because I am taught to set such terms apart from my usual vocabulary, words used as agencies of social control may have an intrinsic force—and, if so, I may very well distort the key terms of social conflict, commitment, and control if I think of them as parts of a proposition rather than as basic units of analysis…What "rule of law" means is the series of propositions, all of them, that could be manufactured to justify a Whig/Liberal order. (pp. 6–7)

In spite of, or perhaps because of, the fact that an ideograph stands in for multiple propositions (i.e., it is "ill-defined"), people come to embrace the term as a normative goal. The term can then be used in political discourse to "[warrant] the use of power, [excuse] behavior and belief which might otherwise be perceived as eccentric or antisocial, and [guide] behavior and belief into channels easily recognized by a community as acceptable and laudable" (p. 15). For McGee, ideographic analysis involves two approaches: synchronic analysis, which explores an ideograph's interaction with other related terms at a particular point in time, and diachronic analysis, which considers the term's meaning at different points in time (pp. 10–14).

The discourse surrounding the operation of the SATRC was replete with ideographs, the two most prevalent, of course, coming from the Commission's title: "truth" and "reconciliation." Not surprisingly, much of scholarship on the SATRC has revolved around the meaning and function of these two terms. For the purposes of this chapter, I focus primarily on demonstrating, through scholarship about the SATRC, that reconciliation has functioned as an ideograph—a finding that lends support to my claim that the practices of transitional justice have given rise to a rhetorical tradition. Conceptualizing reconciliation as an ideograph has scholarly precedent. In his book *Race and Reconciliation: Redressing Wounds of Injustice*, John B. Hatch (2009) developed a theoretical framework that enables critics to better understand reconciliation discourse by considering it in light of four motives for reconciliation: truth, agency, justice, and peace (p. 149). Hatch acknowledged that such terms are ideographs, and his theory was similar to McGee's "in its focus on key orienting terms of society, their relations to each other, and their development…over time" (p. 150). While Hatch ultimately distinguished his approach from McGee's, he noted, "[O]ne could readily perform ideographic analysis of reconciliation discourse" (p. 150).

It is not my intent to conduct an *ideographic analysis* of reconciliation; rather, the next sections of this chapter highlight reconciliation's *ideographic characteristics* to highlight this facet of the rhetorical tradition of transitional justice. As patterned ways of using language, ideographs are part of the fabric of rhetorical traditions, and they serve as one of the "characteristic devices" that subsequent rhetors are able to reaccentuate to meet the contingent demands of their own rhetorical context. In what follows, I synthesize the work of other scholars to highlight the following characteristics of reconciliation discourse in South Africa, which are consistent with McGee's (1980) definition of ideographs: reconciliation represented collective commitment to ill-defined yet normative goals; its meaning was tied to a multiplicity of underlying propositions; its meaning intersected with a constellation of related terms; and it was used to warrant the use of power, excuse behavior, and guide belief (i.e., it was used rhetorically).

Collective Commitment to Reconciliation as a Normative Goal

At the national level, at least, the formation of the SATRC expressed a collective commitment to reconciliation as a normative goal—a key feature of ideographs. However, though reconciliation was sought after as a normative goal at the national level, calls for reconciliation in South Africa were by no means universally accepted by all constituencies: some worried about the religious associations of the term (Dwyer, 1999, p. 2); others feared that reconciliation—and related practices advocated by the SATRC—denied the demands of justice. Journalist Antjie Krog (1998) expressed this worry in her book *Country of My Skull: Guilt, Sorrow, and the Limits of Forgiveness in the New South Africa*: "The word 'reconciliation' is used most often by Afrikaner politicians. Although you might expect them to use it as a cover-up for their fear that they alone will be held responsible for the country's shameful past, they mainly prefer to use it as a threat…They use reconciliation to dictate their demands" (p. 143). Another oft-cited example, which called the legality of the SATRC's authority into question, was the court case *Azanian Peoples Organisation (AZAPO) and Others v. President of the Republic of South Africa and Others* (1996). In the case, supporters of murdered political activists attempted to demonstrate that the Promotion of National Unity and Reconciliation Act, which established the SATRC, was unconstitutional. Ultimately, though, the constitutionality of the Act was upheld: the approach of the SATRC—including its aim of reconciliation—was reaffirmed by the State. In the legal opinion following the court's ruling, Justice J. P. Mahomed wrote, "It was wisely appreciated…that the task of building such a new democratic order…could not be achieved without a firm and generous commitment to reconciliation" (AZAPO, 1996, p. 676). The state's defense of reconciliation ensured that, despite some critics and detractors, its status as a normative goal was maintained.

The Ambiguity of Reconciliation

Part of reconciliation's potential to function as a normative goal was tied to its connotations, which, according to Dwyer (1999), were "almost exclusively positive" (p. 2). Although Dwyer questioned reconciliation's religious connotations, she noted that reconciliation suggested "an end to antagonisms, the graceful acceptance of disappointment or defeat, the healing and repair of valuable friendships, and so on" (p. 2). These positive connotations, however, did not ensure clear, precise, and agreed-upon denotations of the term. Dwyer asked, "But what is reconciliation? Curiously, given the frequency with which the term 'reconciliation' is used, no one is saying" (p. 1). Like Dwyer, many scholars have commented on the fact that, throughout the operation of the SATRC, the term's meaning was ambiguous or, in McGee's terms, ill-defined—another key feature of ideographs.

According to SATRC scholar Hugo van der Merwe (2001), the ambiguity of the term was rooted in two pieces of legislation that established the SATRC: the "National Unity and Reconciliation" section of the interim Constitution and the Promotion of National Unity and Reconciliation Act. Such legislation, claimed van der Merwe, attempted to appease everybody, addressing the demands of political parties and non-government organizations alike (p. 87). In attempting to meet the demands of multiple constituencies, the terms of the South African transition were necessarily ambiguous. Van der Merwe wrote that "nowhere in the Act [was] the meaning of reconciliation given any real substance" (p. 88). This lack of precision about reconciliation in the SATRC's founding documents continued during the Commission's operation and hindered the efficacy of the outreach strategies and public policy of the SATRC; van der Merwe cited a 1997 personal interview with a South African NGO staff member, who claimed that the SATRC lacked "a coherent vision of where it [was] taking people" (p. 99).[3] SATRC scholar Rosemary Nagy (2002) agreed with van der Merwe's assessment, insisting that the SATRC's failure to adequately define reconciliation resulted in a lack of direction for efforts to promote it: "Projections as to what would constitute a successful project of reconciliation, or what a reconciled people or persons ought to look like are generally hazy" (p. 326).

For Hamber and van der Merwe (1998), this ambiguity led, in turn, to definitional variations among members of the public:

> [D]espite the Truth and Reconciliation Commission (TRC) popularizing the term, the [SATRC] has not provided the country with a clear definition of what it really means...The result is that very seldom is anyone in South Africa talking about the same thing when they refer to reconciliation. Equally so, the final outcome of a so-called reconciled South Africa means different things to different people. (para. 2)

Nagy's (2004) findings were consistent with Hamber and van der Merwe's claims: she reported that, according to a 2003 survey, nearly one-third of the South

---

[3] According to the NGO staff member, "The [SATRC's] approach to reconciliation is very vague… It lacks an organized strategy to reach out to communities and involve them. Victims do not know what to expect and they are absent from any participation in the policy process" (van der Merwe, 2001, p. 99).

Africans polled were unable to explain the concept of reconciliation (p. 719). For Nagy, the SATRC's failure to define reconciliation was not simply bad policy; it was also potentially dangerous. She wrote, "Without basic agreement on its meaning, reconciliation remains at best an elusive goal; at worst, it is empty rhetoric subject to political and ideological manipulation" (2002, p. 326). Her remark, with its emphasis on reconciliation as an ambiguous goal connected to ideology, suggests that the term is, in fact, an ideograph.[4]

Reconciliation's Many Meanings: A Multiplicity of Propositions

The term's ambiguity may have been the result of a surplus of definitions, as opposed to a lack of them (VanAntwerpen, 2010, p. 46).[5] As McGee (1980) noted of the phrase "rule of law," what a given ideograph "means is the series of propositions, all of them, that could be manufactured to justify" a particular ideological position (p. 7). Erik Doxtader—who has written extensively on reconciliation from a rhetorical perspective (2001, 2003, 2004, 2007, 2009)—highlighted the link between reconciliation's overabundance of meanings and the fact that it remains ill-defined. Doxtader noted, "Charles Villa-Vicencio, former director of research for the TRC, contends that South African reconciliation has many faces and voices. If so, the study of reconciliation brings us into a labyrinth in which reference is far from certain, a puzzle that obliges us to concede that we may not know what reconciliation *is*" (2001, p. 224).

SATRC scholars have made various attempts to catalog reconciliation's many definitions. Hamber and van der Merwe (1998) outlined five conceptions of reconciliation that emerged during the SATRC, each of which was tied to different South African constituencies. The five conceptions they identified included the dissolution of racial identities (para. 4); understanding between communities in opposition to one another (para. 5); confession, forgiveness, and new birth (para. 6); "social interaction" and the "prevention of violence" through the rule of law (para. 7); and "community building" at the local level among individuals (para. 8). Likewise, Posel (2002) noted several characteristics of reconciliation that emerged in South Africa, which were "inspired by a cluster of meanings around the idea" (p. 150). Her short list included individual, interpersonal, and collective healing that recognized others' humanity; nation-building that was rooted in the construction of "a 'shared' history"; and compromise (p. 150). Nagy (2002) defined reconciliation as

---

[4] Hamber and Van der Merwe (1998) commented on the term's connections to ideology as well, referring to reconciliation's "hegemonic ideologies" (para. 18). Other scholars have, however, offered a more sympathetic analysis of reconciliation's ambiguity. Verdoolaege (2008), for one, contended that such ambiguity was intentional, allowing for a more inclusive process (p. 167).

[5] About this point, VanAntwerpen (2010) wrote, "[T]he extensive usage of the word 'reconciliation' continues to hide a great diversity of meaning… The wonder of reconciliation is not an absence of definitions but an abundance of meanings" (p. 46).

"building solidarity," and she highlighted the presence of "thick" accounts of solidarity that require the moral transformation of individuals and "thin" accounts that are closer to mediated compromise or agreement (pp. 326, 329).

The Constellation of Terms Surrounding Reconciliation

As these definitions reveal, reconciliation's meanings and functions were tied to a cluster of related terms, and—in ways not inconsistent with McGee's description of synchronic analysis—many scholars have explored the relationship between reconciliation and these terms.[6] For the purposes of this chapter, I briefly survey a few scholars' remarks about three of the terms: amnesty, forgiveness, and *ubuntu*. A more complete survey is beyond the scope of the present work; however, my point is not to be comprehensive but to provide enough evidence to demonstrate that reconciliation served as an ideograph during the South African transition.

Janet Cherry, John Daniel, and Madeleine Fullard (2002)—who noted that, in developing a truth commission, "much time was spent on the arduous process of developing definitions"—explained that the call for reconciliation dovetailed with a call for amnesty, which "was seen largely as a sop to the right wing, an attempt to sweeten the pill for those opposed to the very creation of the Commission" (pp. 25–26). Likewise, Doxtader's (2001) analysis of the postamble of the South African interim Constitution pointed out that this legislation substituted reconciliation for amnesty when it stated the following: "In order to advance…reconciliation and reconstruction, amnesty shall be granted in respect of acts, omissions and offences associated with political objectives and committed in the course of the conflicts of the past" (p. 247).

Reconciliation was also conflated with forgiveness, and, as many have noted, the merging of these terms privileged Christian notions of reconciliation, both during the Commission's operation and in its report. Graeme Simpson (2002) claimed that the language of forgiveness pervaded the discourse surrounding the SATRC to such an extent that the Commission itself had a religious quality (pp. 239–240). The result, Simpson said, was that the TRC cultivated the "onerous expectation" that "reconciliation depended on the victim's ability to forgive" (pp. 239–240). Similarly, Njabulo Ndebele (2001) argued that the Commission's conflation of reconciliation and forgiveness hampered dialogue. He wrote, "The linking of reconciliation directly with forgiveness closed off many other angles of discussion" (p. 152). Many scholars and commentators, including Nbelele, have contended that reconciliation's religious

---

[6] While much of the scholarship surveyed in this chapter is more consistent with McGee's (1980) notion of synchronic analysis, there are scholars who have analyzed reconciliation diachronically. Jonathan VanAntwerpen (2010), for example, investigated reconciliation's meaning over time and beyond the South African context, and he contended that there "has been a trend towards the attempted 'liberalization' and 'secularization' of reconciliation discourse, especially among elite international actors, the globetrotting cosmopolitans who occupy influential positions within global civil society" (p. 34). Such findings are consistent with Teitel's (2002) observations about the liberalizing trajectory of transitional narratives (p. 252).

connotations were emphasized because Archbishop Desmond Tutu served as the SATRC's chairperson. "The more I read the Commission's Report," Ndebele wrote, "the more I become convinced that the predominance of religious connotation in the public discourse on reconciliation resulted from a tendency for many of us to focus on the Chairperson of the Commission as a man of God" (p. 152). Along these lines, Yadh Ben Achour (2002) remarked how, because of Tutu, the SATRC's processes "bore a strong resemblance to the act of repentance" (p. 132); and Avishai Margalit (2002) suggested that Tutu associated reconciliation with the Christian doctrine of atonement (p. 63).

The South African notion of *ubuntu*—which has often been translated as "a person is a person through other persons" and defined in terms of human interdependence—was also associated with reconciliation during the operation of the SATRC.[7] This association was established, in part, through the postamble to South Africa's interim Constitution. According to the postamble, reconciliation was a necessity—i.e., it claimed that unity and peace "required" reconciliation—and this necessity entailed "a need for understanding but not for vengeance, a need for reparation but not for retaliation, a need for *ubuntu* but not victimization" (Tutu, 1999b, p. 45). Throughout the life of the Commission, Chairperson Desmond Tutu reinforced the connection between *ubuntu* and reconciliation. The concept was central to his theology (Battle, 1997), and he frequently employed the term when defending the Commission's emphasis on reconciliation and restorative justice. This emphasis on *ubuntu* during the truth and reconciliation process has been explored from a number of angles. Some, like philosopher Augustine Shutte (2001), viewed the emphasis as a positive one. Shutte claimed that *ubuntu* offers an ethic for all of life, and he attempted to develop an ethical framework that explored the relationship between *ubuntu* and gender, sex and the family, education, healthcare, work, politics, and religion. "[It] is my view," he wrote, "that the understanding and vision of humanity embodied in the concept of *ubuntu* is something of vital importance to the contemporary world, not just to contemporary South Africa but to all the rest of the nations as well, developed or undeveloped" (p. 2). Others, like Christoph Marx (2002), argued that *ubuntu* was being used to cultivate a new cultural nationalism that uncritically replaced the nationalism promoted by many Afrikaners during the apartheid era. Demonstrating the parallels between the development of Afrikaner nationalism and the nation-building project of the "new" South Africa, Marx claimed that *ubuntu* was being used to promote conformity inimical to the development of democracy (pp. 50, 52).

Using Reconciliation Rhetorically

Another key feature of ideographs is that they have rhetorical force. While reconciliation was, of course, employed for many different rhetorical purposes in South Africa, this section focuses on one particularly forceful way that reconciliation was used rhetorically: as a prompt to encourage people to engage in dialogue. Doxtader (2003) claimed that reconciliation was a "call for rhetoric and a form of

---

[7] Chapter 3 provides a more thorough analysis of *ubuntu* and its connotations.

rhetorical activity" (p. 268). For him, reconciliation's ambiguous meanings were tied to the fact that one of the term's key functions was redefinition: calls for reconciliation in South Africa were calls to reinvent the past, which allowed acts of redefinition to take place, including redefinitions of reconciliation itself (pp. 268–269). Put another way, as reconciliation was employed in public discourse, it invited more discourse, including discourse about what the term itself meant.[8]

Reconciliation's power to reinvent and redefine the past had the rhetorical potential to enable dialogue between adversaries (Doxtader 2003, pp. 268–269). Doxtader (2009) contended that, through calls for reconciliation, opposing parties may have been able to realize that they shared together in something—their opposition to one another (pp. 3–4, 90–91). Without negating "adversarial discourse," a call for reconciliation "fashions its potential in distinction to that violence, which forecloses on those history-making words that invite human beings to begin in relation" (Doxtader, 2004, p. 379). Van der Merwe (2001) touched upon this rhetorical function of reconciliation as well. He wrote, "Rather than leading to greater unity, disagreements about what reconciliation means and what an appropriate [reconciliation] process would be, have led to greater visibility of differences and increased tension" (p. 100). While such outcomes could have been viewed negatively, van der Merwe saw them in terms of their potential:

> [The SATRC] thus almost acted as a lightening rod by attracting controversy, and in this process provided a forum for the articulation of different views about the basis of the new social and moral order that is envisioned by these groups. In terms of viewing the TRC as a reconciliation process, it may thus be most constructive to regard it as a starting point, a vehicle that has managed to bring out the various viewpoints, values, needs, and interests and put them on the table. (p. 101)

In sum, the call for reconciliation was a rhetorical move that, in Doxtader's (2009) terms, created the possibility for a series of "beginnings." Such a claim lends support to the notion that reconciliation functioned as an ideograph, and it is consistent with the larger arguments that this chapter is making—namely, that the field of transitional justice has given rise to a rhetorical tradition and that the patterned ways of using language that circulate in the field provide resources for subsequent discourse.

The *Ethos* of the SATRC

In addition to these patterned ways of using words, the discourse surrounding the SATRC contained patterned ways of constructing *ethos*, which, as I define it in the previous chapter, is the rhetor's subject position as it is constructed through one's

---

[8] Doxtader (2009) has explored other ways that reconciliation was used rhetorically as well. Analyzing the 1995 Promotion of National Unity and Reconciliation Act, which established the SATRC, Doxtader noted, "Among some 30 others, reconciliation was cast as a way to open up the past, close the book on history, establish the truth of individual experience, support the catharsis of confession, exorcise evil, account for the nation's collective responsibility, engender ubuntu, revive moral conscience, rejoin law and morality, spur voluntarism, redress motivations for violence, undertake human reconstruction, heal victims, liberate institutions, support transition, and contribute to the development of democracy" (p. 270).

rhetorical performances. By positioning itself in patterned ways in relation to audiences in and outside of South Africa, the SATRC developed a model of institutional *ethos* that subsequent truth commissions—including the Greensboro Truth and Reconciliation Commission—could reaccentuate in their own rhetorical performances. This section of the chapter surveys scholarship that brings the SATRC's constructions of *ethos* into relief. Doing so provides further demonstration that the field of transitional justice has given rise to a rhetorical tradition.

It is not possible to consider the institutional *ethos* of the SATRC without reference to its chairperson, Archbishop Desmond Tutu.[9] When speaking of Tutu's influence, many scholars and commentators—with varying degrees of apprehension—have noted ways that his religious identity shaped the TRC's work (Ben Achour, 2002, p. 132; Bharucha, 2002, p. 371–372; Margalit, 2002, p. 63; Philpott, 2006, p. 31).[10] Philpott (2006), for example, highlighted the effect that Tutu's presence had on the Commission's hearings: "Religious language and ritual pervaded the proceedings. In publicly presenting the Commission through speeches and writings, Tutu and other commissioners explained it in explicitly theological terms" (p. 31). Philpott also noted that, in addition to Tutu's theological explanations, the Archbishop began and ended each public hearing with prayers and hymns—an act of framing that may have indirectly affected the ways audience members responded to testimony. Words would sometimes fail commissioners after listening to accounts of human suffering, and, oftentimes, at these moments, "the people in the hearing room, participants and onlookers alike, would break out into hymns, thus acknowledging, ritualizing, marking, honoring, and strengthening wounded victims and witnesses" (Philpott, 2006, pp. 31–32). One important facet of this religious emphasis was that Tutu often positioned the Commission as a stand-in for other individuals and groups in South Africa. Like a priest in the role of intercessor or mediator, the SATRC was positioned as an entity that could act on behalf of others in the reconciliation process.

Several scholars have reflected on the Commission's role as a kind of surrogate or proxy for others. Cole's (2010) book *Performing South Africa's Truth Commission: Stages of Transition*—which explored the SATRC's "public enactment" (p. xv)—highlighted one important way that the Commission functioned in this manner:

> Those who gave testimony before the commission ostensibly did so for the commissioners: it was they who would make findings, determine amnesty cases, decide who would be counted a victim of gross violations of human rights and thus be eligible to receive whatever reparations the government might decide to dole out. But the audience for the TRC was far greater than the commissioners. They, I argue, were surrogates, standing in for a larger audience, one more central to the TRC's mission: the nation at large. (pp. 92–93)

---

[9] Cole (2010) is one of many scholars who have commented on Tutu's importance to the Commission: he was, she wrote, "the unquestioned master of ceremonies, a brilliant showman. Without his talents, it could be argued, the commission would surely have broken down at several particularly fraught junctures. His ability to stage-manage, to orchestrate contending forces, to shift abruptly the tone, style, language, and mood of the proceedings kept the audience and all participants slightly off guard" (pp. 16–17).

[10] For more on the *ethos* that Tutu established for the SATRC, see Beitler (2012).

Similarly, Sanders (2007) argued that, in representing "the national public," the SATRC was able to function as a substitute for "victims, bystanders, and beneficiaries" and, perhaps most importantly, for perpetrators (p. 40). He wrote, "[F]aced with the reality that perpetrators would not come forward en masse to make good for what they had done, the Truth Commission generalized responsibility across the body politic by making itself a proxy for the perpetrator vis-à-vis victims whose testimony it solicited" (p. 9). The SATRC's *ethos* as surrogate for the nation extended beyond the hearings as well. Salazar (2002) claimed that, when Tutu publicly presented the SATRC's report to Nelson Mandela, the Commission's chairperson "acted as a plenipotentiary proxy, with the full powers granted to him by law, to speak on behalf of the constituent parts of the nation, which until then were estranged and divided, foreign to one another, torn between past and present" (p. 77–78).

What made the Commission's role as proxy possible was, I think, a more fundamental set of contrasting, institutional subject positions, which were held in tension with one another: the Commission positioned itself as both representative and unrepresentative. An *ethos* of representivity enabled the Commission to stand-in for a number of different groups in South Africa, while an *ethos* of unrepresentivity attempted to ensure that, while speaking on behalf of a particular group, the Commission would still be perceived as fair and unbiased by other groups.[11]

Alex Boraine, the Commission's deputy chairperson and one of its principle architects, helped to construct and reinforce the SATRC's *ethos* of representivity (Beitler, 2012, pp. 12–15). In his book *A Country Unmasked*, Boraine (2001) constructed the SATRC's representivity according to race, ethnicity, and gender: "Among the seventeen commissioners there were seven women, ten men, seven Africans, two 'coloureds', two Indians, and six whites. It was, therefore, a fairly representative group that had been appointed by President Mandela" (p. 75). Tutu, too, positioned the SATRC as representative, and—as I have noted elsewhere—he did so in a number of different ways: he talked about how the commissioners, whom he referred to as "wounded healers," had been affected by apartheid; he described the Commission as a "microcosm" of South African society; and he called attention to the group's political representivity (Tutu, 1999a, p. 22; Beitler, 2012, pp. 12–15).

The SATRC constructed an *ethos* of representivity for itself in other ways as well. Cole (2010) highlighted how, for example, the SATRC established this *ethos* through the public hearings of the Human Rights Violation Committee, which took place in cities and towns throughout South Africa. The hearings were, Cole contended, a "major stage production" (p. 9): they were "scripted, produced, rehearsed, stage-managed, and represented" (p. xv). In this production, Cole argued, the Commission "served as the casting director, choosing which victims would have the

---

[11] I discuss these subject positions in greater detail in Chap. 4.

opportunity to appear in public" (p. 9). What matters most for my argument is how victims were chosen:

> The commission tried to get a fair distribution of men and women, different races and ethnicities, abuses perpetrated by the state and those committed by people in the liberation movements, extreme atrocities and less serious violations. The approximately twenty people chosen to testify would, it was hoped, "somehow reflect the totality of the experience of that particular region or that particular city," said [commissioner Mary] Burton. (Cole, 2010, p. 9)

The SATRC's goal, then, was that those testifying would provide a kind of regional representation—a rhetorical move that reinforced the Commission's *ethos* of representivity. As Cole's comments indicate, this representivity was constructed in terms of gender, race, and ethnicity; political affiliation of the perpetrator; and magnitude of the human rights violation.

Even as the SATRC positioned itself as representative, it also positioned itself as unrepresentative. In the Chairperson's Foreword, for instance, Tutu repeatedly attempted to demonstrate the Commission's impartiality—a characteristic that suggested that the Commission was not representative of anyone (1999a, pp. 11, 13, 15; Beitler, 2012, pp. 8–11). "[W]e are," he wrote, "politically independent and not biased in favour of any particular political party or group" (p. 11). One concrete way in which the Commission attempted to establish this objectivity was through its interpreters. Those testifying in the public hearings were permitted to give testimony in their language of choice, and, as they testified, the remarks were translated into a number of different languages by interpreters hired by the SATRC. Cole (2010) has recounted some of the instructions given to the interpreters:

> [Interpreters] were "to reproduce the speaker's account as reliably as possible" and in the first person, yet they were supposed to maintain neutrality and emotional distance, even when the witness's demeanor was intensely emotional. Emotional expressiveness was somehow not considered part of the witness's narrative truth. "We had it drummed into us the fact that as interpreters we are merely supposed to be in the background," recalls Sobrey, "we are supposed to be invisible, with an invisible, monotone, low-key voice. And it was even taken to the extreme of us being told, as ladies, that we shouldn't even wear bright colors." No reds, but dull colors; no shouts or lilting tonalities, but rather a monotone; no crying, but neutrality without affect. Be inconspicuous, the interpreters were told." (p. 74)

Interpreters were, in other words, meant to be transparent, a conduit for information. While such a stance was, of course, impossible, instructions like these allowed the Commission to construct its *ethos* of objectivity and impartiality.

Whether these rhetorical moves were efficacious or not is another question. Citing a number of research surveys, Theissen (2008) reported, "There is no public consensus on whether the TRC was impartial. While more than 60 percent of all African respondents felt that the TRC was fair to everybody, only a minority of white South Africans shared this view" (pp. 200–201). But measuring public opinion about the SATRC's impartiality is not the only way to evaluate the rhetorical efficacy of the Commission's *ethos*. Another measure might be its contribution to the rhetorical tradition of transitional justice: in constructing the SATRC's *ethos*, the commissioners established additional patterned ways of using language that subsequent rhetors could take up to bring about change elsewhere.

The Genre of the TRC's *Final Report*

In addition to the patterns at the level of words and argument, rhetorical traditions contain patterned ways of using language at the level of entire texts. One way to look at these patterns is to consider the field's genres. James Slevin (1988) has defined genre as a "received form, part of a cultural code, that synthesizes discursive features (e.g., subject matter, meaning, organization, style, and relations between writer and implied/actual audience) in recognizable ways" (p. 4). Such forms—which include but are not limited to patterns at the level of words and argument—are sites of social action (Miller, 1984). That is, language users draw on these (temporarily) stable cultural codes to do things in the world. With regard to truth commissions, some prominent genres that have developed are the mandate, the public hearing, written testimony, the amnesty application, and the final report.[12] This section surveys several scholars' analyses of the final report—the genre that a truth commission is usually charged with producing at the conclusion of its inquiry.

While the final report is, in many ways, a distinctive genre, it does share some of the discursive features of other genres, and several scholars have sought to understand the final report by comparing and contrasting it with similar genres. Sanders (2007) contrasted the SATRC's *Final Report* with the testimony given at the Commission's public hearings, noting that—unlike the interpersonal nature of the hearings—the report was more aptly characterized as a history (p. 24). Sanders based this distinction on differences between the genres' purposes. He wrote, "The commission's report, in contrast to its hearings, does not assume the task of restoring human dignity to victims by facilitating their speaking, but sets out instead to establish a full picture of human rights violations" (p. 24). The authors of the report, in other words, did not give victims a voice in the same way that the hearings did; rather, the authors wrote *about* victims, creating a critical distance that, for Sanders, gave the report a historical quality. Gready's (2011) analysis of the genre of the SATRC's *Final Report* in his book *The Era of Transitional Justice* productively complicated this perspective. Citing Bhatia (2004, p. 23), Gready defined genre as "'language use in a conventionalized communicative setting in order to give expression to a specific set of communicative goals of a disciplinary or social institution, which give rise to stable structural forms' by imposing constraints through language, texts, discourse and context" (p. 28). Unlike Sanders, who maintained that the genre of the report was history, Gready (2011) suggested that the SATRC's report was a particular kind of history—an official history (p. 45). Given that official histories aim to legitimize the state, they result in the "marginalization of history, if history is understood as contested, contextual, interpretive and explanatory, exploring patterns of social relations and institutional dynamics" (p. 49).

---

[12] Mack (2012) has highlighted additional genres associated with the SATRC, including the novel and the photographic essay (p. 6).

Furthermore, Gready (2011) maintained that the SATRC's *Final Report* was not simply an official history. The report was actually a "hybrid genre," composed of "the coming together of three tributary genres: the state inquiry, the human rights report and the official history" (pp. 12, 27). According to Gready, this generic synthesis had not been achieved effectively. He noted that, despite some methodological similarities among its three tributary genres, the SATRC's report "failed to achieve a hybrid or synthetic coherence" (p. 56). The writers of the report had aimed to achieve different (often competing) purposes using a variety of (often incompatible) research methodologies, and, as a result, the report's contents were "characterized by description, fragmentation, repetition and multiple messages" (p. 50).[13] For Gready (2011), some of the SATRC's limitations and failures were partly a result of this lack of genre coherence (p. 27). However, he also noted that, where he saw fragmentation and a lack of coherence, other scholars—like Teresa Godwin Phelps (2004)—had seen a productive polyvocality:

> Some argue that the weakness of the report's meta-narrative may be a strength, inviting rather than curtailing further debate (Posel 2002: 168–69; Posel and Simpson 2002: 12–13). Certain analyses map ways in which commissions combine meta-narrative and multiple voices…The inclusion of such stories in the master narratives of truth commission reports 'allows for the *carnivalization* of history, an entirely new kind of history telling and nation making' (Phelps 2004: 69). (p. 51)

In other words, the genre of the final report—with all of its fragmentation—may have functioned much like the ideograph reconciliation: as a prompt for future dialogue and discussion.

Another recurring feature of the genre of the truth commission final report is a neutral stance; authors of the reports have typically aimed to position themselves as unbiased. Charles Villa-Vicencio and Wilhelm Verwoerd (2000)—both of whom served on the SATRC's research team—wrote of the need for reports to be "impartial and objective" (p. 285). Such a stance, others have noted, helps a truth commission to achieve its goals: "If the body is considered to be impartial, fair, and competent, a truth commission's report can offer a basis on which to build a shared history" (Chapman & van der Merwe, 2008, p. 3). Without the perception of impartiality, a commission's history—as well as its recommendations—is less likely to be accepted. To establish this unbiased stance, the authors of the SATRC's *Final Report* employed several rhetorical techniques. According to Gready (2011), the authors attempted to construct objectivity "via established methodologies of data collection, corroboration techniques, references to legal standards and report-writing formats" (p. 33). They also did so by corroborating evidence, reporting facts (while keeping judgments to a minimum), and using "measured language and a transparent

---

[13] The evidence Gready (2011) provided to support this claim included "the failure [in the report] to integrate testimonies and statistical analysis; the need to relate things treated separately (time periods, regional profiles, categories of abuse, parts of individual stories); and the treatment of sector hearings and related structural issues in a separate volume…To this list should be added the decision to begin, and therefore frame, the whole report with a chairperson's foreword (genre: sermon)" (p. 50).

acknowledgement of sources" (p. 34). At the grammatical level, such objectivity was reinforced through the use of the third person (Sanders, 2007, p. 24).

Given the genre's fragmentation, polyvocality, and impersonal stance—as well as its customary cost and size—final reports have often been difficult texts for audiences to engage. These factors, along with literacy and/or language constraints, have tended to limit the genre's circulation and reception. Most reports have been—to quote from Salazar's (2002) comments about the five volumes of the SATRC's *Final Report*—"not intended for public consumption…they are just as illegible to citizens as most bills or laws are—and just as incontrovertible" (p. 77). Consequently, to date, final reports have not been very effective tools for facilitating change.[14] On this point, Madeleine Fullard and Nicky Rousseau (2011) noted, "The fate of most truth commission reports is retirement to libraries, limited bookshops, and study by academics" (p. 85). While some groups and organizations have attempted to translate the content of reports into other media formats, many of these attempts have been unsuccessful (Gready, 2011, p. 35). Nevertheless, final reports often serve important social functions in the wake of political transition. For example, according to Salazar (2002), the SATRC's *Final Report* served as a kind of fulfillment of the country's new Constitution:

> The *Report* gives life and shape to the Constitution. It imparts rhythm and imagery to the abstract text of the fundamental law. The dance makes political music—for all to see, to hear, to visualize. The intention was for citizens to find the will to enunciate, to voice (this term is often used in the *Report*), and to materialize the boundaries of the polis and of the social contract, boundaries which were abstractly presented in the fundamental law. (pp. 91–92)

For Salazar, the very existence of the report—as witnessed during Desmond Tutu's ceremonial delivery of it to then-President Nelson Mandela—was "a demonstration of the nature of the new social contract" (p. 79).

While final reports have not enjoyed large readerships in their immediate contexts, the genre is an important feature of the rhetorical tradition of transitional justice. As with the tradition's ideographs and constructions of *ethos*, the genre of the final report contains reoccurring patterns and argumentative devices that provide rhetors with resources to bring about change in their own contexts.

The patterns of language that I have highlighted in this chapter are only a tiny facet of the rhetorical tradition of transitional justice.[15] Many other patterns emerged during the SATRC's operation and during the operation of other transitional justice initiatives. With regard to truth commissions, these patterns have included commonplaces (truth-telling is necessary for reconciliation), political styles (the repentant

---

[14] *Nunca Más*, the final report of Argentina's truth commission, was an exception to this rule: an abbreviated version of the report was a best seller in the country (Gready, 2011, p. 35). Most final reports do not enjoy this sort of public reception.

[15] It is worth noting, for example, that the rhetorical tradition has been performed in other types of texts than the ones surveyed in this chapter. Salazar (2002) explored the rhetorical aspects of rituals (such as Tutu's dance accompanying the public delivery of the SATRC's *Final Report* to Mandela), South African newspaper inserts and advertisements, South African voting ballots, *Elle* magazine covers, and geographic spaces like Robben Island.

perpetrator, the forgiving victim), speech acts (confession, testimony), acts of dissociation (distinguishing "retributive justice" from "restorative justice"), and metaphors (the bridge, the rainbow). The tradition also has given rise to its own idioms (phrases like "come to terms with"), additional ideographs (terms such as truth and justice), diverse genres (the mandate, the public hearing), and meta-narratives.[16]

Conclusion

Reaccentuating the elements of a rhetorical tradition is never a morally neutral action—a fact that I was recently reminded of while rereading Antjie Krog's (1998) moving textual mosaic *Country of My Skull*. One of the many things Krog did in her book was to offer a sustained meditation on language's power to both liberate and oppress. On the one hand, Krog brought language's liberating power into relief by weaving together testimonies from the SATRC's public hearings. For example, in one of the testimonies Krog recounted, the speaker talked about the murder of a child named Sonnyboy. The account ended this way: "Sonnyboy, rest well, my child. I've translated you from the dead" (p. 40). Another testimony that Krog included was that of Lucas Baba Sikwepere, who had been blinded from a gunshot. Krog reported that, at the end of his testimony to the truth commission, Mr. Sikwepere said, "I feel what—what has brought my sight back, my eyesight back is

---

[16] With regard to meta-narratives, Teitel (2002) reflected on the patterns that circulate in the field of transitional justice. He wrote, "Transitional narratives follow a distinct rhetorical form: beginning in tragedy, they end on a comic or romantic mode" (p. 252). Unlike "classic" tragic tales in which the revelation of knowledge foretells the demise of one or more characters, in narratives of transition "the revelation of knowledge actually makes a [positive] difference. The country's past suffering is…reversed, leading to a happy ending of peace and reconciliation" (p. 252). There has typically been a liberalizing political shift implicated in this narrative trajectory; that is, transitional narratives have often told the stories of nations and societies that transition from authoritarian or totalitarian regimes toward democratization (Teitel, 2000, p. 5). Teitel's arguments lend support to the presupposition that, in the activities and inquiries that comprise the field of transitional justice, there are patterned ways of using language.

While there are undoubtedly many reasons why the emphasis on liberalization that Teitel described has become commonplace in the field of transitional justice, Kritz's (1995) field-defining compilation—*Transitional Justice: How Emerging Democracies Reckon with Former Regimes*— may have been a contributing factor. As Charles D. Smith (1995), the former Director of the Rule of Law Initiative for the United States Institute of Peace, noted in the Introduction to Kritz's anthology, "These volumes are limited, as the subtitle indicates, to the way that emerging *democratic* societies address the legacy of their repression of their own people. This approach has excluded consideration of non-democratic successor states (for example, the transition from the Pahlavi to Khomeini regimes in Iran, or from Somoza to the Sandinistas in Nicaragua) It has also excluded most material on the transitional policies of occupation authorities (such as post-World War II Japan)" (p. xvi). For more on liberalization within the field of transitional justice, see Ní Aoláin and Campbell (2005, p. 173).

to come back here and tell the story. But I feel what has been making me sick all the time is the fact that I couldn't tell my story. But now I—it feels like I got my sight back by coming here and telling you the story" (p. 43). Quoting Tutu, Krog showed how these testimonies, and others like them, prevented denial about past atrocities in the country by revealing the "depth of depravity" (p. 60).

On the other hand, Krog demonstrated language's coercive power. When discussing the politicians' testimonies at the SATRC's public hearings, she wrote, "The posters that read 'The Truth Sets You Free' are suddenly drained of meaning," and she contrasted these testimonies with the more heart-felt victims' testimonies:

> Gone is the dearly bought language. Over months we've realized what an immense price of pain each person must pay just to stammer out his own story at the Truth Commission. Each word is exhaled from the heart; each syllabus vibrates with a lifetime of sorrow. This is gone. Now it's the hour of those who scrum down in Parliament. The display of tongues freed into rhetoric—the signature of power. The old and new masters of foam in the ears. (p. 132)

Krog's reflections about the various uses of language surrounding the SATRC are not inconsistent with Murphy's (1997) claim that rhetorical traditions provide rhetors with "enabling constraints": language both constrains our actions and enables them (p. 85).

Many of the studies surveyed in this chapter implicitly explored how the patterns of the rhetorical tradition of transitional justice have functioned to constrain. To recount a few examples, scholars have claimed that the goal of reconciliation perpetuated hegemonic ideologies; that the conflation of reconciliation and forgiveness limited the range of acceptable responses to the SATRC; that the fusion of reconciliation and amnesty denied some the opportunity to seek justice; that the Commission's Christian *ethos* undermined its efficacy; and that the genre confusion of the SATRC's *Final Report* limited its potential to bring about change. But rhetorical traditions do not simply constrain, and other studies surveyed in this chapter highlighted the rhetorical tradition's capacity to enable action: calls for reconciliation invited adversaries to begin to talk with one another; the Commission's *ethos* allowed the organization to present itself as unbiased; and the polyvocal genre of the SATRC's *Final Report* opened up a space for multiple voices to be heard.

Moreover, such patterns circulate—and have power—beyond their immediate contexts. Shaffer and Smith (2004) have noted, for example, that well-to-do readerships may consume testimonies of suffering in order to "reinvent imagined securities" (p. 25). But stories can be used in more positive ways as well: "In the midst of the transits that take stories of local struggle to readerships around the world, NGOs and activists enlist stories from victims as a way of alerting a broader public to situations of human rights violations" (p. 27). Mack (2012), too, has investigated the circulation of the SATRC's rhetorical activity, highlighting various *topoi*—i.e., places of argument—generated by the SATRC and showing how each "sprouted in its travels from the TRC mandate to the commissioners' statements during the public hearings and finally to the *Report*" (pp. 8–9). From there, she examined "varied receptions of the Commission's process that stem from these *topoi*, including those of participants in the public hearings and select literary and photographic texts that represent or explicitly reference the TRC process" (p. 9). These considerations of the "migration" of the SATRC's discourse to other contexts help to set the stage for the central argument of my book (p. 11). Subsequent chapters of *Remaking Transitional Justice in the United States* expand upon and develop this intellectual trajectory, demonstrating how the people of Greensboro—including the members of the Greensboro Truth and Community Reconciliation Project and the Greensboro Truth and Reconciliation Commission—reaccentuated facets of the rhetorical tradition of transitional justice in their performances, in an attempt to establish their own authority in the city.

References

Azanian Peoples Organisation (AZAPO) and others v President of the Republic of South Africa and Others, (4) SA 671 (1996).

Battle, M. (1997). *Reconciliation: The ubuntu theology of Desmond Tutu.* Cleveland, OH: Pilgrim.

Beitler, J. (2012). Making more of the middle ground: Desmond Tutu and the *ethos* of the South African Truth and Reconciliation Commission. *Relevant Rhetoric, 3,* 1–21. Retrieved June 1, 2012, from http://relevantrhetoric.com/wp-content/uploads/making-more-of-the-middle-ground.pdf.

Ben Achour, Y. (2002). The order of truth and the order of society. In O. Enwezor (Ed.), *Experiments with truth: Transitional justice and the processes of truth and reconciliation: documenta 11_ platform 2* (pp. 123–134). Ostfildern-Ruit: Hatje Cantz.

Bharucha, R. (2002). Between truth and reconciliation. In O. Enwezor (Ed.), *Experiments with truth: Transitional justice and the processes of truth and reconciliation: documenta 11_platform 2* (pp. 361–388). Ostfildern-Ruit: Hatje Cantz.

Bhatia, V. (2004). *Worlds of written discourse: A genre-based view.* London: Continuum.

Boraine, A. (2001). *A country unmasked: Inside South Africa's Truth and Reconciliation Commission.* Oxford: Oxford University Press.

Butler, J. P. (1997). *Excitable speech: A politics of the performative.* New York, NY: Routledge.

Chapman, A. R., & van der Merwe, H. (2008). Introduction: Assessing the South African transitional justice model. In A. R. Chapman & H. van der Merwe (Eds.), *Truth and reconciliation in South Africa: Did the TRC deliver?* (pp. 1–22). Philadelphia, PA: University of Pennsylvania Press.

Charland, M. (1987). Constitutive rhetoric: The case of the *Peuple Québécois. Quarterly Journal of Speech, 73*(2), 133–150. doi:10.1080/00335638709383799.

Cherry, J., Daniel, J., & Fullard, M. (2002). Researching the 'truth': A view from inside the Truth and Reconciliation Commission. In D. Posel & G. Simpson (Eds.), *Commissioning the past: Understanding South Africa's Truth and Reconciliation Commission* (pp. 17–36). Johannesburg, South Africa: Witwatersrand University Press.

Cole, C. M. (2010). *Performing South Africa's Truth Commission: Stages of transition.* Bloomington & Indianapolis, IN: Indiana University Press.

Doxtader, E. (2001). Making rhetorical history in a time of transition: The occasion, constitution, and representation of South African reconciliation. *Rhetoric & Public Affairs, 4*(2), 223–260. doi:10.1353/rap. 2001.0023.

Doxtader, E. (2003). Reconciliation—a rhetorical concept/ion. *Quarterly Journal of Speech, 89*(4), 267–292. doi:10.1080/0033563032000160954.

Doxtader, E. (2004). The potential of reconciliation's beginning: A reply. *Rhetoric & Public Affairs, 7*(3), 378–390. doi:10.1353/rap. 2005.0005.

Doxtader, E. (2007). The faith and struggle of beginning (with) words: On the turn between reconciliation and recognition. *Philosophy and Rhetoric, 40*(1), 119–146. doi:10.1353/par.2007.0011.

Doxtader, E. (2009). *With faith in the works of words: The beginnings of reconciliation in South Africa, 1985–1995.* East Lansing, MI: Michigan State University Press.

Dwyer, S. (1999). Reconciliation for realists. *Ethics & International Affairs, 13*(1), 81–98. doi:10.1111/j.1747-7093.1999.tb00328.x.

Fletcher, L. E., & van der Merwe, H. (2007). Editorial note. *The International Journal of Transitional Justice, 1*, 1–5. doi:10.1093/ijtj/ijm012.

Fullard, M., & Rousseau, N. (2011). Truth telling, identities, and power in South Africa and Guatemala. In P. Arthur (Ed.), *Identities in transition: Challenges for transitional justice in divided societies* (pp. 56–86). Cambridge: Cambridge University Press.

Gready, P. (2011). *The era of transitional justice: The aftermath of the truth and reconciliation commission in South Africa and beyond.* New York, NY: Routledge.

Hamber, B., & van der Merwe, H. (1998). What is this thing called reconciliation? *Reconciliation in Review, 1*(1), 3–6. Retrieved March 1, 2012, from http://www.csvr.org.za/wits/articles/artrcbh.htm.

Hatch, J. B. (2009). *Race and reconciliation: Redressing wounds of injustice.* Lanham, MD: Lexington Books.

Hayner, P. B. (2001). *Unspeakable truths: Confronting state terror and atrocity.* New York, NY: Routledge.

Kritz, N. J. (Ed.). (1995). *Transitional justice: How emerging democracies reckon with former regimes.* Washington, DC: United States Institute of Peace Press.

Krog, A. (1998). *Country of my skull: Guilt, sorrow, and the limits of forgiveness in the new South Africa.* Johannesburg, South Africa: Random House.

Mack, K. (2012). *A generative failure: The public hearings of South Africa's Truth and Reconciliation Commission.* Manuscript in preparation.

Margalit, A. (2002). Is truth the road to reconciliation? In O. Enwezor (Ed.), *Experiments with truth: Transitional justice and the processes of truth and reconciliation: documenta 11_platform 2* (pp. 61–64). Ostfildern-Ruit: Hatje Cantz.

Marx, C. (2002). Ubu and ubuntu: On the dialectics of apartheid and nation building. *Politikon: South African Journal of Political Studies, 29*(1), 49–69. doi:10.1080/0258934022014943.

McGee, M. C. (1980). The "ideograph": A link between rhetoric and ideology. *Quarterly Journal of Speech, 66*(1), 1–16. doi:10.1080/00335638009383499.

Miller, C. R. (1984). Genre as social action. *Quarterly Journal of Speech, 70*(2), 151–167. doi:10.1080/00335638409383686.

Murphy, J. M. (1997). Inventing authority: Bill Clinton, Martin Luther King, Jr., and the orchestration of rhetorical traditions. *Quarterly Journal of Speech, 83*(1), 71–89. doi:10.1080/00335639709384172.

Nagy, R. (2002). Reconciliation in post-commission South Africa: Thick and thin accounts of solidarity. *Canadian Journal of Political Science, 35*(2), 323–346. doi:10.1017/S0008423902778268.

Nagy, R. (2004). The ambiguities of reconciliation and responsibility in South Africa. *Political Studies, 52*(4), 709–727. doi:10.1111/j.1467-9248.2004.00504.x.

Ndebele, N. (2001). Of lions and rabbits: Thoughts on democracy and reconciliation. In W. James & L. Van de Vijver (Eds.), *After the TRC: Reflections on truth and reconciliation in South Africa* (pp. 143–156). Cape Town: David Philip.

Ní Aoláin, F., & Campbell, C. (2005). The paradox of transition in conflicted democracies. *Human Rights Quarterly, 27*(1), 172–213. doi:10.1353/hrq. 2005.0001.

Olsen, T. D., Payne, L. A., & Reiter, A. G. (2010). Transitional justice in the world, 1970–2007: Insights from a new dataset. *Journal of Peace Research, 47*(6), 803–809. doi:10.1177/0022343310382205.

Phelps, T. G. (2004). *Shattered voices: Language, violence, and the work of truth commissions.* Philadelphia, PA: University of Pennsylvania Press.

Philpott, D. (2006). Beyond politics as usual: Is reconciliation compatible with liberalism? In D. Philpott (Ed.), *The politics of past evil: Religion, reconciliation, and the dilemmas of transitional justice* (pp. 11–44). Notre Dame, IN: University of Notre Dame Press.

Posel, D. (2002). The TRC report: What kind of history? What kind of truth? In D. Posel & G. Simpson (Eds.), *Commissioning the Past: Understanding South Africa's Truth and Reconciliation Commission* (pp. 147–172). Johannesburg, South Africa: Witwatersrand University Press.

Salazar, P. J. (2002). *An African Athens: Rhetoric and the shaping of democracy in South Africa.* Mahwah, NJ: L. Erlbaum.

Sanders, M. (2007). *Ambiguities of witnessing: Law and literature in the time of a truth commission.* Stanford, CA: Stanford University Press.

Shaffer, K., & Smith, S. (2004). *Human rights and narrated lives: The ethics of recognition.* New York, NY: Palgrave Macmillan.

Shutte, A. (2001). *Ubuntu: An ethic for a new South Africa.* Pietermaritzburg, South Africa: Cluster.

Simpson, G. (2002). "Tell no lies, claim no easy victories": A brief evaluation of South Africa's Truth and Reconciliation Commission. In D. Posel & G. Simpson (Eds.), *Commissioning the Past: Understanding South Africa's Truth and Reconciliation Commission* (pp. 220–247). Johannesburg, South Africa: Witwatersrand University Press.

Slevin, J. F. (1988). Genre theory, academic discourse, and writing within disciplines. In L. Z. Smith (Ed.), *Audits of meaning: A festschrift in honor of Ann E. Berthoff* (pp. 3–16). Portsmouth, NH: Boynton/Cook.

Smith, C. D. (1995). Introduction. In N. J. Kritz (Ed.), *Transitional justice: How emerging democracies reckon with former regimes* (pp. xv–xvii). Washington, DC: United States Institute of Peace Press.

South African Truth and Reconciliation Commission. (1999). *Truth and Reconciliation Commission of South Africa report* (Vol. 1). New York, NY: Grove's Dictionaries.

Teitel, R. G. (2000). *Transitional Justice.* New York, NY: Oxford University Press.

Teitel, R. G. (2002). Transitional justice as liberal narrative. In O. Enwezor (Ed.), *Experiments with truth: Transitional justice and the processes of truth and reconciliation: Documenta 11_ Platform 2* (pp. 241–260). Ostfildern-Ruit: Hatje Cantz.

Theissen, G. (2008). Object of trust and hatred: Public attitudes toward the TRC. In A. R. Chapman & H. van der Merwe (Eds.), *Truth and reconciliation in South Africa: Did the TRC deliver?* (pp. 191–216). Philadelphia, PA: University of Philadelphia Press.

Tutu, D. (1999a). Foreword by chairperson. In *Truth and Reconciliation Commission of South Africa Report* (Vol. 1, pp. 1–23). New York, NY: Grove's Dictionaries.

Tutu, D. (1999b). *No future without forgiveness.* New York, NY: Doubleday.

van der Merwe, H. (2001). National and community reconciliation: Competing agendas in South African Truth and Reconciliation Commission. In N. Bigger (Ed.), *Burying the past: Making peace and doing justice after civil conflict* (pp. 85–106). Washington, DC: Georgetown University Press.

VanAntwerpen, J. (2010). Reconciliation reconceived: Religion, secularism, and the language of transition. In W. Kymlicka & B. Bashir (Eds.), *The politics of reconciliation in multicultural societies* (pp. 25–47). New York, NY: Oxford University Press.

Verdoolaege, A. (2008). *Reconciliation discourse: The case of the truth and reconciliation commission.* Philadelphia, PA: John Benjamins.

Villa-Vicencio, C., & Verwoerd, W. (2000). Constructing a report: Writing up the "truth". In R. I. Rotberg & D. Thompson (Eds.), *Truth v. justice: The morality of truth commissions* (pp. 279–294). Princeton, NJ: Princeton University Press.

Chapter 3
"A Person is a Person Through Other Persons": Reaccentuating *Ubuntu* in Greensboro

Abstract This chapter analyzes the discourse surrounding the Greensboro Truth and Reconciliation Commission's (GTRC) Swearing In and Seating Ceremony—focusing on a speech delivered by Reverend Bongani Finca, a former commissioner on the South African Truth and Reconciliation Commission—to show how advocates of the GTRC reaccentuated the South African notion of *ubuntu* in order to build solidarity between Greensboro and South African stakeholders and thereby establish the GTRC's authority. Through his speech, Finca endorsed the GTRC commissioners, entrusted the people of Greensboro with the truth commission model, and established the GTRC's status in the community. As he did so, he also called community members to embrace *ubuntu*, both explicitly and implicitly. The chapter concludes by analyzing the front and back covers of the GTRC's *Final Report*, noting how the commissioners drew upon the notion of *ubuntu* to position themselves and the covers' viewers.

J.E. Beitler III, *Remaking Transitional Justice in the United States*,
Springer Series in Transitional Justice, DOI 10.1007/978-1-4614-5295-9_3,
© Springer Science+Business Media New York 2013

"In our language, we have a saying that a person is a person because of other persons. In that saying we recognize that a person is not complete until she embraces other persons and struggles to make them complete also. We recognize that a person cannot be fulfilled until she finds fulfillment for others also. We recognize that we can not have real peace until we move in isolation and find peace for those on our side and for those who live on the other side."

Reverend Bongani Finca (2004)

Introduction

Discourse travels. When the group of Greensboro citizens who were concerned about the legacy of November 3, 1979 was put in touch with the International Center for Transitional Justice (ICTJ), a network began to form between people in Greensboro, New York, and South Africa; and the Greensboro citizens were given an institutional model for addressing the past: the Truth and Reconciliation Commission (TRC). But the gains to the people of Greensboro went beyond a network of support or an institutional model. Viewed in rhetorical terms, the group was connected to the rhetorical tradition of transitional justice. This chapter begins to show how this rhetorical tradition was performed in Greensboro by offering close readings of speeches delivered at the Greensboro Truth and Reconciliation Commission (GTRC)'s Swearing In and Seating Ceremony and other events in Greensboro by former members of the South Africa Truth and Reconciliation Commission (SATRC). It focuses primarily, though not exclusively, on the speeches of Reverend Bongani Finca, a member of the SATRC who traveled to Greensboro to observe the work of the GTRC and to speak on its behalf (Finca, 2004; GTRC, 2005b).[1] Through his reaccentuation of the rhetorical tradition of transitional justice, Finca helped to constitute the GTRC's authority. Most notably, his speeches—especially his remarks at the Swearing In and Seating Ceremony—built authority by reaccentuating the South African notion of *ubuntu* in the Greensboro context. Before demonstrating this point through an analysis of Finca's remarks, it is necessary to describe the concept of *ubuntu* and highlight one of the ways that it made its way to Greensboro.

Defining *Ubuntu*

Ubuntu has been described, aptly, as "a multidimensional concept" (Kamwangamalu, 2008, p. 114) that "defies a single definition or characterization" (More, 2004, p. 156). The term is derived from the Bantu languages, and there are phonological variants in a number of African languages, including, for example, the Sotho word

---

[1] At various points throughout the chapter, I make connections between Finca's (2004) keynote address and other rhetorical performances that occurred in Greensboro, including Desmond Tutu's (2005) speech at Guilford College and Finca's remarks following the Commission's first public hearing (GTRC, 2005b). This chapter, then, provides insights into how individuals associated with past truth commissions and, more broadly, with the field of transitional justice helped to authorize the GTRC.

botho (Kamwangamalu, 2008, pp. 114, 120). According to Michael Battle (1997), the term is the plural form of the word *Bantu*, which, Battle noted, was recorded by nineteenth-century German linguist Wilhelm Bleek and subsequently used to describe the "similar linguistic bond among African speakers" (p. 39). It is sometimes translated as "humanity" or "humanness"; however, this definition does not do justice to the semantic richness of *ubuntu*. Sociolinguist Nkonko Kamwangamalu (2008) highlighted this complexity in his study of the term's use, noting that *ubuntu* connotes "respect for any human being, for human dignity and for human life, collective sharedness, obedience, humility, solidarity, caring, hospitality, interdependence, [and] communalism" (p. 114). Likewise, philosopher Mabogo More (2004) claimed that *ubuntu* "has been variously equated with African communalism or African humanism, and has been associated with values such as caring, sharing, hospitality, forgiveness, compassion, empathy, honesty, humility, or 'brotherhood'" (p. 156).[2] The term, moreover, has often been used synecdochically for the Zulu expression, "*umuntu ngumuntu nganbantu*," which in English has been rendered as, "each individual's humanity is ideally expressed in relationship with others," or, more commonly, "a person is a person through other persons" (Battle, 1997, p. 39; More, 2004, p. 157).[3]

Though such definitions have led some to reduce *ubuntu's* meaning to notions of human interdependence and interconnectedness, Mark Sanders (2007) has persuasively argued that the term does not exclude individual identity (p. 27). Disputing the accuracy of the common translation "people are people through other people," Sanders noted the following:

> The Zulu phrase *umuntu ngumuntu ngabantu* has, in its tropic movement, an economy of singular and plural not captured in the banal "people are people through other people." *Umuntu* is the singular form of *-ntu*, or human being. The prefix *-ngu* is copulative. *Nga-* is a noun prefix for forming instrumental adverbs and combines with *abantu*, the plural of *-ntu*, to form *ngabantu*. A preliminary translation might thus be: a human being is a human being through human beings; or the being-human of a human being is realized through his or her being (human) through human beings...*ubuntu*, if it is an imperative, demands that responsibility begin with singularity. If we preserve that moment of singularity we do not simply reduce *ubuntu* to group solidarity or loyalty. (p. 27)

---

[2]The many meanings associated with the term are often said to come from the values that circulated within the structure of the African village, although this explanation is by no means universally accepted; historian Christoph Marx (2002), for example, called this explanation an "invented tradition" (p. 59). *Ubuntu* has also often been used to contrast Western and Africa views of personhood (Battle, 1997, p. 39). Kamwangamalu (2008), for example, wrote, "Interdependence is valued highly in Africa, much as it is in Asia. However, in the West, independence rather than interdependence is the norm. Consequently, these two values, independence and interdependence, tend to clash when those who hold them come into contact" (p. 116). Similarly, Augustine Shutte's (2001) call to an ethic of *ubuntu* hinged on this distinction: "Both [African and European traditions] base their ethics on their understanding of humanity. For both the moral life is intrinsically connected to human flourishing and fulfillment. But they present us with different insights into human nature. The African insight is into our communal nature, persons depend on persons to be persons. The European insight is into the freedom of the individual" (p. 51). Marx noted (2002) that such generalizations about cultures are seldom based on evidence (pp. 59–60).

[3]The equivalent Sotho expression—"*Motho ke motho ka batho ba bang*," which has been translated "I am, because we are"—has also contributed to the fact that *ubuntu* has often been associated with notions of interdependence and connectedness (More, 2004, p. 157).

Ubuntu, in other words, preserves the notion of individual identity, even as it emphasizes that the constitution of individual identity depends on corporate identity. Jomo Kenyatta's explanation of the term captured this point. Kenyatta wrote, "[N]obody is an isolated individual. Or rather, his uniqueness is a secondary fact about him; first and foremost he is several people's relative and several people's contemporary" (as cited in Kamwangamalu, 2008, p. 115).

Ubuntu was one of the commonplaces underpinning the operation of the South African Truth and Reconciliation Commission (SATRC). Reasons for the Commission's emphasis on *ubuntu* were undoubtedly myriad, but chief among them was the term's importance in the Commission's discursive architecture. In 1993, before the SATRC was established, the authors of the postamble to South Africa's interim Constitution used the term to describe what the country's transition from an apartheid regime to a democracy needed to look like. "There is a need," they wrote in their historic postamble, "for understanding but not for vengeance, a need for reparation but not for retaliation, a need for *ubuntu* but not victimization" (as cited in Tutu, 1999, pp. 45–46). It was this threefold call for understanding, reparation, and *ubuntu* that prompted the South African Parliament to pass the "Promotion of National Unity and Reconciliation Act" (1995), the legislative act responsible for establishing the SATRC. Once the Commission was underway, Desmond Tutu and many of the other commissioners frequently deployed the term to support their emphasis on restorative, as opposed to retributive, justice; it was on the premise of the interconnectedness of all humans that members of the SATRC claimed that the restoration of victims depended upon the restoration of perpetrators. Tutu's (1999) discussion of *ubuntu* in *No Future Without Forgiveness* illustrated this point: "We are bound up in a delicate network of interdependence because, as we say in our African idiom, a person is a person through other persons. To dehumanize another inexorably means that one is dehumanized as well" (p. 35).

In its *Final Report*, the SATRC (1999) claimed, "[A] spontaneous call has arisen among sections of the population for a return to *ubuntu*" (p. 127). Judging from the many different ways the term has been applied in post-apartheid South Africa, this assessment would seem to be accurate. *Ubuntu* has been taken up by the South African business sector as a framework for revamping managerial paradigms and increasing productivity through a return to "traditional African values" (Kamwangamalu, 2008, p. 118).[4] It has also been embraced by educators such as Philip Higgs and Elza Venter, who argued that the goal of African pedagogies should be to foster *ubuntu* (Enslin & Horsthemke, 2004, p. 548). And non-governmental organizations, such as Ubuntu Africa and the Ubuntu Education Fund, have drawn upon the concept to warrant their educational and health-related community action programs (Ubuntu Africa, 2012; Ubuntu Education Fund, n.d.).[5] The term's

---

[4] *Ubuntu*-informed business practices focus on mentoring as opposed to managing, teamwork as opposed to competition and individualism, diversity as opposed to uniformity, and affirmative action as opposed to discrimination (Kamwangamalu, 2008, p. 118).

[5] Given such developments, and many others like them, it is little wonder that More (2004) cited the recent emphasis on *ubuntu* as one of the "three most important developments in African society" (p. 156).

circulation has extended beyond national boundaries as well: it has been deployed internationally by religious groups, software companies, and sports teams. Moreover, and more importantly for my purposes, the term has also been used by other truth commissions, including the GTRC.

Reaccentuating *Ubuntu*

The ICTJ provided a path by which *ubuntu* and other facets of the rhetorical tradition of transitional justice made their way to Greensboro. Until it was connected with the Greensboro community through the Andrus Family Fund, the ICTJ had primarily focused its efforts at the level of the nation-state—in Peru, Liberia, and elsewhere. But despite this prior focus, the organization agreed to work with the people of Greensboro to assist it in fostering transitional justice in their community. One important way they did so was to connect the GTRC with other practitioners of transitional justice from around the world. As a result of the ICTJ's networking, Dr. Peter Storey, the former prison chaplain to Nelson Mandela, served on the Greensboro Truth and Community Reconciliation Project (GTCRP) and attended the GTRC's Report Release Ceremony; Sofia Macher, a member of the Peruvian TRC, traveled to Greensboro to assist the Commission in planning their public hearings; Eduardo Gonzalez, the coordinator of the Peruvian TRC's public hearings, visited to help commemorate the 24th anniversary of November 3, 1979; and Reverend Bongani Finca—a minister within the South African Presbyterian Church and former member of the SATRC[6]—came for the 24th anniversary of the Greensboro massacre, the GTRC's Swearing In and Seating Ceremony, and the Commission's first public hearing.

Each of these individuals—along with Desmond Tutu, who also made two visits to Greensboro[7]—introduced facets of the rhetorical tradition of transitional justice in the city.[8] With the exception, perhaps, of Desmond Tutu, Bongani Finca was arguably the most visible of the GTCRP's and GTRC's international guests, and, therefore, he played a pivotal role in reaccentuating *ubuntu* and other facets of the rhetorical tradition of transitional justice in Greensboro. Whereas Macher and others primarily strategized with the Commission in private, Finca spoke publicly

---

[6]Bongani Finca was also one of the signers of *The Kairos Document*—a statement by South African theologians and clergy that called for an end to apartheid in South Africa (Kairos theologians, 1986, p. 54).

[7] Although Tutu had contact with both the GTCRP and the GTRC, neither of his visits to Greensboro were arranged by the ICTJ.

[8]Desmond Tutu's daughter Naomi Tutu also came to Greensboro. Speaking at a news conference at North Carolina A&T University on the 25th anniversary of the Greensboro massacre, she said, "If we say we are those who want to pass on a better world to the next generation, we have to come up with a better way, and we know the only way for healing is for us to listen to one another's stories and to incorporate those stories into a bigger whole" (McLaughlin, 2004, p. B1).

each time he was in Greensboro.[9] And his most important speech in terms of the GTRC's authorization was his keynote address at the GTRC's Swearing In and Seating Ceremony—the public event, organized by the GTCRP, in which the seven individuals selected to serve on the Commission were formally installed as commissioners and charged with their mandate.[10]

The Swearing In and Seating Ceremony took place on June 12, 2004 in the city's historic train depot. With over 500 people in attendance, the depot's main assembly room was filled to capacity. Commissioners sat on a stage at the front of the room, surrounded by features of the rhetorical tradition of transitional justice. A banner, much like those used by the SATRC during its public hearings, was draped behind them, and the slogan fastened on the stage's podium—which read, "Facing Our Past, Shaping Our Future"—could well have served as a motto for the GTRC's predecessor. To the right and left of the stage, a number of flags were displayed, each of which represented a country where a truth commission had taken place or was currently taking place. After a processional and opening remarks, the master of ceremonies, Gregory Headen, introduced Bongani Finca and invited him to the podium (GTCRP, 2004).

Rhetorical performances always draw upon multiple rhetorical traditions, and Finca's (2004) speech was no exception: he quoted Neil Armstrong one moment and Desmond Tutu the next. Not surprisingly, though, Finca relied most heavily on rhetorical tradition of transitional justice. In addition to quoting Tutu, he read a poem from the day that he himself was installed as a commissioner, mentioned Nelson Mandela's release from prison, referred to the oft-quoted postamble to the South African interim Constitution, and conveyed a number of commonplaces that were central to the SATRC, including the notion that "the past will continue to haunt the present" until the truth is told. The ways in which Finca deployed each of these facets of the rhetorical tradition helped to establish the *ethos* of the soon-to-be-constituted GTRC; however, of all of these facets, the most important to the Commission's authorization—and most integral to the speech as a whole—was his reaccenutation of the notion of *ubuntu*.

Finca explicitly mentioned *ubuntu* twice; however, his speech reaccentuated the concept in another way as well. To see how this is so, it is helpful to trace some of the other ways Finca authorized the commissioners. As I reveal in what follows, the first third of Finca's speech functioned as an endorsement of the Commission; the second third symbolically entrusted commissioners with the truth commission model; and the final third positioned the people of Greensboro as subordinate to, yet in collaboration with, the Commission. My close readings illustrate that the way in which Finca positioned the GTRC in relation to the members of the Greensboro

---

[9] Finca served on a public discussion panel with Gonzalez, gave the keynote at the GTRC's Swearing In and Seating Ceremony, spoke at New Light Baptist Church on the night before the GTRC's first public hearing, and offered concluding remarks at the first public hearing (Steadman, 2003, p. B4; Swensen, 2005, p. B1).

[10] Finca's (2004) keynote address is central to my argument in this chapter, and the entirety of the address is reprinted with permission in the Appendix.

audience was not static; he identified them with a variety of other individuals, organizations, and groups as the speech unfolded. As a result of these identifications and re-identifications, the primary subject position that emerged in the speech was a position of positions, consistent with the notion of *ubuntu* as Finca himself defined it. Put another way, the speech, in its entirety, was a call to the Greensboro commissioners and audience members alike to embrace *ubuntu* as a way of viewing themselves and their relationships with others.[11]

Endorsing the Commissioners

The first third of Finca's (2004) address belonged to the epideictic branch of oratory, which, in distinction from oratory whose purpose is either to judge past actions or deliberate about future ones, aims at ceremoniously demonstrating a present state of affairs. Finca's epideictic display aimed, primarily, to demonstrate praise of and support for his audience. He began, "I bring you all greetings, very warm greetings. I also bring you a lot of respect and admiration and a message of congratulations, solidarity, and encouragement from South Africa." In his next lines, Finca developed this rhetorical display by shifting the object of his praise from those attending the Swearing In and Seating Ceremony to the ceremony itself:

> I bring it [this praise and support] to this occasion which is unique, an occasion which is indeed the first of its kind in the history of our struggle to build reconciliation based on truth. As South Africans we believe that this occasion perhaps better deserves to be referred to as one small step for a man and one giant leap for mankind.

In these lines, Finca built up the significance of the ceremony by using the word "occasion" three times, an act of repetition that served to amplify the event's importance. Furthermore, each time he repeated the term he ascribed value to it—first by describing it as distinctive, then by suggesting that the event was historic, and finally by associating it with Neil Armstrong's famous quotation, which he deployed in the Greensboro context to suggest that, for South Africans, the Swearing In and Seating Ceremony was as momentous as a moon landing. The praise and support Finca conveyed in these introductory remarks was contingent upon the existence of the Commission and, thus, doubled as a tacit expression of praise and support for the Commission itself—an implicit endorsement of the Commission, which helped to reinforce its legitimacy.

---

[11]Finca (2004) was not the first person to reference *ubuntu* in Greensboro. Writer Mark Mathabane—who was born in Johannesburg, South Africa—delivered a lecture in the Greensboro area on September of 1999, entitled, "Discovering the Importance of *Ubuntu*—Our Common Humanity" ("Author," 1999, p. 6). Later, in 2001, Greensboro's *News & Record* published a story on Mathabane's writings (Caranna, 2001, p. D1). The piece touched on Mathabane's work of fiction *Ubuntu*, and it described the concept as follows: "*Ubuntu* is a Zulu word that means 'soul' or the 'quality of being human.' 'You cannot be a human being just by yourself,' Mathabane says to put the word in context. 'How you treat other people is how you become a human being'" (Caranna, 2001, p. D1).

The *source* of Finca's endorsement of the GTRC is worth noting. In the space of a few opening lines, Finca used the grammatical resources of projection repeatedly. Instances of projection are usually comprised of a *projecting* clause that attributes speech or thought to a particular source (e.g., "she says" or "Desmond Tutu thinks") and a *projected* clause that presents a locution or idea (Christie, 2002, p. 25).[12] Finca (2004) used the projecting clause "I bring" to introduce projected clauses, which, in this case, were a series of semiotic nouns (i.e., nouns like "greetings" and "message," which referred to other texts). By using the projecting clause "I bring" followed by semiotic nouns, Finca was able to position himself as a messenger—or, perhaps more accurately, as a kind of ambassador—speaking to his Greensboro audience *on behalf of* other South Africans. Thus Finca's expressions of praise—first for his audience and then for the Swearing In and Seating Ceremony—were not simply framed as his own expressions; they were said as if they had the weight of the people of South Africa behind them, and they served to align—to rhetorically connect or join—the people of South Africa with the people of Greensboro.

But moments later, Finca took a different tack. Rather than reinforcing the connection he had just constructed between South Africans and his audience, he created different connections:

> To the commissioners about to be inaugurated into office, I bring a special message of support of love and solidarity from the members of the Truth and Reconciliation Commission of South Africa, from our esteemed chairperson, his grace the Archbishop Desmond Tutu, who writes in his personal letter to yourselves as commissioners, and I quote, "The task of a Commission such as this is to bring to life the truth in order to promote reconciliation." He continues to say, "You have the additional burden of initiating the first TRC in the U.S. Many will be looking to you to assess whether similar commissions might be helpful in other communities also."

Here Finca continued to position himself as a messenger, using projecting clauses such as "I bring" and "I quote," followed, respectively, by a semiotic noun and a quotation from a letter. However, at this point, he spoke on behalf of different sources—the SATRC and Desmond Tutu—and he addressed a different audience: the commissioners themselves. In this passage, then, Finca began by aligning the Greensboro commissioners with the South African commissioners around a shared message of solidarity from the latter. As the passage unfolded, Finca introduced the "personal letter" to the Greensboro commissioners from Tutu, realigning the former with the latter. Another realignment followed this one. Speaking now on his own behalf, Finca said, "Let me begin my own remarks with the words I wrote in December 1995, when I stood, as these commissioners will stand today, and took my oath to be a commissioner in the South African Truth and Reconciliation Commission." In this moment, Finca suggested that he and the GTRC commissioners were aligned—i.e., they shared a stance—in two senses: they stood in a similar place and took a similar oath. Thus, in the space of a few lines, Finca repositioned the GTRC commissioners no less than three times: he aligned them first with the entire SATRC, then with the SATRC's chair, and finally with one of its members,

---

[12] The projecting clause, as linguist Christie (2002) noted, "takes something said or thought before and reinstates it" (p. 25).

himself. There was a kind of movement here, a narrowing of scope, which reinforced the connection between the SATRC and the GTRC on multiple organizational levels—institution, chair, and member.

Furthermore, it must be remembered that even as Finca was directly addressing the GTRC commissioners in this passage he was also indirectly addressing the audience attending the Swearing In and Seating Ceremony. Looked at from the perspective of those attending the ceremony, Finca's positioning work functioned as an endorsement—a public display of support—for the GTRC commissioners from the SATRC, Tutu, and Finca. And, to the extent that the people of Greensboro acknowledged the status of these entities, such rhetorical moves helped to warrant the installation of the Commission and to justify the Commission's subsequent attempts, as Finca put it, "to do the task that you [the people of Greensboro] have set for it to do."[13]

---

[13] Finca's (2004) remarks at the Swearing In and Seating Ceremony were not his only public endorsements of the Commission. One year after Finca's first visit to Greensboro for the Swearing In and Seating Ceremony, he returned, this time to attend the first of three public hearings that the Commission held in the summer and early fall of 2005. Each public hearing was a 2-day event, in which the seven commissioners called experts and eyewitnesses to offer testimony related to the 1979 killings (GTRC, 2005b). Much like at the South African public hearings, the commissioners sat behind a long table in the front of an auditorium, while those offering testimony sat at a separate table nearby. At the beginning and end of each day of the hearings, the GTRC observed eighty-eight seconds of silence, the same length of time that the violence lasted on November 3, 1979. To mark this time of silence, Reverend Mark Sills—one of the seven GTRC commissioners—rang chimes.

At the end of the first public hearing, after all of the testimonies had been given, Finca took a seat at the witness table. From start to finish, Finca's remarks that evening functioned as an endorsement of the Commission. He began, "I feel very uncomfortable speaking from here [the witness table]. I'm used to speaking from there [the commissioners' table]. I hope, however, I'm not going to be asked any difficult questions from yourselves" (GTRC, 2005b). Finca's humor here, which prompted chuckles from the audience, played upon the genre conventions of the public hearing; the fact that he delivered his remarks to the commissioners from the witness table was incongruous with his identity as a former commissioner of the SATRC. By highlighting this incongruity, Finca aligned himself, at least in the eyes of the audience, with those sitting behind the commissioner table. This move was reinforced by a subsequent remark: "Commissioners," Finca said, "have a certain family relation, whether they are here or anywhere else in the world, and there is a sense where, if there is going to be a hearing, we sense discomfort or anxiety about how it's going to turn out." Having thus aligned himself with the commissioners, Finca continued:

> [A]s you began your hearings, in some village back home in South Africa, there was an activity of bells which were ringing to mark our solidarity with you at two o'clock your time, at nine o'clock our time. Those bells were meant to indicate that we were beginning this process in solidarity with yourselves. But having participated in these hearings as an observer yesterday and today, I have a feeling that it is not sufficient that we [South Africans] should ring bells when [you] start your hearings. I think we have to do more than that. We should light a candle and maintain a vigil, because the task that you face requires that we continue to be in solidarity with you.

The theme of Finca's remarks on this occasion was solidarity—a term that Finca used no less than three times in this passage alone. But he did not simply mention solidarity; he also helped constitute it between the GTRC and the people of South Africa.

He did so by calling attention to the shared practice of tintinnabulation between the Greensboro commissioners and South Africans. Then, as if to construct some permanence for this solidarity,

Entrusting the People of Greensboro
with the Truth Commission Model

The second third of Bongani Finca's (2004) address served to extend the truth commission model to the people of Greensboro and, considered in light of the entire speech, to entrust the Greensboro community with the model. Finca began this part of the speech by reflecting on the origins and authorship of the truth commission model:

> We, as the South African Truth and Reconciliation Commission, are humbled and honored that the Greensboro Truth and Reconciliation Commission has been established using the *model* [emphasis added] of South Africa. As we think of that *model* [emphasis added], we pay tribute to Nelson Mandela, who became the author and the pioneer of that *model* [emphasis added]. As you will remember, he emerged out of prison, having spent twenty-seven past years of his life, crushing stones and confined in cells. But he emerged with a *message* [emphasis added], which was later adopted as *a preamble* [*sic*] *to our constitution* [emphasis added]. And I quote from that preamble [*sic*]: "We need to find understanding, but not vengeance. We need to find reparation, but not retaliation. We need to find *ubuntu*, but not victimization." These are the *pillars* [emphasis added] of the route you have chosen to deal with the shame of November 3, 1979, eleven hours [and] twenty-three [minutes], at the corner of Carver and Everitt Street.

In the opening sentences of this passage, Finca referred to the SATRC as a "model" for the GTRC, and, as the passage unfolded, he explained the model's origins and development using a progression of terms: the "model" began as a "message" that was incorporated into a "constitution," the content of which became the "pillars" of the method employed by the people of Greensboro. At each point in this progression, Finca ascribed rhetorical significance to the concept of the truth commission. The "model" was, for example, attributed to Nelson Mandela, who, in reality, neither authored the truth commission model nor was the first to suggest its use in South Africa (Boraine, 2001, p. 11). However, associating the model with Mandela—an internationally respected, iconic figure—increased its value, as did

---

(continued)

Finca suggested that the one-time practice of bell ringing was insufficient. As indicated by the verbs that Finca employed in the last sentence (e.g., "maintain," "continue"), he suggested that a symbolic gesture indicating continuity and duration was needed: a candlelit vigil. Moreover, he framed the relationship between South Africans and the Greensboro commissioners as increasingly intimate. At the beginning of the passage, Finca had used passive constructions to describe South African action (e.g., "there was an activity of bells which were ringing"; "Those bells were meant to indicate…"). By the end of the passage, however, he had shifted to the active voice and used the modal verb "should" to express obligation. The trajectory of this passage culminated in the following pledge to the Greensboro commissioners: "I just wish to pledge to you, on behalf of the fellow commissioners in South Africa and indeed in other parts of the world, our solidarity, our support, and our prayers."

Like Finca's address at the Swearing In and Seating Ceremony, the rhetorical situation at this event was complex. While Finca ostensibly directed his remarks to the Greensboro commissioners, an audience made up of Greensboro citizens was present to witness the comments. What they witnessed might accurately be described as a public pledge of allegiance—that is, an endorsement.

the suggestion that the model was born out of adversity, the product of Mandela's 27-year tenure in prison "crushing stones and confined in cells" (Finca, 2004). Next Finca associated the model—now referred to in the speech as Mandela's "message"— with Mandela's release from prison, one of the defining political events of the twentieth century. As the passage continued to unfold, Finca associated the model with the postamble to the South African interim Constitution.[14] The line that Finca quoted from the constitution called for understanding, reparation, and *ubuntu*. Describing these norms as "pillars" framed them as foundational, thereby giving them added significance.

Even as Finca invested the truth commission model with increasing value, he highlighted its movement from one context to another. In doing so, Finca affiliated the model more and more closely with Greensboro, linking the people of Greensboro to the model first by their memory of its origins ("As *you will remember* [emphasis added], he emerged from prison") and then by their choice to use it ("These are the pillars of the route *you have chosen* [emphasis added]"). Next Finca affiliated the people of Greensboro even more closely with the model. With the help of yet another iteration, he transformed the model into the following series of commonplaces:

> *You have awakened, as we did* [emphasis added], to the truth that bygones will not be bygones until they are confronted honestly, truthfully, and responsibly addressed. *You have realized, as we did* [emphasis added], that the tears on the eyes of those who were victimized will not be dry. No amount of ignoring those tears will make them dry. They will only be dry when we stop and face them and confront our shame and dry them. *You have found, as we did* [emphasis added], that the truth must be told, that the record must be set straight, that forgiveness must be asked for and pardon must be given, before we can move together as communities and as nations. *You have learned, as we did* [emphasis added], that our past will continue to haunt our present, until we agree to face that past with all its shame and address it.

Up until this point in the address, Finca had located authorship for the truth commission model in South African sources—Nelson Mandela and the South African interim Constitution. Here, however, Finca attributed the authorship of the model, at least in part, to the people of Greensboro themselves. He did so by employing four parallel projections—which took the general form "You have [mental projecting verb], as we did"—to introduce a series of commonplace statements. The implication here was that the people of Greensboro and the people of South Africa had co-authored these aspects of the model. Thus, the trajectory of these two paragraphs functioned as a rhetorical passing of the baton, through which Finca extended the authorship of the truth commission model from South Africans to the people of Greensboro. Authorship and authority are, as noted in Chap. 1, linked etymologically, and this etymological link points to the fact that authorship tends to carry with it certain rights and entitlements. In the case of Finca's address, the extension of

---

[14] South Africans involved in the TRC process would have likely recognized Finca's (2004) reference from the interim Constitution, which has probably been quoted more often than any other line from the document. Whether or not the people of Greensboro knew the line, the association of the TRC model with a constitution probably rendered it more legitimate.

authorship helped to entitle the GTCRP to use the model and helped to warrant the installation of the commissioners as commissioners.

Considered in the context of the entire speech, Finca's comments here also functioned to entrust the people of Greensboro with the model. The letter from Tutu that Finca read charged the community with responsibility for it. Quoting from the letter, Finca said, "You have the additional burden of initiating the first TRC in the USA. Many will be looking to you to assess whether similar commissions might be helpful in other communities also." Finca implied, by way of the letter, that as the first truth commission in the USA, the GTRC bore some responsibility for the national development of the field of transitional justice. Later in the address, Finca elaborated upon this notion, suggesting that, because the GTRC was the first TRC in the USA, it was also responsible for the development of the field of transitional justice all over the world:

> [The GTRC] is the first of its kind in the U.S. It *must* [emphasis added] set a model that *must* [emphasis added] succeed. If it does succeed, it will give us all hope that one day there will be truth commissions on Iraq, that there will be truth commissions on Ireland, that there will be truth commissions on the Middle East. If it [does] succeed, as it *must* [emphasis added], it will give us hope that one day we will know the truth of Rwanda and know the truth of Burundi and know the truth of Angola. If it [does] succeed, as it *must* [emphasis added], it will give us all hope that one day we will know the truth on neighborhoods and ghettos on villages and towns and cities, where the blood of the innocent has been spilt, and the cloud of silence has hovered over the national shame.

Finca's use of the modal verb "must" no less than four times in this passage suggested that the GTRC was obligated to succeed. By this point, which came near the end of Finca's address, authorship of and responsibility for the truth commission model had been fully extended to Greensboro. The GTRC, said Finca, "must set a model" for other regions, countries, and communities all over the world: for Iraq, Ireland, the Middle East, Rwanda, Burundi, and Angola.

Establishing the Commission's Stature in the Community

The first and second sections of Finca's (2004) speech primarily highlighted the relationship between the people of Greensboro and South Africans, including members of the SATRC, Tutu, Mandela, and Finca himself. In the third part of the speech, Finca focused more explicitly on the relationship between the people of Greensboro and the Greensboro commissioners. In terms of the Commission's authority, this shift was important, and, significantly, it was precisely at this point that Finca chose to deploy the South African notion of *ubuntu* explicitly. He began by describing the English rendering of *ubuntu ungamntu ngabanye abantu*. "In our language," he said, "we have a saying that a person is a person because of other persons." He elaborated as follows:

> In that saying we recognize that a person is not complete until she embraces other persons and struggles to make them complete also. We recognize that a person cannot be fulfilled

until she finds fulfillment for others also. We recognize that we cannot have real peace until we move in isolation and find peace for those on our side and for those who live on the other side.

The subject position that Finca constructed here—which emphasized complementariness—used *ubuntu* to prompt audience members to see their identities as defined in relation to one another, despite any prior differences they may have had. Finca then nuanced his description of *ubuntu* to help construct the commissioners' authority in the Greensboro community:

> But *ubuntu* goes further than that. It says if you appear a bit taller than others who stand with you, it is not because you are really taller than them, but it is because others are carrying you [on] their shoulders. For this Commission to fulfill its mandate, and to do the task that you have set for it to do, we urge you as the community of Greensboro, to carry the commissioners on your shoulders, to support them, to encourage them, to be with them, and to pray fervently for them.

These remarks were consistent with a facet of Michael Battle's (1997) description of *ubuntu*. *Ubuntu*, Battle claimed, "excludes competitiveness" (p. 41). For Finca (2004), *ubuntu* excludes competitiveness—it even exposes the falsity of comparisons (e.g., I am "a bit taller" than you)—because, insofar as "a person is a person through other persons," one's achievements are wrapped up with those of others. This explanation, however, did not exclude or discredit positions of authority; rather, the image of some individuals sitting atop the shoulders of others acknowledged the necessity of authority. According to Finca, *ubuntu* recognized human interdependence, but, in doing so, it did not involve the dissolution of the hierarchical relationships. Conversely, Finca used *ubuntu* to exhort the people of Greensboro to accept those relationships, thereby helping to establish the Commission's stature in the community.[15]

---

[15] It is worthwhile to note that, throughout the rest of the Swearing In and Seating Ceremony, other subject positions were constructed that were incongruous with *ubuntu*. Take, as just one example, US Congressperson Melvin Watt's comments at the event. While Watt mentioned the SATRC in conjunction with his role at the Faith and Politics Institute, he framed the citizen-led effort in Greensboro as an outgrowth not of the South African political transition, the interim Constitution, or *ubuntu* but of the United States political transition, the Declaration of Independence, and civil rights. Watt's remarks, like Finca's, helped to establish authority for the Commission; however, unlike Finca's remarks, they did so by "attaching" it to a series of "ongoing efforts initiated by citizens to secure and maintain the rights of life, liberty, and the pursuit of happiness" (GTCRP, 2004). The subject position of *ubuntu* (as Finca described it) was a different thing than this subject position, which was characterized by equality and inalienable rights. Watt privileged individual personhood and self-determination, while Finca emphasized community fulfillment or wholeness. Furthermore, Finca did not emphasize equality among persons; rather, he affirmed the differences and complementariness of people. My point in bringing these different emphases into relief is *not* to highlight a fundamental or essential difference between South African culture and Western culture; rather, it is simply to highlight the fact that, in the context of the Commission's Swearing In and Seating Ceremony, there were subject positions constructed that challenged the subject position constructed by Finca.

Constructing Ubuntu *as a Subject Position*

Though Finca only mentioned *ubuntu* twice is his speech, his use of the term was rhetorically forceful because he reinforced his explicit remarks about *ubuntu* with an implicit reaccentuation of the concept as the speech unfolded. More precisely, the speech functioned constitutively by calling audience members to adopt a subject position consistent with *ubuntu*—"a person is a person through other persons."

In his article "Constitutive Rhetoric: The Case of the *Peuple Québécois*," Maurice Charland (1987) claimed that conceptualizing rhetoric simply as *persuasion* incorrectly assumes that audiences are "extra-rhetorical" (p. 133). But Charland saw in rhetorician Kenneth Burke's (1967) work on *identification* a generative alternative for thinking about rhetoric and the rhetorical situation. Calling identification the "key term" of rhetoric, Burke had downplayed the emphasis in rhetorical studies on persuasion and the "deliberate design" of rhetorical activity (p. 63). Through the concept of identification, Burke had suggested that rhetoric is not simply about strategic attempts to persuade, but about all the ways in which speakers and writers "induce cooperation" in their audiences (p. 63). Rhetorical identification allows individuals to achieve what Burke referred to as "consubstantiality," "a type of mixed ontological state in which people are…part of a community of shared interests while remaining autonomous individuals" (Jasinski, 2001, p. 306). Charland (1987) wrote, "Burke's stress on identification permits a rethinking of judgment and the working of the rhetorical effect, for he does not posit a transcendent subject as audience member, who would exist prior to and apart from the speech to be judged, but considers audience members to participate in the very discourse by which they would be 'persuaded'" (p. 133). Rhetoric, in short, not only persuades but also constitutes audience members' identities—often unconsciously. Drawing on key phrases from Louis Althusser's (1970) essay "Ideological State Apparatuses," Charland (1987) contended that through identification individuals are interpellated—or hailed—into subject positions by rhetorics that "'always already' presume the constitution of subjects" (p. 134).

In sum, audiences are always hailed in the initial moment of their address. Thus when Finca (2004) saluted the "people of Greensboro" on behalf of South Africans, or when he conveyed a "special message" of "love and solidarity" to the GTRC commissioners, he helped to constitute these groups as such. That said, according to Charland (1987), the rhetoric of identification is also an ongoing phenomenon (p. 138).[16] As texts unfold in time and/or space, they can constitute subject positions in a multiplicity of ways: subject positions may be altered, reified, contradicted. Or,

---

[16] The rhetoric of identification is, Charland (1987) said, "not restricted to one hailing, but [is] usually a part of a rhetoric of socialization" (p. 138). Rhetorician Michael Leff also commented on this point. In his piece "Textual Criticism: The Legacy of G. P. Mohrmann," Leff (2000) emphasized the importance of acknowledging a text's temporality (pp. 553–554). The temporality of texts—the fact that they unfold in time—offers possibilities for rhetors to shape or fashion subject positions within a given text.

as was the case with Finca's (2004) address, they may be forged. Understanding how Finca forged a subject position for the GTRC and the people of Greensboro requires analyzing how he identified his audience with multiple individuals and groups as the text unfolded.

As noted earlier in the chapter, Finca began his address by identifying various people in Greensboro with South Africans, the SATRC, its chair Desmond Tutu, and one of its members (himself). Note that there was, in this first third of the speech, a contraction in the scope of identification, from nation to institution to chair to individual member. This movement, however, gave way to an expansion, when Finca read the words he wrote on the day he was installed as a SATRC commissioner:

> When hope decays there is a particular stench in the air, of bitterness, of strife, of holding on for dear life to things that neither heal nor help. When hope decays there is anger that pulls down what others try to build. There is frustration with those who build, with those who dream, and with those who think, for how dare they dream and hope and think, because our hope has decayed. But when hope is reborn, we dream the dreams which others scorn. We sing the songs of birds that fly. We embrace our past with all its shame, and say to it you, too, belong to us. We hope, we dream, we think, because our hope is reborn.

Here Finca identified his Greensboro audience with the whole of humanity. The "we" in the passage was a universal we, transcending specific nationalities, institutions, or individuals. Following this poem, in the second third of the speech, the scope of the identification that Finca constructed once again contracted and then expanded, as he identified the people of Greensboro first with Nelson Mandela and then with all South Africans. In the final third of the speech, Finca attempted to establish identification at a local level, between the two groups sitting in his audience: the people of Greensboro watching the ceremony and the GTRC commissioners. Then, at the end of his speech, Finca expanded the scope of identification again by attempting to identify the people of Greensboro with those living in other parts of the world: Iraq, Ireland, the Middle East, Rwanda, Burundi, and Angola.

What Finca seems to have done here relates back to the notion of *ubuntu* as he himself described it. Finca identified the people of Greensboro with others—and each other—in a multiplicity of ways as his speech unfolded and, by doing so, called attention to their positionality. One's identity, he implied, is inextricably linked to and defined by others. In other words, the individual ways in which Finca positioned his audience, taken together, forged a subject position consistent with the logic of *ubuntu*: "I am who I am because of who we all are." I would argue that this emergent subject position, coupled with Finca's explicit description of the concept, gave the speech its rhetorical force. Understanding the importance of this subject position to Finca's address also helps to clarify one of his concluding remarks. "Today," he said, "I am proud to be South African, but today I am also proud to be a little tiny part of Greensboro."

On November 2, 2005, over a year after the Swearing In and Seating Ceremony, Desmond Tutu came to Greensboro to meet privately with the GTRC commissioners and encourage them in their work. The next day, on the 26th anniversary of the Greensboro massacre, Tutu (2005) delivered an address entitled "Reconciling

Love: A Millennium Mandate" at Greensboro's Guilford College as part of the college's Bryan Series lectures. Throughout his remarks, which received a standing ovation, Tutu—arguably the most prominent "author" of TRC discourse—publicly endorsed the work of the GTRC and prompted his audience to do the same. Such comments, from such a prominent source, helped to establish the Commission's authority. Furthermore, he positioned the audience in ways that reinforced the rhetorical action of Finca's remarks.

In the address, Tutu discussed the "delicate network of complementarity" between people, calling to mind both Martin Luther King, Jr.'s (1963/2004) memorable statement that humans are "caught in inescapable network of mutuality" (p. 693) as well as Finca's (2004) articulation of *ubuntu*. Tutu (2005) then went on to describe the concept of *ubuntu* explicitly:

> At home we have something that is very difficult in fact to render into English—*ubuntu*. *Ubuntu*—the essence of being human. And we say, "A person is a person through other persons." I am human ultimately only because I belong. I would never know how to be able to speak as a human being; I wouldn't know how to think as a human being; I wouldn't be able to walk as a human being; yes, I wouldn't know how to be human. I need other human beings to help me to become human. And *ubuntu* says my humanity is caught up in your humanity. When you are dehumanized—whether or not I like it—inexorably, when you are dehumanized, I am dehumanized.

Much like in Finca's address, Tutu's explicit description of *ubuntu* here was complemented by an implicit attempt to position his audience in ways consistent with the concept. One of the key moments came toward the beginning of the speech when Tutu thanked the international community for its help in overcoming apartheid in South Africa. "We wouldn't have made it without the international community," Tutu said. He then added, "I speak on behalf of millions of my compatriots when I say, even now, thank you for that remarkable support: thank you, thank you, thank you." Tutu's expression of gratitude here prompted light applause from the Guilford College audience, but Tutu stopped them and, in mock disgust, said, "No, no, no." He continued, "You are very shy and reserved, and so I discovered that I, in fact, had a special magic wand. When I wave it over people, they turn into instant South Africans." Amidst audience laughter, Tutu proceeded to wave his hand over the audience, remarking, "So I wave it over you and so say to you, fellow South Africans, let's give these Americans a real humdinger of an applause." At this point, the audience erupted into applause (for itself); and, when the applause subsided, Tutu added, "Thank you. Oh, yes, and I wave it again over you, and you revert to your normal shy selves."

Tutu's performance called attention to the differences between South Africans and the people of Greensboro, but it also momentarily pretended that those differences did not exist by positioning the audience as "fellow South Africans" with Tutu. There were, in fact, three subject positions constructed for the audience in this brief excerpt from Tutu's speech: Tutu first positioned the people of Greensboro as members of the international community (which supported South Africans during their transition from apartheid), then as honorary South Africans, and finally as their "normal shy selves." In these alignments and realignments, Tutu highlighted the audience's positionality; he prompted them, perhaps, to acknowledge their interdependence with others.

In his oft-cited piece "Declarations of Independence," Jacques Derrida (1986) raised a question relevant to this discussion of Bongani Finca's address—which came moments before the commissioners took their oath and thereby established the Commission. Derrida asked, "[W]ho signs, and with what so-called proper name, the declarative act which founds an institution?" (p. 8). Reflecting on the United States Declaration of Independence, he contended that such declarative acts are "fabulous" events, in that the signer of such acts does not exist in his authorizing capacity until he has signed the act. "The signature," as Derrida put it, "invents the signer" (p. 10). Such acts are, therefore, self-authorizing: the signature, Derrida noted, "opens *for itself* a line of credit, *its* own credit, for itself *to* itself" (p. 10). In many ways, the founding of the GTRC was an event similar to those events about which Derrida theorized. Because the GTCRP and the GTRC both lacked state-sponsored support, the Swearing In and Seating Ceremony was a kind of self-authorizing "fable"—a performance in and through which the Project attempted to open a line of credit for the Commission.

Given that events like the Swearing In and Seating Ceremony are "fables," their authority can be called into question, as Derrida (1986) playfully did with the Declaration of Independence. Bongani Finca's (2004) speech, however, worked against those who attempted to expose the authority of the GTRC as a "fabulous" act at self-authorization.[17] It did so by providing an answer to the question, "[W]ith what so-called proper name" did the seven individuals take their oath to be commissioners? According to Finca's speech, the GTCRP was entitled to form a truth commission on the grounds that it had shared in the authorship of the truth commission model with Nelson Mandela and the people of South Africa. Moreover, when, moments after Finca's address, the chosen individuals stood, raised their right hands, and took the oath to become members of the GTRC, they stood—thanks, in part, to Finca's address—as individuals endorsed by South Africans; and they stood—again, thanks to Finca—upon the shoulders of the citizens of Greensboro. Reinforcing all of these endorsements was the fact that Finca had positioned his audience in a way that was consistent his understanding of *ubuntu*.

Reaccentuating *Ubuntu* Again

What of the effects of Finca's address? Was the constitutive rhetoric of *ubuntu* that Finca constructed successful in hailing audience members? Measuring the success of the speech with regard to the Greensboro public is, of course, difficult to do, especially given the fact that it is difficult to know who was in attendance at the Swearing In and Seating Ceremony and how they have (or have not) responded to

---

[17]In Chap. 5 of this project, I show that the Commission's opponents called the Commission's authority into question by accusing it of bias toward the group that established it, the GTCRP. Such accusations of bias attacked the legitimacy of the Commission's founding moment: they essentially called the GTCRP's declaration of the Commission's independence into question.

Finca's address since its delivery. What can be said with some certainty, however, is that Finca's address—in conjunction with his many other public appearances in Greensboro—had the effect of reinforcing the association between the GTRC and the SATRC in the public eye.[18] In the days surrounding his visits to Greensboro, Finca was mentioned several times in Greensboro's newspaper; and, in each case, associations were made between the GTRC and the SATRC. For example, in the days leading up to the 24th anniversary of the Greensboro massacre, the *News & Record* reported the following:

> The [anniversary] events begin Friday with a devotion, panel and audience discussion that includes the Rev. Bongani Finca, who serves on the model South African Truth and Reconciliation Commission formed to help that country heal wounds left by the struggle for independence. (Steadman, 2003, p. B4)

The SATRC was described here as a "model" for Greensboro. Similar remarks were made in the paper on June 14, 2004, two days after the Swearing In and Seating Ceremony:

> The Greensboro commission, considered by many to be a first of its kind in the United States, is modeled after groups in South Africa and Peru. "There is no alternative to truth for us to be healed. We need it," said the Rev. Bongani Finca, a member of the South African Truth and Reconciliation Commission, which sought to heal racial division in post-apartheid South Africa. (Church, 2005, p. B1)

And on June 16, 2004, the *News & Record* suggested that the truth commission process taken up in Greensboro originated in South Africa:

> [T]he renovated Depot was the starting point for another kind of journey Saturday – seating of Greensboro's Truth and Reconciliation Commission, formed to revisit the Nov. 3, 1979 deaths of five anti-Klan protestors. Filling the terminal beneath the old Southern Railway clock, VIPs [e.g. Bongani Finca] from as far away as South Africa, where the reconciliation process was born, spoke of communities outside Greensboro that will be watching this process – from Wilmington, Montgomery and Philadelphia to Belfast, Baghdad and Kigali, Rwanda. (Ahearn, 2004, p. B1)

These excerpts from the *News & Record*—which do not cite Finca at length, if at all—suggest that one of Bongani Finca's greatest gifts to the GTRC may have simply been his repeated presence in Greensboro. As a former member of the SATRC, Finca embodied the rhetorical tradition of transitional justice, and his presence reinforced his endorsement of the GTRC in his address.

The commissioners themselves acknowledged the importance of Finca's presence in Greensboro in remarks they delivered at their first public hearing. At the hearing, a little more than a year after the Swearing In and Seating Ceremony, GTRC co-chair Cynthia Brown spoke directly to Finca, who was in attendance at the event:

> Thank you very much Reverend Finca. We certainly appreciate…the support that you have provided…since we were installed. I remember even prior to our installation, before any of us knew what we would be doing, I remember your speaking…during a ceremony where…

---

[18] In Chap. 5 of this project, I demonstrate how the commissioners themselves attempted to reinforce the association between the SATRC and the GTRC, while most of their opponents tried to downplay such connections.

you tried to make the community aware of the kind of challenge that we face. And I really appreciate, and I think that the full Commission appreciates, the fact that you have stayed the course in terms of this journey that we're on as a community. (GTRC, 2005b)

Later, in a letter from the Greensboro commissioners to Finca—dated August 16, 2005, exactly one month after the first public hearing—the commissioners again acknowledged how important it was that Finca attended the first public hearing: "Your presence alone," they wrote, "added great meaning and legitimacy to the hearing" (GTRC, 2005c). At the end of the letter, they added, "By traveling to, observing, and commenting on our first public hearing you reminded us of the distinguished company we keep, and we thank you for your support, wisdom, and presence" (GTRC, 2005c). These observations by the Greensboro commissioners were, I think, on the mark: it mattered greatly to the Commission that Bongani Finca chose to be, as he himself put it, "a little tiny part of Greensboro" (2004).

But Finca gave another resource to the GTRC as well—namely, the concept of *ubuntu*. In the months following Finca's address at the Swearing In and Seating Ceremony, the members of GTRC reaccentuated the concept again: they made use of it for their own ends. On February 22, 2005, eight months after the Swearing In and Seating Ceremony, the GTRC began publishing a weekly e-mail newsletter to inform the Greensboro community of their progress and to notify them about the Commission's upcoming events. They titled their newsletter "*Ubuntu* Weekly" (GTRC, 2005a). By the time that the GTRC finished its work in May of 2006, the newsletter had over 800 subscribers.

The concept was reaccentuated in at least one other important way as well: it was represented visually on the front and back covers of the GTRC's *Final Report*, which was distributed to the Greensboro public at a ceremony in Bennett College's Annie Merner Pfeiffer Chapel on May 25, 2006 (see Fig. 3.1). Chapter 5 looks at the Commission's *Final Report* in more detail; however, I want to conclude this chapter with a brief reading of the report's covers.

As Fig. 3.1 shows, the five victims of November 3, 1979 circle the center of the front cover of the *Final Report*. Proceeding counter-clockwise from the top left corner are images of Sandra Neely Smith, César Cauce, Michael Nathan (holding daughter Leah), James Waller, and William Sampson. Completing the circle, in the top-right corner, is an image of another person impacted by the events of November 3, 1979—César Weston, whose mother Floris Weston was César Cauce's wife. Centered on the front cover are images taken from events surrounding the operation of the GTRC. Just right of center is an image of five roses placed on five empty chairs—a gesture that the commissioners made at each of their public events. Right of that image is a picture of one of the Commission's volunteers, standing before a banner, between the words "Past" and "Present." Left and up from center are images of the commissioners: Mark Sills, Muktha Jost, and Barbara Walker gaze right across the page, and Robert Peters, Cynthia Brown, Patricia Clark, and Angela Lawrence each stand with their right hands raised as they take the oath at the Swearing In and Seating Ceremony. Above these four commissioners, the Commission's logo is prominently displayed: two doves, one black and one white,

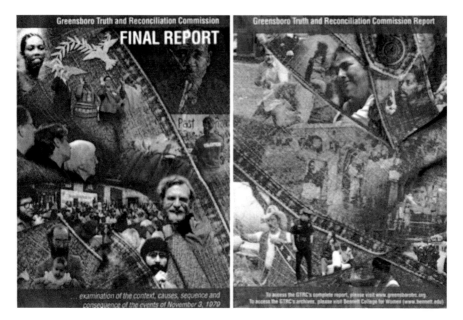

Fig. 3.1 Front and back covers of the GTRC's *Final Report*. From the *Greensboro Truth and Reconciliation Commission Final Report: An examination of the context, causes, sequence and consequence of the events of November 3, 1979*, by the Greensboro Truth and Reconciliation Commission, 2006, Greensboro, NC. Copyright 2006 by GTRC Executive Director Jill E. Williams on behalf of the Greensboro Truth and Reconciliation Commission. Reprinted with permission

holding an olive branch between them. Just below center is an image of Bongani Finca giving his address at the Swearing In and Seating Ceremony.

The back cover of the *Final Report* is a mosaic of images from the events surrounding November 3, 1979, which, for the most part, progress chronologically, starting in the lower left corner and moving clockwise. The back cover includes images of a KKK member hoisting a confederate flag at a showing, a few months before the killings, of D. W. Griffith's racist film *The Birth of a Nation* (bottom left); a member of the Klan/Nazis firing at a CWP protester on November 3, 1979 (top left); a survivor clutching one of the victims (top middle); CWP survivor Martha Nathan, who was widowed on November 3, 1979 (top middle); CWP survivor Nelson Johnson, describing the shootings after the event (top right); and the Greensboro police, lining the streets after the killings (bottom right).

In *Reading Images: the Grammar of Visual Design*, Gunter Kress and Theo van Leeuwen (2006) presented a framework for reading visual images, grounded in M. A. K. Halliday's functional grammar, which provides useful resources for analyzing the front and back covers of the *Final Report*. Kress and van Leeuwen described three principles of visual composition—framing, information value, and salience—that help to realize the meanings of a given image (p. 177). The first of these, framing, was central to the positioning work that the GTRC did in creating the report's covers. Framing devices, according to Kress and van Leeuwen, create unifying and dividing lines, and "the presence or absence of [these] devices…disconnects or connects elements of the image, signifying that they belong or do not belong together in some sense" (p. 177). The central framing device of the report's covers—which organizes the two collages and also thematically connects the front and back covers—is the denim background; and this framing device serves as a kind of visual reaccentuation of *ubuntu*. The folds and stitching of the dark blue denim fabric present a visual argument about the connectedness and interdependence of those implicated in November 3, 1979—victims, perpetrators, survivors, and police—as well as the people of Greensboro, the GTRC commissioners, the Commission's staff, and Bongani Finca. In other words, the covers tie participants together in "a single garment" (King, 1963/2004, p. 693), which symbolically weaves together perpetrator and survivor, commissioner and victim, and—as the banner on the front cover suggests—past and present. It is not, I think, a coincidence that one of the central images on the front cover is of Finca delivering his speech about *ubuntu* at the Swearing In and Seating Ceremony.

However, *ubuntu* was not represented on the covers of the *Final Report* simply in order to make a case for interconnectedness. Much like Finca's reaccentuation of *ubuntu* in his address, the commissioners' reaccentuation of *ubuntu* helped them establish their authority. Here again it is instructive to introduce another distinction put forward in *Reading Images*. Commissioners structured the images according to a conceptual scheme that Kress and van Leeuwen (2006) referred to as a network:

> Networks seek to show the multiple interconnections between participants. Any participant in a network ("node") can form an entry-point from which its environment can be explored, and the vectors or lines ("links") between these participants can take on many different values, the value of signification ("a means b"), of combination ("a goes with b"), of composition ("a contains b"): the essence of the link between two participants is that they are, in some sense, next to each other, or close to each other, associated with each other. (p. 84)

Understood in this way, both the front and back covers of the report present viewers with a network of images, with each image functioning as a node that offers viewers a different entry point for exploring the relationships of the network. Although such networks may appear to be value-neutral, they always operate according to a particular logic:

> [Networks] on the one hand provide the reader with many choices, many paths to follow, but on the other hand tend to obscure the fact that the range of choices is ultimately pre-designed and limited. As such, networks are, in the end, just as much modeled on forms of social organization in which everything has its pre-ordained place in a grand scheme unified by a single source of authority. (p. 84)

What is important to note for my purposes is that the commissioners' two visual networks on the front and back covers of the report were created according to two different schemes, and commissioners identified themselves with the scheme on the front cover, while distancing themselves from the scheme on the back.

The back cover bears witness to the violence surrounding November 3, 1979. The violence, symbolically demonstrated in the hoisting of the confederate flag in the lower left corner, is displayed explicitly in the top left, as a CWP protester doubles over, after having been shot at close range. The posture of the KKK/Nazi killer is mirrored on the opposite side of the page by Nelson Johnson as he lifts a bandaged hand in the form of a gun. Situated between the two is Marty Nathan, mourning the loss of her husband Michael. And the picture in the lower right corner of police lining a Greensboro street testifies to the violence inflicted on the community itself. The images on the front cover operate according to a different logic; commissioners used this space to display images related to their two primary modes of action—talking and listening. Such images include Bongani Finca speaking to the people of Greensboro, three of the victims speaking into microphones, and four of the commissioners performing their oath. The three remaining commissioners who are pictured stand in silence, their eyes directed at the five roses and five empty chairs. It is almost as if the back and front covers were meant to perform, respectively, the Commission's two great aims—truth and reconciliation.

In considering how the commissioners constructed their authority through these networks, it is important to note where they did and did not position images of themselves on the pages. In keeping with the notion that their inquiry into the truth of November 3, 1979 should maintain a critical distance, they did not place themselves on the back cover. Rather, they placed themselves on the front cover. In doing so, they wrote themselves into the story of November 3, 1979 in a way that identified with the victims and reaffirmed their particular approach to addressing the atrocities represented on the back cover—not with additional violence, but through acts of speech and silence.

It is also worth considering how *viewers* of the covers are positioned. Kress and van Leeuwen (2006) noted two kinds of participants that one must consider when analyzing images: represented participants (i.e., the people depicted in the images) and interactive participants (i.e., "the people who communicate with each other *through* images, the producers and viewers of images") (p. 114). Both kinds of participants are connected through vectors, which often—though certainly not always—take the form of sight lines between represented participants or between represented participants and interactive participants. On the back cover, most of the represented participants' gazes are directed at unknown sources outside of the camera's frame. (The exception to this is the policeman talking to a mother and her two children.) However, there are important vectors established between represented and interactional participants—namely, the vectors created by the KKK member's gun and Nelson Johnson's bandaged hand, which takes the form of a gun. Viewers of the back cover are, in other words, positioned as targets of the violence.

On the front cover, commissioners constructed a network of gazes that functions as a kind of visual memorial, and there are several vectors constructed between represented participants that help to constitute this memorial. First, César Weston (who testified at the public hearings) glances from the upper right quadrant across the page to victim Sandra Neely Smith in the upper left quadrant, and this vector is reinforced by the similar reddish tone of these two images. Second, three of the commissioners gaze across the page at the rose-filled empty chairs. This gaze, too, is reinforced by similar tones: both images are black and white. These vectors seem to symbolize acts of remembering—as does the downward vector between Michael

Nathan and daughter Leah, as well as the inward vector established between the Commission's volunteer and the banner's words: "Past and Present."

This visual memorial is not, however, something that the observer of the front cover stands outside of, insofar as there are two additional vectors, which emerge outward from the page. These vectors are what Kress and van Leeuwen (2006) referred to as a "demand": "[T]he participant's gaze (and the gesture, if present), demands something from the viewer, demands that the viewer enter into some kind of imaginary relation with him or her" (p. 118). In this case, William Sampson and baby Leah look outward at viewers, establishing vectors between represented and interactive participants. Such vectors function to identify viewers with the scheme of the front cover, to align viewers with the victims and draw them into the network of memorializing gazes, and—perhaps most importantly—to call viewers, much like Finca's speech called its audience members, into the logic of *ubuntu*.

References

Ahearn, L. (2004, June 16). On the street: Losing bearings on "new" I-85. *News & Record*, p. B1.

Althusser, L. (1970). *Lenin and philosophy and other essays* (B. Brewster, Trans.). New York, NY: Monthly Review Press.

Author, anti-apartheid activist to give speech. (1999, September 26). *News & Record*, p. 6.

Battle, M. (1997). *Reconciliation: The ubuntu theology of Desmond Tutu*. Cleveland, OH: Pilgrim.

Boraine, A. (2001). *A country unmasked: Inside South Africa's Truth and Reconciliation Commission*. Oxford: Oxford University Press.

Burke, K. (1967). Rhetoric—old and new. In M. Steinmann (Ed.), *New Rhetorics* (pp. 60–76). New York, NY: Charles Scribner's.

Caranna, K. (2001, February 19) Mathabane explores a life without hatred; "No good can come out of hating," writer Mark Mathabane says. *News & Record*, p. D1.

Charland, M. (1987). Constitutive rhetoric: The case of the *Peuple Québécois*. *Quarterly Journal of Speech, 73*(2), 133–150. doi:10.1080/00335638709383799.

Christie, F. (2002). *Classroom discourse analysis: A functional perspective*. New York, NY: Continuum.

Church, Ellica. (2005, April 16). Panel seeking truth compared to one in Peru; a member of the Peruvian Commission shares her experiences with the local group. *News & Record*, p. B1.

Derrida, J. (1986). Declarations of independence (T. Keenan & T. Pepper, Trans.). *New Political Science: A Journal of Politics and Culture, 15*, 7–15.

Enslin, P., & Horsthemke, K. (2004). Can *ubuntu* provide a model for citizenship education in African democracies? *Comparative Education, 40*(4), 545–558. doi:10.1080/0305006042000284538.

Finca, B. (2004, June 12). Keynote address at the Swearing In and Seating Ceremony of the Greensboro Truth and Reconciliation Commission [DVD]. Copy in possession of author.

Greensboro Truth and Community Reconciliation Project. (2004, June 12). Swearing In and Seating Ceremony of the Greensboro Truth and Reconciliation Commission [DVD]. Copy in possession of author.

Greensboro Truth and Reconciliation Commission. (2005a, February 22). *Ubuntu Weekly*. Retrieved January 15, 2008, from http://www.greensborotrc.org/ubuntu_weekly.php.

Greensboro Truth and Reconciliation Commission. (2005b, July 15–16). First public hearing: What brought us to November 3, 1979? [DVD]. Available March 1, 2012, from http://www.greensborotrc.org/index.php.

Greensboro Truth and Reconciliation Commission. (2005c, August 16). [Letter to Rev. Bongani Finca]. Greensboro Truth and Reconciliation Commission Archive, Bennett College Library, Greensboro, NC.

Greensboro Truth and Reconciliation Commission. (2006). *The Greensboro Truth and Reconciliation Commission final report: An examination of the context, causes, sequence and consequence of the events of November 3, 1979.* Retrieved March 1, 2012, from http://www.greensborotrc.org/.

Jasinski, J. (2001). *Sourcebook on rhetoric: Key concepts in contemporary rhetorical studies.* Thousand Oaks, CA: Sage.

Kairos theologians. (1986). *The kairos document: Challenge to the church: A theological comment on the political crisis in South Africa.* Grand Rapids, MI: W. B. Eerdmans.

Kamwangamalu, N. (2008). *Ubuntu* in South Africa: A sociolinguistic perspective to a pan-African concept. In M. K. Asante, Y. Miike, & J. Yin (Eds.), *The global intercultural communication reader* (pp. 113–122). New York, NY: Routledge.

King, M. L., Jr. (1963/2004). Letter from Birmingham jail. In D. McQuade & R. Atwan (Eds.), *The writer's presence: A pool of readings* (pp. 692–707). Boston, MA: Bedford/St. Martin's.

Kress, G., & van Leeuwen, T. (2006). *Reading images: The grammar of visual design* (2nd ed.). New York, NY: Routledge.

Leff, M. C. (2000). Textual criticism: The legacy of G. P. Mohrmann. In C. Burgchardt (Ed.), *Readings in rhetorical criticism* (pp. 546–557). Strata: State College, PA.

Marx, C. (2002). Ubu and ubuntu: On the dialectics of apartheid and nation building. *Politikon: South African Journal of Political Studies, 29*(1), 49–69. doi:10.1080/0258934022014943.

McLaughlin, N. (2004, November 13). Confronting past is first step toward healing, professor says; the daughter of a Nobel Prize winner and others re-examine the Klan/Nazi shootings that left five dead in 1979. *News & Record*, p. B1.

More, M. P. (2004). Philosophy in South Africa under and after apartheid. In K. Wiredu (Ed.), *A Companion to African Philosophy* (pp. 149–160). Oxford: Blackwell.

Parliament of the Republic of South Africa. (1995, July 19). *Promotion of national unity and reconciliation act 34 of 1995.* Retrieved March 1, 2012, from http://www.justice.gov.za/legislation/acts/1995-034.pdf.

Sanders, M. (2007). *Ambiguities of witnessing: Law and literature in the time of a truth commission.* Stanford: Stanford University Press.

Shutte, A. (2001). *Ubuntu: An ethic for a new South Africa.* Pietermaritzburg, South Africa: Cluster.

South African Truth and Reconciliation Commission. (1999). *Truth and Reconciliation Commission of South Africa report* (Vol. 1). New York, NY: Grove's Dictionaries.

Steadman, T. (2003, October 29). Project revisits Nazi-Klan shootings; the Truth and Community Reconciliation Project will commemorate the 24th anniversary of the Nazi- Klan shootings. *News & Record*, p. B4.

Swensen, E. (2005, July 11). About 50 people watch a movie about the South African panel that's a model for the committee on the Klan-Nazi shootings. *News & Record*, p. B1.

Tutu, D. (1999). *No future without forgiveness.* New York, NY: Doubleday.

Tutu, D. (2005). Reconciling love: a millennium mandate. *2005–2006 Bryan series lectures on spirit and spirituality* [videocassette]. Hege Library, Guilford College, Greensboro, NC.

Ubuntu Africa. (2012). Ubuntu Africa homepage [Website]. Retrieved July 7, 2008, from http://ubafrica.org/.

Ubuntu Education Fund. (n.d.). Ubuntu Education Fund homepage [Website]. Retrieved July 7, 2008, from http://www.ubuntufund.org/.

Chapter 4
Reaccentuating Representivity in Greensboro

Abstract This chapter analyzes the discourse surrounding the Greensboro Truth and Reconciliation Commission's public events—its calls for participation, Swearing In and Seating Ceremony, three public hearings, and Report Release Ceremony—to demonstrate how the commissioners reaccentuated the organizational rhetoric of past truth commissions to position the Commission, and the truth commission process in general, as representative of the Greensboro community at large. However, even as they established their representivity, commissioners also highlighted the ways in which they were unrepresentative of the community. Creating this tension enabled commissioners both to identify themselves with community members and to establish themselves as a model of interaction and reconciliation for the community.

J.E. Beitler III, *Remaking Transitional Justice in the United States*,
Springer Series in Transitional Justice, DOI 10.1007/978-1-4614-5295-9_4,
© Springer Science+Business Media New York 2013

"The Commission has...been harshly criticized for being loaded with so-called 'struggle'-types...We want to say categorically we did not choose ourselves, nor did we put our own names forward. We were nominated in a process open to anyone – whatever their political affiliation or lack of it. We were interviewed in public sessions by a panel on which all the political parties were represented. Moreover, when the President made his choice from a short list, it was in consultation with his Cabinet of National Unity, which included the ANC, the IFP and the National Party. No one, as far as we know, objected publicly at the time to those who were so appointed. Indeed, many of us were chosen precisely because of our role in opposing apartheid – which is how we established our credibility and demonstrated our integrity. I am myself, even today, not a card-carrying member of any political party. I believe, on the other hand, that some of my colleagues may have been chosen precisely because of their party affiliation, to ensure broad representivity."

Archbishop Desmond Tutu (1999, p. 9)

Introduction

In the Foreword to his Commission's *Final Report*, Archbishop Desmond Tutu (1999) described the make-up of South African Truth and Reconciliation Commission (SATRC) in terms of its "representivity" (p. 9). He supported this claim by highlighting how commissioners' different political affiliations represented those of the South African population as a whole, by suggesting that commissioners were "wounded healers" who had shared in the violence of apartheid, and by bringing into relief conflicts among commissioners, which, he suggested, typified the conflicts among South Africans from different backgrounds (pp. 9, 22; Beitler, 2012). "We in the Commission," he wrote, "have been a microcosm of our society, reflecting its alienation, suspicions and lack of trust in one another" (p. 22). Tutu's threefold construction of representivity served to warrant the SATRC's judgments and recommendations as detailed in their *Final Report*: positioning the Commission as representative of the South African society helped to ensure that, as Tutu put it, the Commission's "work and report should gain the widest possible acceptance" (p. 15). As Chap. 2 noted, this stance of representivity has been an important facet of the *ethos* of truth commissions and a recurring feature of the rhetorical tradition of transitional justice.

The International Center for Transitional Justice facilitated the transmission of the concept of representivity from South Africa to Greensboro.[1] In a memorandum dated June 26, 2002, ICTJ Senior Associate Lisa Magarrell exhorted the GTRC's architects—the GTCRP—to carefully consider what the composition of the Commission should be, which, she claimed, was one of the "key decisions" that they needed to make (p. 2). She advised the GTCRP to sketch "a general logic for the commission's overall make-up," and she provided a series of questions to help them develop that logic:

---

[1] Peter Storey, the former prison chaplain to Nelson Mandela, may also have been involved in bringing the notion of representivity to the Greensboro process. Storey served on the National Advisory Committee, which helped to draft the GTRC's defining documents. In an e-mail to Lisa Magarrell, he wrote, "To get a commission that has broad acceptance, you have to involve the widest number of different constituencies" (Magarrell & Wesley, 2008, p. 57).

Should the commission be somehow representative? If so, representative of what? (Community? Economic, political, geographic, racial, ethnic, gender balance? Interested parties? Neutrality? Diverse but opinionated voices on the issue?)…A decision must be made about the local vs. national composition. (All local? All national? Mixed in some proportion?) (pp. 2–3)

Despite the fact that Magarrell introduced the concept of representivity in the form of a question, she seemed to suggest it was of paramount importance: it was the first criterion she listed for determining the Commission's make-up, and she returned to it again later in the memo when discussing who should select the commissioners. She wrote that the panel that selected the commissioners should be "a broader coalition of people representative of the community" (p. 3). Shortly thereafter she reiterated the point, noting, "A small selection panel could be formed from as wide and representative a group as possible, allowing the selection process to satisfy the need for representation" (p. 3).[2]

Although Magarrell emphasized the importance of representivity, she didn't dictate in the memo what the Commission should be representative of; instead, she offered the GTRC's architects a menu of options from which to choose. One of this chapter's central aims, then, is to explore how the GTCRP and the GTRC chose to position the Commission as representative.[3] In what follows, I trace how the Commission's *ethos* of representivity was constructed diachronically, and I demonstrate that it was constructed in a number of different ways at various times during the Commission's life. At the Commission's inception, members of the Project primarily established the Commission's representivity in terms of demographic categories, but by the end of its operation, commissioners constructed representivity by describing themselves as a microcosm of the Greensboro community and by highlighting their different viewpoints. At the midpoint of the Commission's operation, during its three public hearings, the Commission established representivity by selecting which individuals to invite to offer testimony.[4] These findings are complicated

---

[2] When Magarrell (2002) suggested that GTRC should be "somehow representative," she seemed to be using the term primarily to mean that the Commission should be typical—that is, having the distinctive qualities—of some class, group, or body of opinion. Tutu (1999, p. 9) used the term "representivity" in a similar sense: to highlight the typicality of the SATRC in relation to South Africans.

[3] In exploring how the Commission positioned itself as representative, I am primarily concerned—as Magarrell (2002) seemed to be—with the ways in which the Commission positioned itself as typical of some larger class, group, or body of opinion. This distinction is necessary because there were moments, before and during the life of the Commission, in which various parties were positioned as representative in another sense—namely, as people chosen to act or speak on behalf of a wider group. To prevent confusion, I use the adjective "representative" to mean typical or characteristic of a wider group, unless I explicitly specify otherwise. I also borrow Tutu's term "representivity," which I use, much like Tutu (1999) did, to specify a subject position characterized by typicality in reference to a wider group.

[4] I contextualize my findings with media coverage of these events from Greensboro's newspaper— the *News & Record*. The *News & Record* was one of the main media sources that the Commission used to publicize its events, and—at the time of the Commission's operation—the paper had a fairly wide readership in the city. According to Magarrell and Wesley (2008), the paper claimed "to have a circulation of over 92,000 (rising above 110,000 on Sundays) to a racial demographic that tilts toward white readership but that roughly corresponds to the area's population" (p. 163).

by the fact that, during each stage of its life, the Commission positioned itself—and was positioned by its advocates—as unrepresentative of the wider Greensboro community: commissioners were, for example, described by the GTCRP as independent, extraordinary, objective, and willing to engage in dialogue about November 3, 1979.

As the memo to the Project from Lisa Magarrell indicates, the Commission's advocates were aware of the importance of the GTRC's representativeness to the success of the truth-seeking process in Greensboro. In *Learning from Greensboro*, published after the Commission had concluded its work, Magarrell and Wesley (2008) emphasized that the commissioners' representativeness (p. 57)—along with related notions of diversity (pp. 65–66) and independence (pp. 69, 77–80)—was a key concern throughout the process. What distinguishes my chapter from Magarrell and Wesley's reflections is that I present representivity and unrepresentivity as rhetorically constructed subject positions (i.e., constructions of the Commission's *ethos*), and I seek to explain how, exactly, these features of the rhetorical tradition of transitional justice were reaccentuated at different points during the GTRC's operation. Furthermore, I contend that, although these seemingly contradictory constructions of *ethos* could have attenuated one another, the tension established between the Commission's representivity and unrepresentivity helped to ensure that the GTRC's work was efficacious.[5] It was, I suggest, the interplay between these positions that allowed the Commission to present itself as a model of community for the people of Greensboro—a model that was characterized by unity in diversity.

The Selection Panel

On May 6, 2003, a little over a year before commissioners were installed at the Swearing In and Seating Ceremony, the GTCRP took out a full-page advertisement in three local newspapers—the *News & Record*, the *Carolina Peacemaker*, and the *Rhinoceros Times* (GTCRP, 2003b, p. A9). In the advertisement, the GTCRP described how the commissioners were to be chosen and what their mandate would be. Greensboro citizens would nominate individuals to serve as commissioners, and a selection panel would choose seven commissioners from the list of nominees.[6]

---

[5]As I will show, representivity enabled commissioners to identify with a greater segment of the Greensboro community, while unrepresentivity served as a warrant for their claim that they would evaluate the past fairly. My thinking about the ways in which the GTRC navigated between these constructions of *ethos* was informed primarily by two sources. The first was Ruti Teitel (2000), who noted that most truth commissions are expected to be *both* "politically balanced" *and* "neutral" (p. 81). The second was D. Robert DeChaine (2005), who, when writing about the non-governmental organization Doctors without Borders, noted that the organization has had two "contradictory motivations": they have made use of both a rhetoric of neutrality and a rhetoric of moral-ethical commitment. DeChaine highlighted that Doctors without Borders' practice of *temoignage*—i.e., its practice of "bearing witness to, and speaking out against, perceived human injustices that its volunteers encounter" (p. 83)—demonstrated a "precarious navigation of political neutrality and moral conviction" (p. 77).

[6] For another account of the formation and work of the selection panel, see Magarrell and Wesley (2008, pp. 57–65).

The GTCRP's advertisement also described how the selection panel itself was to be selected: the GTCRP would invite each of Greensboro's interest groups to appoint one individual to serve on the panel. In the weeks that followed the publication of the advertisement, 14 interest groups appointed individuals to serve on the selection panel, and this group began reviewing commissioner nominations in February of 2004 (GTRC, 2006, p. 431).[7]

This selection process—especially the formation of the selection panel—enabled the GTCRP to begin to establish the Commission's *ethos* of representivity. By asking interest groups to each appoint one individual to the selection panel, the GTCRP was able to make the case that the process incorporated the interests and perspectives of the community as a whole. The GTCRP (2003a) acknowledged as much, noting that the various interest groups were chosen because "they reflect the broad range of interests in this community" (para. 3). They continued, "It is hoped that residents of Greensboro can look at this list and see their perspectives at least partially represented by one or more of the groups" (para. 3). The rhetorical efficacy of this construction of representivity—i.e., the extent to which Greensboro's residents *could* "see their perspectives at least partially represented"—hinged, in part, on whether or not the list of interest groups appeared to accurately correspond to the array of perspectives in the city. The rhetorical nature of the process appears to have been clear to the Commission's architects. Writing about the formation of the selection panel after the Commission had concluded its work, Magarrell and Wesley (2008) noted, "There was discussion on how to identify and reach out to different identity groups within Greensboro to tap the community…for selection panel representatives" (p. 53). They continued, "The biggest challenge was to establish an adequate list of sectors [of the community]" (57). It is not surprising, therefore, that the GTCRP's (2003a) list of interest groups included institutions from both the public and private sector; was characterized by a number of different institutional types, including educational institutions, religious organizations, political parties, a labor union, and other interest groups; and contained several parties implicated in the events of November 3, 1979 (para. 4).

The selection process was a noteworthy rhetorical move for several reasons. First, to the extent that the interest groups agreed to appoint a representative (and most did so), they appeared to tacitly endorse the TRC process.[8] Second, by publishing the list of interest groups in local newspapers, the GTCRP encouraged

---

[7] The list of interest groups included the student body chairs, Presidents, and Chancellors of Greensboro's six colleges and universities; the Chamber of Commerce; the Neighborhood Congress; the Police Officers Association; the Truth and Community Reconciliation Project (GTCRP); the Guilford County Democratic Party; the Guilford County Republican Party; the Jewish community; the NAACP; the National Conference for Community and Justice (NCCJ); the Mayor of Greensboro; the Muslim community; the Pulpit Forum of African American Churches; the Sons of Confederate Veterans and the Daughters of the Confederacy; the Triad Central Labor Council; and a consortium of traditional Protestant, Catholic, and Independent churches (GTCRP, 2003b, p. A9).

[8] However, Mayor Keith Holliday clarified that his appointment of Judge Lawrence McSwain to the selection panel did not constitute an endorsement of the GTRC (Dyer, Binker, Buchanan, & Shultz, 2004, p. B1).

participation: the list included several groups that were antagonistic toward one another (or, at the very least, had different viewpoints about November 3, 1979), and this fact probably prompted many of the groups to appoint a representative so as to prevent others from dominating the process. Third, the process allowed the GTCRP to make use of existing institutional frameworks in constructing the selection panel's *ethos*.[9] Put another way, the process positioned Greensboro's citizens as agents of their own persuasion: as each of Greensboro's interest groups appointed individuals to serve on the selection panel, they themselves lent support to the GTCRP's construction of representivity.

That said, the selection process did not simply allow the GTCRP to construct representivity. The creation of the selection panel also allowed the GTCRP to distance itself—and, for that matter, all other politically interested parties—from the GTRC. To reinforce this rhetorical distance, the GTCRP (2003a) mandated that the selection panel would "work independently and free of any outside influence," and it advised the selection panel to carry out its work in private (para. 5).[10] The selection panel, then, was constituted in two seemingly contradictory ways. The panel was to be representative of the interests of the Greensboro community, yet it was to work independently from the community. This twofold subject position was an attempt to garner support for the selection process from members of the community—who, it was hoped, would see themselves represented in the process—while heading off accusations that the process favored the former members of the Communist Workers Party or any other group.

While the GTCRP gave little instruction to the selection panel about how to choose the commissioners, the few stipulations it did give suggested that the Commission should be constituted in a similar way—i.e., according to a twofold subject position. The GTCRP (2003a) said that "strong consideration" should be given to the Commission's "racial, socio-economic, religious, and sexual diversity" (para. 7). It also said that commissioners were to be people of "recognized integrity and principle" and "demonstrated commitment to the values of truth, reconciliation, equity and justice" (GTCRP, 2003b). Each of these positions had a distinct rhetorical purpose: the former enabled the Commission to identify with a broad audience, while the latter held commissioners up as moral exemplars, so that the Commission might do the work of truth-seeking, reconciliation, and justice that the community had not been able to accomplish.

After the selection panel had been formed and the commissioner nominations had been collected, members of the selection panel worked for 3 months. On May 27,

---

[9] That said, as Magarrell and Wesley (2008) recorded, several of the interest groups mentioned in the advertisement—such as the "traditional Protestant, Catholic, and independent churches" and the "Muslim community"—were actually comprised of many groups representing a variety of viewpoints (pp. 60–61). In these cases, work was done to bring these groups together in order to choose a selection panel representative (pp. 60–61).

[10] As Magarrell and Wesley's (2008) account of the GTRC has productively highlighted, the Commission's independence from the Project was an issue that the Commission's architects and the commissioners themselves considered carefully (pp. 70–71, 77–80). Nevertheless, the Commission's independence was contested at a number of points throughout the process (pp. 135, 158).

2004, they released the names of the commissioners: Cynthia Brown, Patricia Clark, Muktha Jost, Angela Lawrence, Robert Peters, Mark Sills, and Barbara Walker.[11] The media coverage of this event suggested that the GTCRP was at least somewhat effective in shaping how the selection process and Commission were perceived. For example, in a May 30th editorial that was otherwise largely critical of the TRC process, the author noted both that commissioners "represent a broad range of occupations and backgrounds" and that the selection panel that chose them was an "independent" body ("In Search," 2004, p. H2). Similarly, a June 11th article reported, "An independent panel chose the seven commission members in May from a list of more than 70 nominations" (Shallcross, 2004, p. B1). For her part, Lisa Magarrell was seemingly satisfied with the outcome: in *Learning from Greensboro*, she and Joya Wesley (2008) wrote, "The selection panel chose a very diverse group that, taken together, represented Greensboro well" (p. 65). To support this claim, Magarrell and Welsey pointed to categories such as gender, race, professional background, residency in and outside of Greensboro, and income (pp. 65–66). After making these points, they quoted Greensboro city councilperson Claudette Burroughs-White, who, after hearing about the Commission's composition, had remarked, "I knew a lot of them, and liked them—thought some of them were strange, thought they were representative" (p. 66).[12]

But despite these successes, the GTCRP's selection process did not quell *all* concerns about the GTRC's composition. According to the *News & Record*, when the selection panel released the names of the commissioners, one of the questions they were asked was "whether the [Commission] was stacked with people who might lean a certain way because of their work on behalf of social justice issues" (McLaughlin, 2004, p. B1). And at least some citizens, upon hearing about the composition of the Commission, lamented the exclusion of any "high-profile names" or "even one high-profile community skeptic," which "would have added considerable weight and credibility to this cause" and given the Commission a more "'bipartisan' flavor" ("In Search," 2004, p. H2).

The Swearing In and Seating Ceremony

On June 12, 2004, sixteen days after the commissioners' names had been released, the Commission's Swearing In and Seating Ceremony took place, and—as this section of the chapter shows—the ceremony's speakers reaccentuated notions of representivity again (GTCRP, 2004). First, Judge Lawrence McSwain, who had chaired the selection panel and formally installed the commissioners during the Swearing

---

[11] The commissioners' names were first listed in the May 28th edition of the *News & Record* (McLaughlin, 2004, p. B1).

[12] Note that claims like these from Magarrell and Wesley's (2008) account are an important part of the rhetoric of representivity surrounding the GTRC. That is, such comments do not simply *describe* a state of affairs (i.e., the Commission's representivity) but help to *constitute* it as such.

In and Seating Ceremony, positioned the Commission as representative of the city of Greensboro's demographics. Then, a number of speakers, each of whom spoke on behalf of a different interest group in the community, endorsed the Commission, thereby demonstrating that the Commission typified a large segment of Greensboro's population.[13] Complicating these attempts at establishing the Commission's representivity was the fact that—at various times throughout the ceremony, including during McSwain's remarks—the Commission was positioned as decidedly unrepresentative of the people of Greensboro. Such complex positioning work, I argue, helped establish the authority necessary for the commissioners to address different aspects of their multi-faceted mandate.

Judge McSwain (GTCRP, 2004) began his remarks by describing how the selection panel chose the commissioners.[14] When describing this process, McSwain referred to the commissioners who were selected using a series of binaries: male and female, professional and non-professional, lower-level workers and upper-level workers, college-educated and un-college–educated, and "of color" and "not of color." Even his explanation about the panel's decision to include a lawyer on the Commission framed the matter in terms of a binary: "There was a long discussion about *whether or not* [emphasis added] we should include a lawyer on the commission." By describing the commissioners in this way, McSwain helped to establish the Commission's representivity: the emphasis on the commissioners' differences implied that the Commission, taken as a whole, would be representative of some particular demographics of the Greensboro community. Representivity was not, however, simply implied. Throughout his description of the process, McSwain used lexemes of the word "representative" twice.

The GTCRP's other attempt to establish the Commission's representivity came later in the ceremony, when the GTCRP (2004) had 18 people from the Greensboro community publicly endorse the newly constituted GTRC. Here are a few relevant excerpts from the speeches:

> I want to tell…the commissioners today there was uniform, unanimous, clear support for this Commission, and I can speak, I think, for the neighbors and the citizens across Greensboro.
>
> Patrick Downs, Co-chair of the Neighborhood Congress

> The Pulpit Forum supports the work of this Commission. It is our belief that we must harmonize the gospel, celebrate signs of these times, and to that end, we greet you, we support you, and we welcome you in the words of the old church fathers, "to the bitters and to the sweets."
>
> Rev. Mazie Ferguson, President, Pulpit Forum

---

[13] As Magarrell and Wesley (2008) put it, the speakers "made it clear that, even though the 'official' city had not taken up the call for truth and reconciliation around the events of November 3, 1979, a significant part of Greensboro saw the Commission as a hopeful and an important step" (p. 67).

[14] Given that the panel conducted the majority of its work in private, Judge McSwain's description of the selection process was instrumental in shaping how the public perceived this process.

I come to you today in my uniform, my teamster uniform. I'm a teamster representative... The truth is I need your help commissioners. I am a man that believes in God, and I promise you that I will go down this path of truth with you; I will go down this path of reconciliation with you, seeking peace and justice and truth in the end.

Chris Roth, North Carolina AFL-CIO

I am...honored to be among those who will speak on this historic and herstoric occasion. I do so for the entire education community and, of course, as the President of Bennett College for Women...May the newly installed Greensboro Truth and Reconciliation Commission do its work well, so that from the darkest and most shameful hour, in the modern history and herstory of Greensboro, truth and reconciliation will pour down upon us, and peace with justice will come in the morning.

Dr. Johnnetta Cole, President, Bennett College

On behalf of the Piedmont Triad region of the National Conference for Community Justice...I bring the best wishes and hopes for the important work that this Commission is about to begin. NCCJ in this community felt honored and even compelled by our mission of fighting bias, bigotry, and racism to join in this effort, to help make is successful, to help make it work.

Steve Simpson, Executive Director, NCCJ

The NAACP has historically, I'm sure you're all aware, the history of defending not only civil rights but human rights, not just for the African-American community, but the community of all peoples of this world. Therefore it is fitting that the NAACP wholeheartedly endorsed this project. It is committed to pledge our continued support.

Viola Fuller, Spokesperson, Greensboro Branch of the NAACP

On behalf of the students of the six institutions in Greensboro, North Carolina, I stand to applaud and to thank the Commission and to accept its charge to seek the truth about a disconcerting event, which occurred on November the 3rd, 1979.

Rashaad Hoggard, Student, North Carolina A&T University

On behalf of the survivors of the Greensboro Massacre, I would like to thank the Local Task Force for making this day possible...These times are times of terrible crimes, mass violence, lawlessness, and torture. Our history is replete with often hidden social, terrible crimes. How can we live together? We wait for you [commissioners] to help us answer that question.

Dr. Martha Nathan, Survivor of November 3rd, 1979, and Executive Director, Greensboro Justice Fund

As these excerpts illustrate, almost all of the speakers, at some point during their speeches, invoked a corporate voice: three individuals began with the phrase "on behalf of"; two claimed to "speak for" their organizations; two others simply spoke for their organizations; and one person explicitly described himself as a "representative." In other words, each of these speakers served as a representative—a spokesperson—who spoke on behalf of a larger interest group. Groups that were represented included, but were not limited to, elected officials, neighborhood organizations, the youth, the religious community, the education community, the labor community, civil rights leaders, college students, tenants of Morningside Homes, and survivors. But these speakers were not simply *representatives* for various interest groups; viewed together as a group, they were also *representative* of an even larger group made up of all of these groups.[15]

What larger group was the group of speakers representative of? The GTCRP's intention was probably to represent the population of Greensboro as closely as possible. For the most part, the groups and institutions represented spanned categories of race, ethnicity, gender, class, age, and profession. It was, I think, the heterogeneity of the group of invited speakers that gave this moment during the Swearing In and Seating Ceremony its rhetorical force. While the 18 individuals who gave speeches did, of course, share characteristics with one another, they also embodied multiplicity in terms of their respective affiliations, identities, etc. In short, the GTCRP created a complex, polyvocal rhetorical situation, which may have established identification between the GTRC and a variety of different audience members.

The Commission, however, was not simply positioned as representative during the Swearing In and Seating Ceremony; it was also positioned as unrepresentative of the community.

McSwain, for one, positioned the Commission as objective and impartial. Toward the end of his remarks, McSwain noted that the Commission would start with a "clean slate" when seeking the truth, meaning it would not be burdened by any one group's agenda. McSwain reinforced this point by reminding the audience that the selection panel had operated "outside" the GTCRP when choosing the commissioners, that there had been no communication between the two groups, and that the GTCRP had first learned who the commissioners were at the selection panel's press conference.

Following these comments, McSwain led the commissioners in their oath, a speech-act that reinforced their unrepresentivity. It did so by sanctifying—literally, "setting apart"—the commissioners for their task. My use of religious discourse here is not accidental. The oath was a highly ritualistic segment of an event steeped in several formal elements, such as a procession, an invocation, special music, and public expressions of acknowledgement. Commissioners were also given symbolic stoles to wear across their shoulders throughout the proceedings. In his book *Discourse and the Construction of Society*, Bruce Lincoln has commented on the rhetorical functions of ritual:

> For over the course of the last two decades, it has gradually become clear that ritual, etiquette, and other strongly habituated forms of practical discourse and discursive practice

---

[15] After all 18 speakers had spoken, Gregory Headen—the master-of-ceremonies of the event—provided a coda that broadened the representivity constructed here: "We want you to know," he said, "that those you have heard today are only a sampling of the many supporters and well-wishers for this project and this process" (GTCRP, 2004). And then he went even further, calling audience members to "autograph the pledge that the commissioners took as a show of your own support for this truth and reconciliation process." Another, related instance occurred when Headen held up a large scroll and remarked, "We...hold in our hands from the community thousands of petitions. Literally thousands of citizens of Greensboro and the greater Greensboro area have signed petitions as a show of support for your [the GTRC's] work and what you will be doing, and we just are so happy [about] the overwhelming support, and I think that alone is a reason for us to clap our hands" (GTCRP).

do not just encode and transmit messages, but they play an active and important role in the construction, maintenance, and modification of the borders, structures, and hierarchic relations that characterize and constitute society itself. (as cited in Jasinski, 2001, p. 496)

Viewed in light of Lincoln's comments, the ritualistic elements of the Swearing In and Seating Ceremony helped to construct "hierarchic relations" between the commissioners and the people of Greensboro, distancing one group from the other. Audience members themselves participated in this construction of the Commission's authority through gestures (e.g., standing and clapping), song, and silence—all of which were prompted by the leaders of the ceremony.

The unrepresentivity of the commissioners was also reinforced by the ways that speakers at the ceremony characterized the event itself (GTCRP, 2004). Take, for example, the remarks delivered by master-of-ceremonies Gregory Headen, which came immediately before and after McSwain administered the oath. Headen introduced the oath by noting, "We pray that all here sense the *potential of this moment* [emphasis added]." After the oath, he asked audience members to reflect on what had just taken place: "I would like to invite you at this time to a *moment of silence* [emphasis added] in recognition of the *significant transition* [emphasis added] we have made by this *historic seating* [emphasis added], and to invoke the Spirit to guide this process." Throughout the ceremony, others referred to the event in similar ways: Headen called the event a "historic moment," Cynthia Nance referred to it as an "amazing event," Bongani Finca described it as "one small step for a man but one giant leap for mankind," Melvin Watt said that it was a "history-making occasion," and McSwain claimed that it was a "historic undertaking" and a "historic step" with "potential for good." Several of these individuals also referred to the Commission as the "first of its kind." These descriptions framed the ceremony—and, in particular, the oath—as an extraordinary moment, a moment set apart from other moments. The distinction constructed here, between extraordinary and ordinary time, is aptly captured by the two terms for "time" used by ancient Greeks—*kairos* and *chronos*. Rhetoricians Sharon Crowley and Debra Hawhee (2004) have explained, "[The ancient Greeks] used the term *chronos* to refer to linear, measurable time, the kind with which we are more familiar, that we track with watches and calendars. But the ancients used *kairos* to suggest a more situational kind of time, something close to what we call 'opportunity.' In this sense, *kairos* suggests an advantageous time" (p. 37). The ceremony and oath, then, was framed as a *kairotic* event, an event outside of the flow of ordinary time, reinforcing the distance between the Commission and the people of Greensboro.

In sum, throughout the Swearing In and Seating Ceremony, representivity and unrepresentivity were constructed in several different ways. Each of these constructions of the GTRC's *ethos* helped the Commission accomplish different facets of its mandate, which involved the following:

1. [Bringing about] healing and reconciliation of the community through discovering and disseminating the truth of what happened [on November 3rd, 1979] and its consequences with the lives of individuals and institutions, both locally and beyond Greensboro.
2. Clarifying the confusion and reconciling the fragmentation that has been caused by these events and their aftermath, in part by educating the public through its findings.

3. Acknowledging and recognizing people's feelings, including feelings of loss, guilt, shame, anger and fear.

4. Helping facilitate changes in social consciousness and in the institutions that were consciously or unconsciously complicit in these events, thus aiding in the prevention of similar events in the future. (GTRC, 2006, p. 16)

Some of these goals were facilitated by constructions of unrepresentivity. Only a Commission that was unbiased and objective—distanced from the community—could do what the community, because of its conflicting interests and opinions, had not yet been able to do: discover the truth and clarify the confusion about the events of November 3, 1979. Other goals were facilitated by representivity. Only a Commission that was able to identify with many different members of the community could reconcile the fragmentation and facilitate changes in social consciousness. In other words, these two positions provided the necessary foundation for commissioners to both understand and transcend the divisions of the community.

The *News & Record's* coverage of the ceremony reinforced the Commission's representivity. The paper reported that a "slate of nearly two dozen speakers encouraged the commission and recognized the efforts of those supporting its work," highlighting that "speakers at the event included government officials, religious leaders, representatives from civil and human rights groups, survivors of the massacre and students" (Church, 2004, p. B1). But not all of the press about the ceremony strengthened the Commission's *ethos*. On June 21st, the *News & Record* ran a letter to the editor, entitled "Commission Pursues One Version of Truth." Editorial writer Ian A. Millar (2004) wrote that the "[Greensboro] Truth and Reconciliation Commission has been designed after the same program hatched by the African National Congress in South Africa. Interesting to note that the ANC is also a communist organization. I urge readers to get on their computers and research every aspect of this event, the people involved, and exactly whose truth these people are pursuing" (p. A8). Millar's implicit claim was that the Commission was not objective because of its ties to former members of the Communist Workers Party. The comment, in other words, attempted to discredit the Commission by suggesting that it was biased in favor of one of the parties involved on November 3, 1979. Greensboro Mayor Keith Holliday also expressed his disapproval of the Commission in the days following the Swearing In and Seating Ceremony, albeit in more nuanced ways. A June 25, 2004 article reported that Holliday viewed the Commission as detrimental to the city's image (Rizzo, 2004, p. A1).[16]

---

[16] 3 months after the Swearing In and Seating Ceremony, the mayor announced a project of his own—the Greensboro Bicentennial Mosaic Partnerships Project (Magarrell & Wesley, 2008, pp. 169–170). The Project, patterned after an initiative in Rochester, NY, was intended to "improve communication among the city's racial and ethnic groups" (Williams, 2004a, p. B1) by pairing "180 top civic leaders across racial lines and encourag[ing] them to become friends and share experiences" (Williams, 2004b, p. A1). According to the *News & Record*, Holliday claimed that "the program wasn't a reaction to the Greensboro Truth and Community Reconciliation Project" (Williams, 2004b, p. A1). But many read it as such, in part because the date for the official launch of the Mosaic Project was set for November 4, 2004—one day after the 25th anniversary of the Greensboro Massacre ("Greensboro Initiative," 2004, p. A8). Moreover, the city stopped funding the Mosaic Project shortly after the Commission completed its work—another indication that the mayor's program may have been at least somewhat reactionary (Magarrell & Wesley, 2008, p. 170).

The Public Hearings

Following the Commission's installation, commissioners rented office space, hired staff members, and held several public events—the most important of which were their three public hearings in the summer and fall of 2005. Each of the hearings was a two-day event, organized around a guiding question.[17] This section of the chapter analyzes the commissioners' opening remarks at the hearings and reflects on who was invited to participate in the hearings. My analysis reveals that, in their opening remarks, commissioners positioned themselves primarily in terms of objectivity and impartiality, instead of representivity. Such positioning work helped to warrant the Commission's goal, at this stage in their operation, to engage in unbiased fact-finding and to listen impartially to the many perspectives pertaining to November 3, 1979. But despite the commissioners' emphasis on their objectivity, representivity was nonetheless constructed at the public hearings: the Commission followed the GTCRP's lead, constructing representivity by inviting people to speak at the hearings.

Commissioners began each day of the public hearings by reading a formal statement (GTRC, 2005a, b, c). In this statement, Commissioner Cynthia Brown called the day's hearing to order, thanking "everyone here for their willingness and openness to listen to the variety of viewpoints on traumatic events in our history." Then each of the other commissioners read prepared remarks. Robert Peters articulated the rationale for their inquiry and summarized the goals of the Commission's mandate. Muktha Jost asked audience members to take notice of the five empty seats at the front of the auditorium, intended to commemorate those who lost their lives on November 3, 1979. Mark Sills acknowledged the ongoing international support for the work of the GTRC, stating during the first hearing, "Just before we came out we received greetings from Archbishop Desmond Tutu, and we have learned that, in a

---

Whether or not the Mosaic Project was a response to the Commission's installation, it generated noteworthy press for the Commission. In the September 14th edition of the *News & Record*, the cover story compared the two initiatives, noting that the efforts shared a common goal—addressing the racial divide in Greensboro—but that they attempted to achieve that goal in different ways: "Holliday's effort will be funded and directed by the community's established institutions and is limiting participation to top leaders of civic groups. Leaders of the reconciliation project say they are taking the opposite strategy, hoping to work with the wider community to face racial problems and to tackle tough truths" (Williams, 2004b, p. A1). Citing Reverend Zeb Holler, an organizer of the Greensboro Truth and Community Reconciliation Project, the article noted, "While Holliday's group aims for its work to 'trickle down,' Holler said the reconciliation project's approach is 'bubble up.' He welcomed the new effort and said there's a need for both approaches to solve the problem" (Williams, 2004b, p. A1). The Mayor's Mosaic Project, in short, offered the Commission's advocates an opportunity to emphasize its own broad appeal and grassroots design in ways not inconsistent with the *ethos* of representivity.

[17] The first, entitled "What brought us to November 3, 1979?", took place on July 15–16; the second, "What happened on, and after, November 3, 1979?", took place on August 26–27; and the third, "What does the past have to do with the present and future?", took place on September 30 and October 1.

village in South Africa, this afternoon, bells are ringing in a church in support and in solidarity with the work of this Truth and Reconciliation Commission" (GTRC, 2005a). Sills then led the audience in 88 seconds of silence, meant to mark the length of time that violence ensued on November 3, 1979. After this time of silence, Barbara Walker petitioned audience members to get involved with the truth and reconciliation process in various ways and described the Commission's research efforts. Then Patricia Clark talked about the format of the hearings. Last to speak was Angela Lawrence, who introduced the topic of the day's hearing and welcomed the invited guests, which, at the first public hearing, included Bongani Finca and Lisa Magarrell (GTRC, 2005a).

In their introductory remarks, commissioners did little to position themselves as representative of the Greensboro community.[18] While they did repeatedly emphasize the value of human life, the stance they took was fundamentally objective. This objectivity was constructed, primarily, by a stated refusal to draw conclusions at this stage in the process. "The Commission," said Patricia Clark, "has not made any findings or conclusions at this point." Barbara Walker added that, as the Commission listened to testimony, there would be "no judgment of presentations given." To reinforce their objectivity, commissioners also distanced themselves from the specific perspectives of the speakers. Angela Lawrence noted that the Commission did not endorse any of the speakers' views, and commissioners twice reminded the audience that the speakers' statements did not represent the final findings of the Commission.[19]

Nevertheless, the GTRC did construct representivity at the public hearings. Much like the GTRCP's attempts to establish representivity, the GTRC did so by inviting a heterogeneous group of individuals to testify at the hearings.[20] The Commission received testimonies from former and current Klan members, former Communist Workers Party members, members of the Greensboro police department, former residents of Morningside Homes (where the shootings took place), attorneys and judges from the trials, city officials, and community activists.[21]

---

[18] Although each member of the Commission spoke, they did not emphasize their individual differences; rather, they emphasized their unity as a body, primarily through the repeated use of the pronoun "we" (GTRC, 2005a).

[19] These statements by Clark and Lawrence were further reinforced by Cynthia Brown's closing remarks, read at the end of each of the public hearings: "We have invited speakers to the hearing based on the contributions they can make to the public's understanding. Such an invitation does not amount to an endorsement by the Commission of that speaker's views or the acceptance of his or her statement as fact....The presentations today are not the Commission's findings but rather just a portion of the evidence we will consider" (GTRC, 2005c).

[20] Magarrell and Wesley (2008) have noted the importance of choosing speakers "who could present a range of perspectives" (p. 101) and "an array of voices to the public" (p. 202) in establishing the credibility of the Commission. Such credibility is grounded in the rhetoric of representation.

[21] Additionally, at each of the hearings, a significant number of academics presented their research on a variety of issues related to November 3, 1979. These researchers, however, may have done less to reinforce the Commission's representivity than they did to reinforce the Commission's objectivity.

To play up the representivity of this group, commissioners called attention to "the variety of viewpoints" of those testifying, and they emphasized that the speakers provided "a range of perspectives" that demonstrated "the complexity of this tragedy" (GTRC, 2005a). In a video summary of the hearings, commissioners claimed that one of main criteria they used for choosing whom to invite to participate in the public hearings was the individual's potential contribution "to [the] complexity and diversity of speakers with regard to: (a) different speakers at each hearing; (b) different viewpoints and perspectives, particularly those that have not been heard previously; (c) race; (d) gender; and (e) age" (GTRC, 2005d).

Inviting a heterogeneous group of speakers to testify about November 3, 1979, was a means of securing tacit endorsement from these individuals for the Commission's work. It also allowed the Commission to appeal to additional groups and individuals in the Greensboro community. Commissioners were aware of these facts, as indicated by a four-page memo from Lisa Magarrell to the commissioners dated 4 days before the first public hearing—titled "Notes on Klan testimony at the public hearings." In the memo, Magarrell reflected on "the significance of the participation of the KKK" in the public hearings:

> As you all have surely noted already, this [the participation of the KKK in the public hearings] is a positive factor for the Commission's credibility, because it points to the seriousness and importance of the Commission's work that even those opposed to it feel that it is important to participate to have their say. Any truth commission process is enhanced, one hopes, by providing space for a broad range of actors to tell their stories and thus giving depth and complexity to the various layers of personal and forensic truth that the Commission is exploring...the Klan's participation reflects the power of the Commission's moral authority, since there is nothing else pushing the Klan to participate. While this participation lends credibility to the Commission's endeavor, it should not be confused with providing credibility to the Klan. (Magarrell, 2005, p. 1)[22]

Magarrell linked the Klan participation—and, more generally, the participation of a "broad range of actors"—to the Commission's credibility. This was one of Magarrell's most explicit acknowledgements of the link between the Commission's *ethos* and its invitations to the Greensboro community to participate in the TRC process. Her comments suggest that the rhetorical moves I have been describing were intentional.

The rhetorical effectiveness of the GTRC's construction of representivity can be gauged by considering the media response to the testimony of Virgil Griffin—the Imperial Wizard of the Cleveland Knights of the KKK and one of the members of the Klan/Nazi caravan on November 3, 1979. In his testimony before the Commission, Virgil Griffin (2005) was recalcitrant and did not show remorse for the killings, nor did he issue an apology. He began by lambasting the TRC process:

> Well first, I'd like to say I don't think this Commission's going to solve anything. I think it's a total waste of time. And...this thing would have been forgotten 20 years ago, if it hadn't been [for] people like this Commission and the news keep bringing it up in the paper. It'd

---

[22] Magarrell and Wesley (2008) make a similar argument about the Klan's participation in *Learning from Greensboro* (pp. 202–203).

have been forgotten after the trials…I think you're hurting Greensboro, and bringing more harm to Greensboro than anything. I think if people here [are] worried about the citizens of Greensboro and worried about Greensboro, you should forget 1979, and go on with your life. The truth was proved in the trials. (Griffin)

Later in his testimony, he indicated that he believed that members of the Communist Workers Party deserved the blame for the massacre: "The blame is on Nelson Johnson [for] putting that ["Death to the Klan"] poster up, and Paul Bermanzohn and the Communist Party for letting him." When asked by commissioners if he thought it strange that no Klansmen were shot during the attacks, he replied, "Maybe God guided the bullets. I don't know."

Perhaps not surprisingly, the *News & Record's* coverage of the hearing focused on Griffin. In the days leading up to the hearing, a number of articles noted that, because Griffin was slated to speak, police security would be tight (Townsend, 2005a, p. A1; Townsend, 2005b, p. B4; Townsend, 2005c, p. B1; Coletta, 2005, p. A1). On the day after the hearing, the paper's headline read, "Klan Leader Remains Defiant; Virgil Griffin Tells the Truth Panel it's a 'Waste of Time' to Study the Shootings" (Townsend, 2005d, A1).

Most of the responses to Griffin's testimony in the *News & Record* suggest that, despite his recalcitrance and troubling ideology, Griffin's very *presence* at the hearings did lend considerable credibility to the Commission, as Magarrell suggested it would. For example, a July 19th editorial stated, "With the first of three public hearings completed, the Greensboro Truth and Reconciliation Commission appears, at least so far, to have put to rest…concerns that this process would be rigged to tell one side of the story" ("Sad Truths," 2005, p. A8). Two articles appearing in the July 24th edition of the paper—one by Allen Johnson; the other by Edward Cone—made similar claims. Johnson (2005) wrote that readers should "give credit" to Griffin for testifying and give credit to the Commission for offering him the invitation to do so; he then added, "Despite widespread skepticism that this was a kangaroo court, the commission seems genuinely committed to a balanced retrospective" (p. H2). Cone (2005) wrote, "So it turns out that the Greensboro Truth and Reconciliation Commission might be interested in the truth after all" (p. H3). His reason for this claim was connected to the multiplicity of perspectives represented at the hearings:

[T]he opening round of public statements showed that the seven-person panel is interested in hearing more than the party line. The party in question – the Communist Workers Party that organized the "Death to the Klan" rally – got plenty of time at the microphone to recount its version of the events leading up to Nov. 3, with talk of government conspiracy and right-wing death squads. But the commission also heard voices that strongly challenged some of the theories used by the victims to explain the context of the killings. (Cone, 2005, p. H3)

Likewise, an August 7th letter to the editor, written on behalf of the League of Women Voters, endorsed the GTRC and commended it for being "inclusive" (Olson, 2005, p. H2). "The commission," the article noted, "now seeks the thoughts and memories of all. We hope the residents of Greensboro will avail themselves of the opportunities to participate" (Olson, 2005, p. H2). These favorable responses to the first public hearing indicate that the Commission's constructions of representivity may have been at least somewhat successful.[23]

The Report Release Ceremony

From the last of the three public hearings on October 1, 2005 until the Report Release Ceremony on May 25, 2006, the Commission kept a low profile, and coverage of the Commission in the *News & Record* was sparse.[24] During the Report Release Ceremony, commissioners continued their attempts to establish their representivity; however, they deemphasized their objectivity and downplayed the notion that they were extraordinary or moral exemplars. Instead, they tried to demonstrate that what set them apart from the community—what made them unrepresentative— was their work toward reconciliation, which primarily involved engaging one another in dialogue. This means of constructing *ethos* was important to the commissioners because it enabled them to identify with their audience, demonstrate that they had performed their mandated task, and position themselves as a model for the Greensboro community.

The Report Release Ceremony was held in the Annie Merner Pfeiffer Chapel at Bennett College for Women (Seel, 2006a). Seated on the stage in the front of the chapel, commissioners wore blue stoles, similar to the yellow stoles they had been given upon taking their oath at the Swearing In and Seating Ceremony. They each

---

[23]There were also a few editorials that criticized the Commission in the days following the hearing. In a letter to the editor entitled, "Is commission really seeking truth?", Donnie Stowe (2005) wrote, "In reading about the self-appointed Truth and Reconciliation Commission 'hearings' in the paper [on] July 27, I was struck by the apparent small part that truth plays in these proceedings" (p. A6). Similarly, a letter to the editor from Marion Griffin (2005) noted, "When those involved have in their majority people who have already decided the outcome beforehand, mutual understanding and an abrogation of prejudice and animosity among the participants are most unlikely to be in the offing" (p. A14). But these two articles aside, most of the blame appearing in the *News & Record* was reserved for members of the Greensboro City Council, for their failure to attend the event (Cone, 2005, p. H3; Flynn, 2005, p. A8; Hummel, 2005, p. A1; Johnson, 2005, p. H2; Manning-Moss, 2005, p. H2; "Sad Truths," 2005, p. A8). Some writers petitioned city leaders to participate. "I would ask our city leaders, and those citizens of Greensboro who share their skepticism, to take another look at the work of the Truth & Reconciliation Commission," wrote Steve Flynn (2005, p. A8). Others expressed disappointment. For example, Cone (2005) wrote, "[T]he silence of the city at the hearings was almost as sad as the silence at the start of the proceedings to remember the dead" (p. H3). And Johnson (2005) issued the following indictment of city leadership: "City officials may have stayed away in droves from the first Truth and Reconciliation hearings last week, but the Ku Klux Klan didn't" (p. H2).

[24]In the days before the Report Release Ceremony, articles about the Commission began reappearing in the paper. These articles highlighted some of the criticism of the Commission that was circulating in Greensboro at the time, including the notion that the Commission was likely to "skim [over] controversial aspects of the deadly incident" (Banks, 2006, p. A1), and that the Commission was "a thinly veiled attempt to recast history in favor of the communist protestors and against the city of Greensboro" (Friedman, 2006, p. A8).

took turns leading the audience through different parts of the ceremony. Mark Sills began by asking the audience to participate in 88 seconds of silence. After the silence, Sills led the audience in an invocation and introduced the special music for the evening. Robert Peters took the podium after the special music to discuss the Commission's mandate. Then Cynthia Brown and Barbara Walker took a few minutes to acknowledge all of the individuals and organizations that had supported the Commission in various ways. Following these expressions of gratitude, the commissioners showed a video chronicling the truth and reconciliation process in Greensboro from its inception to the present. Next Muktha Jost described some of the challenges faced by the Commission, and Angela Lawrence talked about how the Commission went about doing its work. Pat Clark and Angela Lawrence summarized the Commission's findings, and then the commissioners distributed an Executive Summary of the *Final Report* to each audience member. After the Executive Summaries were distributed, several members of the community—including victims of the November 3, 1979, tragedy, a city council person, members of the GTCRP, and representatives from other public bodies in Greensboro—each gave brief remarks, all of them positive, about their experiences participating in the truth and reconciliation process.[25] To conclude the ceremony, the Reverend Peter Storey, one of the architects of the SATRC, delivered a benediction. Mark Sills then dismissed the audience, charging them to continue the work started by the Commission.

The video shown at the ceremony was central to the Commission's construction of *ethos* (Seel, 2006b). With footage taken from the November 3rd killings, the GTCRP's planning meetings, the Swearing In and Seating Ceremony, and the public hearings, it summarized some of the community's responses to the Commission's work, both favorable and unfavorable.[26] Most noteworthy, for my purposes, was the video's conclusion, which was comprised of a short reflection from each of the seven commissioners about the truth and reconciliation process. In many of their statements, commissioners positioned the Commission as representative of the Greensboro community, and they did so, for the most part, by highlighting their own differences. Lawrence noted that the commissioners represented "different parts of the city." Walker commented, similarly, that "each of us [commissioners] came from very different places," and, as a result, there were "different perspectives." Peters remarked on the fact that his fellow commissioners had "quite radically different backgrounds," "significantly different points of view," and "different perspectives" than he did. Brown noted that commissioners had "different vantage points," and she referred to the Commission as "a microcosm of the broader community"—a designation that Desmond Tutu (1999) had used to refer to the SATRC (p. 22). Finally, Clark called attention to the 18 "different representatives" that spoke during

---

[25] Many of the same individuals who spoke at the Swearing In and Seating Ceremony spoke at this time.

[26] For instance, the video showed footage of the Greensboro City Council meeting, in which the council voted not to endorse the Commission's work (Seel, 2006b). I discuss this meeting in more detail in Chap. 5.

the Swearing In and Seating Ceremony (Seel), a series of speech-acts that, as noted earlier in this chapter, helped to establish the Commission's representivity.[27]

In constructing representivity in the video, commissioners avoided demographic categories. Unlike McSwain's explicit description of the commissioners in terms of binaries of race, class, and gender at the Swearing In and Seating Ceremony, commissioners tended to present themselves as different from one another in more ambiguous ways. For example, Angela Lawrence noted that commissioners came from "different parts of the city," but she did not clarify who came from where, nor did she indicate why such differences might matter. Cynthia Brown's claim that the Commission was a microcosm of the Greensboro community highlighted commissioners' differences, without making explicit what those differences were. However, over the course of the evening, commissioners brought the nature of their differences into clearer focus. Instead of relying on binaries, commissioners played up their differences of opinion and their different perspectives to construct their representivity.

Before discussing why this shift in how representivity was constructed matters, it is necessary to unpack how commissioners constructed their unrepresentivity at the Report Release Ceremony (Seel, 2006a). Here again, the way in which they did so looked different than prior constructions of unrepresentivity. Rather than emphasize their objectivity or impartiality, they emphasized their hard work and, in particular, their dialogic engagement with one another. Put another way, it was the actions that commissioners took with regard to November 3, 1979, that set them apart from the community.

Commissioners emphasized the work they had done in their seven video statements (Seel, 2006b). Clark referred to "the magnitude of the [TRC] endeavor," Lawrence talked about the "struggles" commissioners faced, Jost emphasized commissioners' "[work] together," Brown claimed that the commissioners had done "important work," and Sills commented on "what [commissioners had] accomplished."

---

[27] Commissioners reinforced this construction of representivity elsewhere in the ceremony as well. For example, prior to the showing of the video, Brown said, "[It] has become very clear that we have very different perspectives" (Seel, 2006a). Commissioners also strengthened their claims to representivity by positioning themselves as ordinary—not extraordinary—individuals. In a series of remarks describing some of the struggles that the Commission faced, commissioner Muktha Jost referred to the Commission as "a group of ordinary people engaged in something extraordinary." "We [commissioners]," she continued, "have brought deep faith and hope to our work, but naturally, we have brought our human flaws, too." Jost's comments here reinforced representivity to the extent that they identified the commissioners with ordinary Greensboro citizens. Claims to ordinariness attenuated the sanctification of commissioners that had occurred during previous events.

In making this claim, I do not mean to suggest here that commissioners were never positioned as exemplary or extraordinary individuals during the Report Release Ceremony; however, for the most part, such designations came from those outside of the Commission. For instance, when, at the end of the Report Release Ceremony, then-President of Bennett College Johnnetta B. Cole thanked the commissioners for their work, she addressed them as "extraordinary sisters and brothers," adding, "I want to literally bow in acknowledgement of your work, your dedication, your soulfulness" (Seel, 2006a).

This positioning work continued throughout much of the Report Release Ceremony as well (Seel, 2006a). Peters, for example, described the amount of work that the Commission had needed to accomplish; Jost talked about the ways the Commission had carried out that work; and the Executive Summary of the Commission's *Final Report* served as material proof of the work the Commission had done.

The emphasis on the Commission's labors was nowhere more evident, however, than in Angela Lawrence's remarks, which summarized how the Commission did its work (Seel, 2006a).[28] Lawrence framed the process of engaging the community as difficult (e.g., she noted "*how much* it takes to get people to talk" and claimed that "progress was *not easily won*"); the commissioners' research as extensive (e.g., she said, "*much* has already been said and written about November the third, and we went through *a lot* of that information"); and the analysis of the data as intense (e.g., she explained that the commissioners conducted "a phase of *intense* research). The force of these claims was amplified by the modifiers Lawrence used. For example, she noted that the Commission knocked on *countless* doors; investigated *rich and voluminous* archive materials; examined a *wealth* of information; referred to *extensive* media coverage; conducted *intense* research and *intense* analysis; held *frequent, often all-day* meetings; came up with *burning* questions; and spent *countless* hours checking and re-checking facts. The process, she summarized, was *rigorous*. Part of the rhetorical force of these modifiers was their repetition: "At our *intense* research meetings, we held up one finding at a time for *intense* analysis. I really have to say that one more time: It was very *intense*."

One aspect of the Commission's work that all of the commissioners highlighted was the time they spent engaging with one another in discussion. Lawrence reported, "As we looked…for information and evidence, we were mindful of our own differences, diversity, strengths, and hopes. We retreated on several occasions to talk through our own struggles and to stay true to our principles and promises." This point was reinforced by several of the statements in the video (Seel, 2006b). Lawrence's video statement highlighted that the commissioners frequently had to "come together and…talk"; Walker's noted that commissioners had "hardy discussions" and "opened [their] minds" to one another's differences; Jost's mentioned that commissioners "worked together"; and Peters' twice cited the "opportunity to engage" other commissioners as a key element of the process. According to the commissioners, this engagement had positive consequences. Peters, for example, claimed to have "gained personally" and been "enriched" by engaging people with different points of view. Brown echoed his sentiment, noting that such engagement "led each of the seven of us on a journey toward self-reflection and self-transformation." And Jost noted that, through this engagement, commissioners achieved a kind of unity:

> Two years back I came to this process and the people, a stranger…And later this evening when we disband as a group of commissioners, I will feel a great sense of loss because we have become like siblings….We have fought and struggled together and argued and fussed and disagreed and agreed; and, like siblings, we also share a bond. (Seel, 2006a)

---

[28] All of the emphases in this paragraph are my own.

Jost indicated here that commissioners had engaged one another—by fighting and struggling and arguing and fussing and disagreeing—and, in the process, had moved from being strangers to being family, from being a group divided to a group united. Commissioners, in short, constructed their unrepresentivity in relation to the Greensboro community by highlighting how they had engaged one another in dialogue.

Thus, the tension between positions of representivity and unrepresentivity persisted in the Report Release Ceremony. Here, however, representivity was constructed more ambiguously and more in terms of the commissioners' perspectives and opinions than in the previous iterations, and unrepresentivity was constructed in terms of commissioners' activity and engagement with one another and less in terms of their exemplary character or objective judgment. In the context of the Report Release Ceremony, these positions both had important rhetorical functions. Constructions of representivity allowed the commissioners to identify with the many constituencies that made up their audience, which, in turn, helped to ensure that their findings and recommendations would receive broad public support. Constructions of unrepresentivity served as evidence that the Commission had been efficacious in completing its mandate, that it had accomplished the work it had been tasked to do.

More importantly, in the process of establishing these multiform constructions of *ethos*, commissioners constituted a complex model of community action—which might be best described as dialogic engagement among diverse individuals.[29] As I have demonstrated throughout this chapter, this model was performed, in various guises, at nearly every public stage of the Commission's operation: in the coming together of the diverse members of the Selection Panel, in the formation and work of the Commission, and in the gathering of invited speakers at the Swearing In and Seating Ceremony and the Public Hearings. This model, moreover, was meant to be exemplary for the people of Greensboro, as Cynthia Brown's following remark from the Report Release Ceremony indicated:

> You [the audience at the ceremony] have to know that at many points in this process as we have worked together, it has become very clear that we have very different perspectives. And if this work is to be real, from this moment forward, you have to be prepared to take on the challenge of hanging in there when things get tough. That's what we've had to do. This is a microcosm of what will be expected of all of us in this room and the people in this city who we hope you will touch beyond this point. We have struggled together. We have laughed together. We've had fun together. We've left meetings together thinking we may not come back, if I tell you the truth.[30]

---

[29] Magarrell and Wesley (2008) have suggested that one thing that "made it possible for the GTRC's diverse commissioners to stay together through intense discussions" was their prior work together over 2 years—which, Magarrell and Wesley seemed to imply, fostered commissioners' commitment to one another and allowed them to develop skills for interacting productively with one another (p. 121).

[30] Magarrell and Wesley (2008) echoed Brown's sentiments about the Commission: "A microcosm of Greensboro's own diversity, Commission members had a largely successful struggle with the facts before them, providing grounds for optimism that their commitment to truth and integrity and respect for one another could model a new set of relations in the community itself some day" (p. 121).

Brown's comments emphasized both the commissioners' differences from one another and their engagement—a clear articulation of the *ethos* I have been describing. Brown continued: what would make the commissioners' work "real" is what the Greensboro community would do in response to that work. Community members, Brown suggested, must act as the Commission had acted.

One way to read the entire Report Release Ceremony, then, is as a call for individuals to take up the GTRC model for themselves. At one point or another during the ceremony, almost all of the commissioners issued this call.[31] Brown described the Commission as "a model to show what's possible if you give something time to really try to work from different vantage points about a particular issue you might disagree about." Jost invited the people of Greensboro to action, noting, "[T]here's a lot of work that needs to be done by the community, starting with putting the effort to understand what really happened, and to look at our findings, and to look at our recommendations. Agree, disagree, question, critique: do everything that a healthy, critical community would do, but get engaged." Lawrence said that her "greatest hope is that the west side of Greensboro and the east side of Greensboro will come together and at least talk, like we had to do as commissioners." Walker remarked, "We opened our minds, and I hope that what [the people of Greensboro] read in the report and what they garner from it is going to be a similar experience—that they will open their minds to the idea of reconciliation as really a goal to be sought." And Sills, for his part, described the Commission as a model not simply for the Greensboro community but for communities elsewhere: "I'm very proud of what we've accomplished, and I'm thankful that a lot of communities around the U.S. are looking at us for leadership as a model to follow."[32]

Conclusion

At every stage of its operation, from its conception to its conclusion, the Greensboro Truth and Reconciliation Commission positioned itself—i.e., constructed its institutional *ethos*—as both representative and unrepresentative of the Greensboro

---

[31] The members of the Commission "felt strongly that they should model for the community a willingness to seek understanding of each other's differences and persevere through the difficulties and pain that result from such an undertaking" (Magarrell & Wesley, 2008, p. 95).

[32] Moreover, in his opening prayer at the Report Release Ceremony, Sills encapsulated the community model that the GTRC embodied in three different ways. He said that, although we are "unique and separate individuals," we "gather together"; although "we each have our own story," our stories are "interwoven into a social fabric that unites us"; although we are "distinct and different," we are called together into a "shared community" (Seel, 2006a). For those in the audience who had attended the Swearing In and Seating Ceremony, the model of community that Sills articulated should have sounded familiar. It was, after all, strikingly similar to the notion of *ubuntu* that Bongani Finca (2004) articulated in his keynote address. Sills' claim, for instance, that "our stories are interwoven into a social fabric that unites us" (Seel) resonated with Finca's descriptions of human interdependency. And the notion that we become "whole" and "complete" in and through community was seemingly consistent with Finca's definition of *ubuntu*.

community. As this chapter has shown, these features of the tradition were actually reaccentuated several times, and each time they meant different things and served different functions. Representivity was constructed in terms of the selection process's interest groups, McSwain's binaries, the speakers invited to the public hearings, and the commissioners' differing perspectives.[33] Unrepresentivity was constructed in terms of the commissioners' independence, integrity and moral standing, objectivity, and willingness to pursue dialogue with one another. However, none of these positions were new to the GTRC. Tutu and others had constructed them for the SATRC, and Lisa Magarrell and the ICTJ had helped ensure that they found their way to Greensboro.[34] Rather, the positions were *made new* by the GTRC, as they reaccentuated these features of the rhetorical tradition of transitional justice in their own context.

One of the things this chapter's study of representivity and unrepresentivity brings into relief is the fact that the rhetorical tradition of transitional justice—like all rhetorical traditions—contains rich rhetorical resources for organizations as well as individuals. As communication scholar George Cheney (1991) noted, "[M]uch of contemporary rhetoric is organizational in that many of the messages which individuals 'hear' are from 'corporate' or collective sources. Today individuals do much of their speaking to one another through the auspices of corporate or organizational 'persons'" (p. ix). However, speaking or writing with the collective voice of an organization is different than speaking or writing as an individual; institutions, in other words, have different rhetorical possibilities and constraints than individuals do.

To explore these differences, Cheney (1991) conducted a case study of the United States Catholic bishops' 1983 pastoral letter, *The Challenge of Peace*. Drawing upon Kenneth Burke's theory of identification as a framework for analysis, he explored how Catholic bishops "moved from 'I's' to 'we' in constructing a constitutional document" and provided "a framework for analyzing how corporate 'we's' of all sorts are constructed" (p. x). Cheney's observation that groups like the Catholic bishops can position themselves as both "I's" or "we's" clarifies how the GTRC's complex construction of *ethos* worked. Organizations such as the GTRC can utilize the fact that they are both a unity and plurality—a single "we" and a multiplicity of "I's"—to perform *ethos* in ways that emphasize identification among members of the organization, division between members, or both identification and division. Put

---

[33] The *ethos* of representivity was reinforced in other ways as well. Commissioner Mark Sills, for example, helped to reinforce this *ethos* in the way that he described the audience at the Report Release Ceremony. He claimed it was "a pretty darn inclusive audience" and then stated, "I thought it symbolized in many ways the success of what we had accomplished, that that diverse a group would come together to receive our report" (as cited in Magarrell & Wesley, 2008, p. 33). Similarly, representivity was established through "report receivers"—a heterogeneous collection of groups that pledged to read and dialogue about the GTRC's report. Magarrell and Wesley (2008) themselves reinforced this representivity when they noted, "The diversity of the report-receivers provides a view into the growing reach of the Commission's work" (p. 111).

[34] For more on the way in which Tutu established these positions, see Beitler (2012, pp. 14–15).

another way, institutions have the option to position themselves as a single voice and highlight their unity, or as a multiplicity of voices and highlight the identities and interests of individual members. The commissioners' ability to construct representivity hinged upon the fact that they were able to present themselves as a multiplicity of "I's." Correspondingly, the commissioners' ability to position themselves as unrepresentative hinged upon the fact that they were able to present themselves as a unified "we."

One of the risks for commissioners, in performing representivity, was that they would reify the divisions in the community. One of the risks, in performing unrepresentivity, was that they would alienate themselves from the community. It was, therefore, imperative for the commissioners to hold the two positions in tension with one another throughout their operation, thereby enabling them both to relate to community members and to embody what the community should become. In positioning the Commission as representative of the Greensboro community, commissioners were able to identify with a number of different constituencies in the community. Simultaneously, in positioning the Commission as unrepresentative of the Greensboro community, commissioners constructed the critical distance necessary to claim that they were able to adjudicate fairly about what happened on November 3, 1979, and to develop a model for community interaction and reconciliation.

For at least some of Greensboro's residents, the GTRC's constructions of representivity and unrepresentivity were so persuasive that they considered the Commission to be representative in another sense: they considered the Commission to speak and act on their behalf. Johnnetta Cole—who at the time of the Commission's operation was the president of Bennett College for Women—exemplified this position in her speech at the Report Release Ceremony. In her remarks, Cole described the responsibility that Bennett College had to be present at the ceremony. Then she said, "Thank you to seven…sisters and brothers, for speaking up for all of us" (Seel, 2006a). As Cole's remarks indicated, for some in Greensboro, the Commission served as a kind of "proxy" or "surrogate" for them—as a group entrusted to speak and act on their behalf.[35] For people like Cole, the commissioners' construction of *ethos* did more than model what the community should look like; it performed reconciliation in the community.

But not everyone in Greensboro agreed with Cole. There were some in Greensboro who disapproved of the truth and reconciliation process—who, despite the commissioners' best efforts, remained unconvinced of the Commission's objectivity, value, or helpfulness. The next chapter explores some of the resistance that the Commission faced, looking, in particular, at remarks delivered by the members of the Greensboro City Council, who voted 6–3 "to oppose" the work of the Commission at their April 2005 meeting. Chapter 5 also considers the Commission's response to this opposition, as well as the main findings in its *Final Report*.

---

[35] As I noted in Chap. 2, Sanders (2007) highlighted how the SATRC functioned as a kind of proxy (pp. 9, 40, 77–78), and Cole (2010) described the SATRC's commissioners as "surrogates" for the nation at large (pp. 92–93).

References

Banks, M. M. (2006, July 19). City finally joins 'truth' dialogue. *News & Record*, p. A1.

Beitler, J. (2012). Making more of the middle ground: Desmond Tutu and the *ethos* of the South African Truth and Reconciliation Commission. *Relevant Rhetoric, 3,* 1–21. Retrieved June 1, 2012, from http://relevantrhetoric.com/wp-content/uploads/making-more-of-the-middle-ground.pdf.

Cheney, G. (1991). *Rhetoric in an organizational society: Managing multiple identities*. Columbia: University of South Carolina Press.

Church, E. (2004, June 13). A quest for truth; panel hopes to shed light on history. *News & Record*, p. B1.

Cole, C. M. (2010). *Performing South Africa's Truth Commission: Stages of transition*. Bloomington & Indianapolis, IN: Indiana University Press.

Coletta, C. (2005, July 16). Truth panel hears about city's history; security will be tight today when two KKK members speak to the commission. *News & Record*, p. A1.

Cone, E. (2005, July 24). Truth commission makes impressive debut. *News & Record*, p. H3.

Crowley, S., & Hawhee, D. (2004). *Ancient rhetorics for contemporary students* (3rd ed.). New York, NY: Pearson Longman.

DeChaine, D. R. (2005). *Global humanitarianism: NGOs and the crafting of community*. Lanham, MD: Lexington Books.

Dyer, E., Binker, M., Buchanan, B., & Schultz, S. (2004, April 10). Reconciled? *News & Record*, p. B1.

Finca, B. (2004, June 12). Keynote address at the Swearing In and Seating Ceremony of the Greensboro Truth and Reconciliation Commission [DVD]. Copy in possession of author.

Flynn, S. (2005, July 27). Give truth and reconciliation a chance. *News & Record*, p. A8.

Friedman, T. (2006, May 25). The moment of truth. *News & Record*. p. A8.

Greensboro initiative aims to build bridges; A program pairing people of different backgrounds can pull participants out of their comfort zones and perhaps improve personal relationships citywide. (2004, September 14). *News & Record*, p. A8.

Greensboro Truth and Community Reconciliation Project. (2003a). Selection process for the Greensboro Truth and Reconciliation Commission [Web posting]. Retrieved October 5, 2007, from http://www.gtcrp.org/selection.php.

Greensboro Truth and Community Reconciliation Project. (2003b, May 6). Call for nominations for commissioners [Advertisement]. *News & Record*, p. A9.

Greensboro Truth and Community Reconciliation Project. (2004, June 12). Swearing In and Seating Ceremony of the Greensboro Truth and Reconciliation Commission [DVD]. Copy in possession of author.

Greensboro Truth and Reconciliation Commission. (2005a, July 15–16). First public hearing: What brought us to November 3, 1979? [DVD]. Available March 1, 2012, from http://www.greensborotrc.org/index.php.

Greensboro Truth and Reconciliation Commission. (2005b, August 26–27). Second public hearing: What happened on, and after, November 3, 1979? [DVD]. Available March 1, 2012, from http://www.greensborotrc.org/index.php

Greensboro Truth and Reconciliation Commission. (2005c, September 30-October 1). Third public hearing: What does the past have to do with the present and future? [DVD]. Available March 1, 2012, from http://www.greensborotrc.org/index.php

Greensboro Truth and Reconciliation Commission. (2005d). Hearings summary: Segments of 54 speakers' statements to the commission [DVD]. Available March 1, 2012, from http://www.greensborotrc.org/index.php.

Greensboro Truth and Reconciliation Commission. (2006). *The Greensboro Truth and Reconciliation Commission final report: An examination of the context, causes, sequence and consequence of the events of November 3, 1979*. Retrieved March 1, 2012, from http://www.greensborotrc.org/.

Griffin, M. (2005, August 5). Letters to the editor. *News & Record*, p. A14.

Griffin, V. (2005, July 16). Testimony at first public hearing. Retrieved July 22, 2008, from http://greensborotrc.org/hear_statements.php.

Hummel, M. (2005, July 18). Council absent at truth forums, panelist says: The Rev. Mark Sills says he's disappointed the city's lawmakers didn't attend. *News & Record*, p. A1.

In search of truth; in a significant step, the group studying the legacy of Nov. 3, 1979, names seven "commissioners." But are they in danger of preaching to the choir? (2004, May 30). *News & Record*, p. H2.

Jasinski, J. (2001). Sourcebook on rhetoric: Key concepts in contemporary rhetorical studies. Thousand Oaks, CA: Sage.

Johnson, A. (2005, July 24). Nov. 3: More answers, more questions, more clarity, more hope. *News & Record*, p. H2.

Magarrell, L. (2002, June 26). Developing a truth commission mandate and selecting a commission [Memo to Greensboro Massacre Reconciliation Project]. New York, NY: International Center for Transitional Justice Library.

Magarrell, L. (2005, July 26). Notes on first public hearings [Memo to GTRC commissioners and staff]. Bennett College Library, Greensboro, NC: Greensboro Truth and Reconciliation Commission Archive.

Magarrell, L., & Wesley, J. (2008). *Learning from Greensboro: Truth and reconciliation in the United States*. Philadelphia, PA: University of Pennsylvania Press.

Manning-Moss, S. (2005, July 17). Council shuns chance to heal past wounds. *News & Record*, p. H2.

McLaughlin, N. (2004, May 28). Panel forms to review Klan shootings; the panel will examine what happened, and issue a report in 2005. *News & Record*, p. B1.

Millar, IA. (2004, June 21). Commission pursues one version of truth. *News & Record*, p. A8.

Olson, E. B. (2005, August 7). Letters to the editor. *News & Record*, p. H2.

Rizzo, R. (2004, June 25). City cool to U.S. aid for killings; the number of homicides here in 2003 attracts federal attention, but locals fear the help hurts the city's image. *News & Record*, p. A1.

Sad truths revisited; last weekend's first truth and reconciliation hearings successfully delivered compelling testimony and a broad range of perspectives. (2005, July 19). *News & Record*, p. A8.

Sanders, M. (2007). *Ambiguities of witnessing: Law and literature in the time of a truth commission*. Stanford, CA: Stanford University Press.

Seel, L. (Producer). (2006a). Greensboro Truth and Reconciliation Commission report release ceremony [DVD]. Greensboro, NC. (Obtained from Laura Seel.)

Seel, L. (Producer). (2006b). Video shown at the GTRC's report release ceremony [DVD]. Greensboro, NC. (Obtained from Laura Seel.)

Shallcross, L. (2004, June 11). Truth commissioners to be sworn in; the seven members of the truth and reconciliation commission are expected to release a report in 2005. *News & Record*, p. B1.

Stowe, D. B. (2005, August 2). Is commission really seeking truth? *News & Record*, p. A6.

Teitel, R. G. (2000). *Transitional Justice*. New York, NY: Oxford University Press.

Townsend, E.J.S. (2005a, July 14). Wizard in Klan to speak at hearing; A list of people slated to address the truth panel this week will be released today. *News & Record*, p. A1.

Townsend, E.J.S. (2005b, July 15). Truth panel lists speakers' names. *News & Record*, p. B4.

Townsend, E.J.S. (2005c, July 15). Truth panel reveals speakers; security is expected to be tight for a two-day hearing that begins this afternoon in downtown Greensboro. *News & Record*, p. B1.

Townsend, E.J.S. (2005d, July 17). Klan leader remains defiant; Virgil Griffin tells the truth panel it's a "waste of time" to study the shootings. *News & Record*, p. A1.

Tutu, D. (1999). Foreword by chairperson. In *Truth and Reconciliation Commission of South Africa Report* (Vol. 1, pp. 1–23). New York, NY: Grove's Dictionaries.

Williams, M. (2004a, September 9). Mayor to unveil plan for race relations; the project aims to build communication and trust between Greensboro's racial and ethnic groups. *News & Record*, p. B1.

Williams, M. (2004b, September 14). City hopes to repair race divide; Mayor Keith Holliday announces a program to pair top civic leaders of different races. *News & Record*, p. A1.

Chapter 5
Redefining "Truth Commission": Definitional Maneuvering in the Greensboro Truth and Reconciliation Commission's *Final Report*

Abstract This chapter analyzes the Greensboro Truth and Reconciliation Commission's *Final Report*, revealing how the commissioners attempted to lay claim to the title "truth commission" through rhetorical acts of redefinition. Commissioners collapsed the distinction between "official truth commissions" and "unofficial truth projects," described themselves as "victim-oriented" but not "victim-biased," reframed the object of their inquiry as much more than a single event, and suggested that their situation was not qualitatively different from that of other commissions. These acts of redefinition enabled commissioners to identify themselves with past commissions, establish their authority, and respond to perspectives about race that were circulating in Greensboro, North Carolina.

J.E. Beitler III, *Remaking Transitional Justice in the United States*,
Springer Series in Transitional Justice, DOI 10.1007/978-1-4614-5295-9_5,
© Springer Science+Business Media New York 2013

"The GTRC has had the opportunity to meet with and have communication with a number of people associated with truth commissions around the world. We have been struck by the interest they have taken in our small process. From them, we have learned about the value of taking statements from a broad range of people, the positive effect of engaging the public through hearings and discussion forums, and, surprisingly often, what to expect in terms of challenges and opportunities as we moved forward. But perhaps most of all, the GTRC learned that we were not alone in the task of revealing the truth about the past; instead we joined a world in which many people are challenging unfinished and misshapen stories about past abuses and violence that continue to sow distrust and even hate in our nations and our communities today."

GTRC, *Final Report* (2006, p. 12)

Introduction

Louis Bickford (2007) distinguished between two types of approaches to institutional truth-telling: official truth commissions—like those in Argentina, Chile, Guatemala, Peru, and South Africa—and unofficial truth projects—such as the Greensboro Truth and Reconciliation Commission (GTRC), Brazil's Nunca Mais, Uruguay's SERPAJ, Northern Ireland's Arodyne Commemoration Project, and Guatemala's Recovery of Historical Memory Project. One of the key differences for Bickford between official truth commissions and unofficial truth projects related to the matter of authority. Official truth commissions have been entrusted with some form of state-sponsored authority, such as a government-backed mandate, money, and/or subpoena power; unofficial truth projects do not have support from the state, relying primarily, if not solely, on the cooperation of civil society. In writing about this difference, Bickford demonstrated the usefulness of such a distinction as a means of categorizing, describing, and comparing the work of NGOs and grassroots initiatives that have sought "to replicate the goals, and often the form and content, of formal truth commissions" (p. 1002). However, while such a distinction is almost certainly useful to scholars of transitional justice (who often depend on the descriptive mode to make sense of the field's complexity), it is worth reflecting on the effects of Bickford's terminology on the field and, in particular, for the practitioners of transitional justice.

As most contemporary theories of language acknowledge, language does not simply represent the world; it also constitutes it. Thus, while Bickford's terminology has helped scholars classify various institutions, it has simultaneously constructed the field of transitional justice in particular ways. It has, for example, served to widen the umbrella of transitional justice by creating a space in the field for initiatives like the GTRC, Nunca Mais, and the Arodyne Commemoration Projection.[1]

---

[1] One reason why the term "truth commission" will not suffice for all of these initiatives is related to the positive reception to Hayner's (2001) survey of 21 truth commissions. For Hayner, one of the defining features of truth commissions is that they are sponsored by the state (p. 14). Since her book's publication, Hayner's definition has taken on a kind of normative status; however, the definition has not proved expansive enough to account for the array of truth-telling initiatives taken up by countries and communities in recent years. This definitional reification helped create the exigency for Bickford's (2007) article.

On the one hand, this move may have warranted unofficial truth projects' access to the resources and support of organizations like the International Center for Transitional Justice. On the other hand, such a distinction may have hindered stakeholders' access to the title "truth commission" and any cultural capital to be gained from it.

Many might argue that in this case the opportunities for "unofficial truth projects" have far outweighed the constraints. But tellingly, as this chapter demonstrates, the members of the GTRC attempted to maneuver around Bickford's term "unofficial truth project" in their *Final Report*, preferring the label "truth commission." It is not surprising that they did so: Bickford's term's emphasis on an institution's lack of state sponsorship could have undermined the GTRC's authority.

In analyzing how the GTRC maneuvered around Bickford's terminology, my point is not to suggest that we should not embrace Bickford's classification; rather, it is to highlight a rhetorical reality facing those writing about the field of transitional justice and an attendant need. Among scholars and practitioners alike, there has been a tendency to engage in definitional work, i.e., to name, describe, categorize, and compare the activities of transitional justice. Such work has been valuable, especially in light of the relatively young age of the field and the need to establish its domain and scope. That said, in the process of doing this definition work, there is an ongoing need to reflect on the ways that naming, describing, categorizing, and comparing the activities of transitional justice are themselves activities of transitional justice. Such definitional acts function in powerful ways to shape belief, warrant action, and constitute identities. As Edward Schiappa (2003) noted in *Defining Reality: Definitions and the Politics of Meaning*, "[A]ll definitions serve some sort of interests, even if those interests are as simple as coordinating our linguistic behavior so we know how and when to use a word in a socially acceptable manner" (p. 69). Naming, describing, categorizing, and comparing: these, too, are the actions that make up the field.

Titles and the Truth

The Greensboro commissioners completed their work by publishing the *Greensboro Truth and Reconciliation Commission Final Report*. They presented an Executive Summary of the report to the citizens of Greensboro at the Report Release Ceremony on May 25, 2006, and, in the days following the ceremony, they distributed the complete spiral-bound report in the community and made it available online. Like many reports published by other truth commissions, the GTRC's *Final Report* reflects an attempt by commissioners to be thorough. Its 529 pages include an "Introduction & Methodology" section; three sections that correspond to the three public hearings; a "Conclusion & Recommendations" section; and fourteen annexes with timelines, maps, and other "defining documents" (GTRC, 2006, pp. v–vi). The cover of the report is especially noteworthy. Front and back flaps are comprised of images of the five victims of November 3, 1979, the GTRC commissioners, and members of the Greensboro community—all of which overlay an indigo-colored denim pattern. The collage of images, "woven together" by the denim fabric, is, as

I noted in Chap. 3, a kind of visual representation of *ubuntu*. Standing out starkly against this dark background is bold white typeface, which reads, "Greensboro Truth and Reconciliation Commission Final Report." It is this title—or, more specifically, the commissioners' claims to the title "Greensboro Truth and Reconciliation Commission"—that is the subject of the present chapter.

Much like the term *ubuntu* and the notion of representivity considered in Chaps. 3 and 4, the title "Truth and Reconciliation Commission" has been a prominent feature of the rhetorical tradition of transitional justice. The title was first used by Chile's Comisión Nacional para la Verdad y Reconciliación, a Commission instituted by Chilean President Patricio Aylwin in 1990 to investigate the "mass arrests, torture, killings, and disappearances" committed during Augusto Pinochet's seventeen year military rule of the country (Hayner, 2001, p. 35). The South African Truth and Reconciliation Commission (SATRC), with its heavily publicized hearings, popularized the title—one of the results of which has been that "Truth and Reconciliation Commission" has often been used as the generic term for these institutions, despite the preference of many scholars to refer to them generically as "truth commissions" or "commissions of inquiry" (Hayner, 2001, pp. 22–23).[2]

Alex Boraine, the deputy chairperson of the SATRC and subsequent co-founder of the ICTJ, described the decision to title the South African inquiry as a Truth and Reconciliation Commission in his book *A Country Unmasked*. Boraine (2001) recounted a meeting between himself and Dullah Omar, the South African Minister of Justice who brought the proposal for a Truth and Reconciliation Commission to the South African Parliament. He wrote:

> [W]hen we talked about the possibility of a commission, I urged Omar not to call it simply a truth commission, because of the Orwellian overtones of the term, but rather to talk in terms of truth and reconciliation, in the hope that the uncovering of the truth, which could lead to acknowledgement of that truth and accountability, would assist us in bringing about the elusive prize of peace and reconciliation. He agreed almost immediately but said that obviously the final decision about the title would have to be made in consultation with his own colleagues and with Parliament. It may well be that the title promised more than we could ever hope to deliver. (pp. 37–38)

Boraine's recollection here offered insight about the origins of the title of the South African inquiry, and it also acknowledged the rhetorical efficacy of such titles. Titles shape subsequent speech and action, delineating "a limited range of appropriate responses" (Schiappa, 2003, p. 112)—which is to say that titles enable some responses and constrain others. On the one hand, the choice to call the South African inquiry a "Truth and Reconciliation Commission" enabled the use of TRC-specific genres like public hearings and the final report to bring about social and political change in the country. On the other hand, it privileged some responses to the violence of apartheid over others. More specifically, it privileged reconciliation, forgiveness, and dialogue as opposed to retribution, forgetting, and, perhaps, silence.

---

[2] Following the operation of the SATRC, several countries and communities have utilized the title, including Sierra Leone, Liberia, Peru, and Greensboro.

Because they shape perception and action, titles like "Truth and Reconciliation Commission" can be powerful rhetorical resources for constructing (or deconstructing) an entity's authority to act: Schiappa (2003) noted, "To 'entitle' something— 'X'—is not only to give X a title in the simple sense of assigning X a name or label but it is also to give X a particular status" (p. 114). That said, acts of entitlement are not always simply accepted as matters of fact; individuals, wrote Schiappa, "do not always agree on how to describe a given phenomenon, and the degree of denotative conformity obtained in various situations can vary widely and change over time" (p. 111). In such cases, which Schiappa referred to as "disputed entitlements," stakeholders defend or critique the titles in question, often by means of definition arguments.[3] Schiappa's comments here describe well what occurred in Greensboro. According to Magarrell and Wesley (2008), one of the "nagging questions" that the Commission's advocates faced was "whether the Greensboro TRC was even a truth commission at all" (p. 229).

In what follows, I analyze the Commission's *Final Report*, which contained the commissioners' clearest and most detailed attempts to position their inquiry as a truth commission.[4] However, the entitlement was disputed, and I bring this dispute into relief by contextualizing my analysis with comments taken from a Greensboro City Council meeting from April 19, 2005, in which members of the council voted 6–3 to oppose the work of the Commission (Truth and reconciliation: Listen for yourself, 2005).[5] The discursive position—the *ethos*—that the commissioners established for the Commission identified them with other truth commissions and helped to garner authority for their findings and recommendations, as presented in the remainder of their report. The juxtaposition of these two texts, the GTRC's report and the Greensboro City Council meeting, highlights that the definitional debate about the legitimacy of the Commission was connected to beliefs about the role that racism played in the events and aftermath of November 3, 1979—a point I discuss in the latter half of the chapter.

---

[3] Schiappa (2003) persuasively argued that definitions are political and always serve particular interests (pp. 69, 178). Part of the burden of this chapter is to tease out what interests are being served through the definitional arguments constructed by the commissioners as well as by their critics.

[4] I frequently refer to the commissioners as the authors of the *Final Report*; however, they were not the only individuals involved in the writing process of the document. The Commission's research director Emily Harwell drafted several sections of the report and also consolidated the submissions of the commissioners and other staff members. Commissioners then revised and edited these initial drafts (Magarrell & Wesley, 2008, p. 119).

[5] The Greensboro City Council's discussion and vote on April 19, 2005 was a response to a petition, initiated by the GTCRP, asking for the city's support of the Commission. The main portion of the petition, which was signed by over 5,300 Greensboro residents, stated: "We, the undersigned residents of the greater Greensboro area, call upon the Greensboro City Council to endorse, support and fully embrace the truth and reconciliation process and to encourage all residents of the City…to participate in the process" (at cited in Magarrell & Wesley, 2008, p. 154).

Redefining "Truth Commission" in the *Final Report*

The starting point for the commissioners' definitional argument in their *Final Report* was Pricilla Hayner's (2003) definition of "truth commission." In *Unspeakable Truths*, Hayner defined "truth commission" as follows:

> I use the term to refer to those bodies that share the following characteristics: (1) truth commissions focus on the past; (2) they investigate a pattern of abuses over a period of time, rather than a specific event; (3) a truth commission is a temporary body, typically in operation for six months to two years, and completing its work with the submission of a report; and (4) these commissions are officially sanctioned, authorized, or empowered by the state (and sometimes also by the armed opposition, as in a peace accord). (p. 14)

A fifth characteristic that Hayner mentioned a few pages later in her book was that "truth commissions should not be equated with judicial bodies, nor should they be considered a replacement for trials" (p. 16), and, finally, she noted that "all [truth commissions] were created to look into recent events, usually at the point of a political transition" (p. 17).

It is worth noting how, in their *Final Report*, the Greensboro commissioners reaccentuated Hayner's definition. Citing *Unspeakable Truths*, commissioners defined "truth commission" as follows:

> *Generally* [emphasis added], when people talk about truth commissions they are referring to what are *usually* [emphasis added] temporary bodies, officially sanctioned, authorized or empowered by the state. They are non-judicial in nature, and operate independently of government and other outside influences. *Usually* [emphasis added], truth commissions are created within some moment of political transition, focusing on the past and investigating patterns of abuse that have occurred over time, *usually* [emphasis added] referring to violations of human rights. *Typically* [emphasis added], truth commissions complete their work with the submission of a final report that contains conclusions and recommendations. (GTRC, 2006, p. 10)

This passage represented Hayner's definition fairly accurately. Commissioners referenced all of the defining characteristics of truth commissions mentioned by Hayner and, in some cases, did so verbatim. Moreover, the commissioners' additions to Hayner's definition—that truth commissions "operate independently of government and other outside influences" and focus on "violations of human rights"—were not inconsistent with Hayner's description of truth commissions elsewhere in her book. What was notably different, however, was the commissioners' introduction of additional mood adjuncts, such as "generally," "usually," and "typically"—each of which helped to construct what has been called the modality of usuality (Martin, Matthiessen, & Painter, 1987, p. 64). Modality is a grammatical resource that speakers and writers use to express varying degrees of commitment to their propositions; it "sets up," in the words of J. R. Martin and David Rose (2003), "a semantic space between yes and no, a cline running between positive and negative poles" (p. 53). In this case, the commissioners' use of modality introduced an element of possibility into Hayner's (mostly) polarized definition. For example, they modified the claim that truth commissioners are "temporary bodies, officially sanctioned, authorized or empowered by the state" with the mood adjunct "usually" to create a space, within the category of "truth commissions," for institutions that are not "temporary bodies, officially sanctioned, authorized or empowered by the state."

This shift in modality enabled other instances of reaccentuation. Throughout their *Final Report*, commissioners reaccentuated four aspects of Hayner's definition of truth commissions—all of which could have excluded the Greensboro inquiry from laying claim to its title. The first thing that compromised the Commission's ability to lay claim to the title "truth commission" was the fact that the GTRC was not "officially sanctioned, authorized or empowered by the state." Second, the Commission's claims to independence were frequently called into question by those accusing the Commission of bias. Third, the Commission was seemingly called on to investigate a one-time event, as opposed to "patterns of abuse that have occurred over time." Finally, it was not self-evidently the case that the Commission was "created within some moment of political transition." Opponents of the Commission highlighted these discrepancies to discredit the inquiry and to suggest that the Greensboro context did not call for a truth commission; conversely, the Commission attempted to mitigate (and, in some cases, negate) these discrepancies, in order to position itself within the category of "Truth and Reconciliation Commission."[6]

---

[6] It is necessary at this point in my argument to acknowledge the work of Chelsea Marshall (2006), who served as the Commission's public hearing coordinator. At the same time that the *Final Report* was published, Marshall wrote a thesis for the Department of Government at Smith College, entitled "Transitional Justice in 'Non-Transitioning' Societies: Evaluating the Success of the Greensboro Truth and Reconciliation Commission." In Chap. 2 of the thesis, Marshall (2006) considered the GTRC in light of both Hayner's (2001) definition of truth commissions as well as the work of four other truth commissions, and she made the following claim: "the Greensboro Truth and Reconciliation Commission challenges the typical understanding of truth commissions, yet due to the pliability of the [truth commission] model, the GTRC may be considered a truth commission and should be evaluated as such" (p. 18). In short, Marshall's chapter advances the argument of the *Final Report*.

I mention Marshall's thesis here because it helped me to clarify my own argument in this chapter. Seeing Marshall's arguments alongside those in the *Final Report's* introduction confirmed to me the aspects of Hayner's (2001) definition that were at issue for the GTRC (e.g., that truth commissions "address patterns of abuses," "are officially sanctioned by the state," attempt to be "impartial," and "occur during periods of transition"). Moreover, several of my subheadings in this chapter contain phrases that are similar to several of Marshall's subheadings (pp. 34–39). However, it is worth emphasizing that, while our subheadings are similar, our purposes are different. Marshall's primary purpose was, like the commissioners themselves, to make the case that the truth commission model was flexible and that the Greensboro inquiry was, in fact, a legitimate truth commission; my purpose is to unpack the commissioners' definitional arguments, show how they function rhetorically, and explain why they matter.

Furthermore, in Chap. 18 of *Learning from Greensboro,* Magarrell and Wesley (2008) made many of the same points mentioned by Marshall in her thesis and by the commissioners in their *Final Report* (pp. 229–240). The repetition of these arguments has helped to contribute to their rhetorical force. Once again, my purpose is not simply to make these arguments again but to unpack *how* they are made. By analyzing the argumentative moves made in the *Final Report*, it is my hope that we can better understand the rhetorical tradition of the field of transitional justice and how it might (or might not) be reaccentuated elsewhere.

Collapsing Categories to Align the GTRC with State-Sanctioned Initiatives

At the April 19, 2005 Greensboro City Council meeting, before the council voted whether or not to endorse the work of the GTRC, Mayor of Greensboro Keith Holliday read a prepared statement, stating his objections to the truth and reconciliation process (Truth and reconciliation: Listen for yourself, 2005). Central to Holliday's many objections in his statement was the Commission's lack of state sanction. He called attention to the fact that the Commission lacked "authority, sub-poena power, [and] ability to grant immunity" and later emphasized the point, high-lighting that the Commission did not have "the authority or safeguards usually afforded in other judicial proceedings."[7] Such claims, which pertained primarily to the Commission as an institution, were complemented by statements that called into question the commissioners' authority as individuals; Holliday pointed out, for example, that most of the commissioners—with the exception of attorney Robert Peters—lacked "legal training as to the rights afforded under the Constitution of the United States." Furthermore, Holliday reinforced these explicit claims about the Commission's and commissioners' lack of state-sanctioned authority with state-ments that implicitly discredited the Commission: he suggested that the events of November 3, 1979 were, until recently, only the concern of "a few dozen people," and he challenged the Commission's ability to procure witnesses. "I will be sur-prised," he said, "if one could even realistically get Klansmen to come testify."

In the *Final Report*, commissioners responded, directly and indirectly, to several of Holliday's remarks; however, they spoke most forcefully to the issue of state sanction. Commissioners did this by introducing Bickford's distinction between "truth commissions" and "truth projects" (GTRC, 2006, p. 10).[8] They noted that, for Bickford, the term "truth commission" referred to official institutions established by the state, whereas "truth projects" were unofficial institutions emerging from civil society. However, the commissioners dropped Bickford's distinction within a few paragraphs of introducing it, subsuming both truth commissions and truth projects into the category of truth commissions; they wrote, "All of these truth commis-sions—whether official or unofficial, whether they emerge in new democracies or well-established ones—tell a version of history that includes the victims' experi-ences and voices, recognizes their humanity and rights, and seeks to come to terms with abuse in all of its many dimensions" (p. 11). An important shift takes place in this passage: the defining characteristics ("official" and "unofficial") that, in

---

[7]Another council member also raised the issue of the Commission's lack of state-sponsored author-ity. Councilperson Don Vaughan remarked that he agreed with Mayor Holliday, noting, "Many of the red flags as far as a formal endorsement [do] come up: there's no subpoena power here, there's no governmental immunity, there's no process to compel testimony" (Truth and reconciliaton: Listen for yourself, 2005).

[8]With regard to this quotation, the commissioners cited a March 2004 draft of Bickford's *Unofficial Truth Projects: a discussion paper*, written for the ICTJ.

Bickford's formulation, distinguish different categories ("truth commissions" and "truth projects") from one another are reconstituted as characteristics of the same category ("truth commissions"). "Official" and "unofficial" are no longer presented as category-defining characteristics; they are rendered incidental to the definition of truth commissions as opposed to essential. Note that, according to both Hayner's (2001) definition and Bickford's (2007) categories, an "unofficial truth commission" would qualify as a contradiction in terms. But, by explicitly introducing new categories and, subsequently, by implicitly collapsing these categories back under the label of "truth commission," commissioners expanded the definition of "truth commissions" to make room for the GTRC, for themselves.

Commissioners addressed the issue of state sanction in another way as well. They wrote, "While truth commissions can accomplish many things and set a country—or a community—on a path to a stronger and more respectful future, it is important to recognize that expectations for truth commissions can run too high" (p. 12). The commissioners' addition of the parenthetical phrase "or a community" to this sentence was an implicit act of redefinition: it suggested that truth commissions need not be instituted at the national level and, therefore, served as an attempt to broaden the notion of "truth commissions." This parenthetical remark was reinforced in a subsequent paragraph of the report: "[W]e joined a world in which many people are challenging unfinished and misshapen stories about past abuses and violence that continue to sow distrust and even hate in our nations *and our communities* [emphasis added] today" (p. 12).

Commissioners also responded to Holliday's claim that the Commission lacked the power to compel testimonies or produce evidence. They wrote, "[Some in Greensboro] have criticized our Mandate and suggested that we cannot operate as a truth commission because we have no power to compel testimonies or the production of evidence. It is true that this was a limitation, but it is one shared by a number of other truth commissions, including El Salvador, Guatemala and Peru" (p. 15).[9] Here the commissioners utilized one of the criticisms leveled against them—one of their supposed limitations—to align themselves with other truth commissions, thereby reinforcing their claim to their title and, thus, their authority. Likewise, in a subsequent paragraph, they called attention to the fact that the GTRC was "like many others" in terms of its inability to enforce recommendations (p. 15). They continued, "Many truth commissions, even officially sanctioned ones, are undertaken without a prior commitment that recommendations will be put into immediate effect" (p. 15). Such comparisons were rhetorical moves that served to position their inquiry as a legitimate truth commission.

---

[9] Writing about the GTRC's lack of government sponsorship, Magarrell and Wesley (2008) made a similar argument (pp. 236–237). More specifically, they used the grassroots status of the GTRC to identify the initiative with other commissions: "[T]he GTRC did not have the powers that some government-sponsored truth commissions have wielded…But other important truth commissions have managed quite well operating solely on the basis of moral suasion and persistence; such were the truth commissions in Chile, Guatemala, and Peru" (p. 237).

Responding to Accusations of Bias

A second objection raised by council members was that the truth and reconciliation process in Greensboro was biased toward Communist Workers Party (CWP) interests (Truth and reconciliation: Listen for yourself, 2005). This accusation stemmed from the fact that the GTCRP, the group that instituted the Commission, included former CWP members. The claim that the truth commission was biased was voiced publicly at the Greensboro City Council meeting by Councilperson Sandy Carmany, one of the six members of the council who voted not to endorse the work of the Commission: "If [the Commission] had been initiated by a totally unbiased group that had nothing to do with [November 3rd, 1979]…I could have been more comfortable with it. But knowing how it began…it was quite obvious what the intent, or what the outcome, is expected to be from this effort" (Truth and reconciliation: Listen for yourself, 2005). In raising this concern, Carmany echoed and reinforced the sentiments of a number of Greensboro residents (Magarrell & Wesley, 2008, pp. 78, 132–133, 137, 158).[10]

Commissioners, in their *Final Report*, once again used these accusations to align the GTRC with other truth commissions around the world. They did so by identifying their own experiences with the experiences of other truth commissions:

> Some in Greensboro have questioned the role that the survivors of November 3rd, 1979, played in creating the GTRC. In looking at other commission experiences around the world, including South Africa's, which has earned so much attention and credibility, we observe that those most affected – accompanied by others who share their concerns – have almost without fail been the moving force behind truth-seeking initiatives. Truth commissions are victim-oriented – able to offer an outlet for people affected to tell their stories and to be heard in a new setting with new possibilities for understanding. But we are not victim-biased; we operate independently of the influence of the victims and their supporters. (GTRC, 2006, pp. 14–15)

Identification was constructed in this passage through the use of the antithesis in the final two sentences. The first sentence in this antithesis was written in the third-person, setting forth a general principle about truth commissions; the second, however, shifted to a first-person plural perspective. Through the introduction of the pronoun "we" in the second colon of the antithesis, the authors of the report aligned themselves with other truth commissions, reifying their identity as a truth commission.

To address accusations of bias more directly, and distance themselves from any associations with the CWP, commissioners attempted to make the case that they

---

[10]One such resident was John Young, who had been a member of the GTCRP (and signed the Declaration of Intent to form the Commission) but came to believe that the Commission showed partiality to the Project (Magarrell & Wesley, 2008, p. 137). Some residents worried, in particular, about the role that former CWP member Nelson Johnson—a vocal advocate for the Commission and member of the Project—would play in the process (pp. 78, 158). Moreover, many residents expressed concerns about the GTCRP's influence over the GTRC when the two groups held a joint press conference to announce where the Commission's archives would eventually be held (pp. 132–133).

were an independent entity, without commitments to the organization that founded them. They reiterated that the commissioner selection process was "independent" of the GTCRP (p. 15). In the interest of full disclosure, they then explained the specific ways that the GTCRP supported their work, which included "gathering signatures on a petition asking the City Council to endorse the truth and reconciliation process, soliciting grassroots financial donations, organizing various worship services prior to some of our public events, and making a commitment to foster dialogue and work towards the other recommendations in this report" (p. 24). But immediately after making this list, the commissioners again distanced themselves from the GTCRP: "[T]hey have no prior knowledge of what is included herein. We affirm that we have conducted our research and community engagement in accordance with our mandate to operate independently of any external influence, including the GTCRP" (p. 24).[11]

The commissioners also used the Greensboro City Council's 6–3 vote to construct their independence. They noted, "[T]he City Council voted, along racial lines, to oppose the truth and reconciliation process. We chose to view this opposition as an affirmation of our independence" (p. 24). Elsewhere in the report, they reiterated the point, noting that, because they did not receive the support of the City Council, they were "in some ways... even less fettered than 'official' commissions, which may feel pressured by authorities even when nominally independent" (p. 15).

Reframing the Object of Inquiry Beyond a Single Event

As with the first two of the council's objections to the truth commission process in Greensboro, the third also attacked the GTRC on definitional grounds. This objection, however, focused not on the Commission's origins but on its object of inquiry. Recall that both Hayner's (2001) definition of truth commissions and the Commission's (2006) definition indicated that truth commissions investigate a pattern of abuses over a given period, and, additionally, Hayner's (2001) definition specified that truth commissions do not focus on "a specific event" (p. 14). It was, therefore, noteworthy that Mayor Holliday referred, multiple times, to the object of the Commission's inquiry as a specific event: he said, "I believe everyone would agree that November 3rd, 1979 was a tragic event in the history of Greensboro," and he later reiterated the point, remarking, "November 3rd, 1979 was a tragic event" (Truth and reconciliation: Listen for yourself, 2005). These remarks framed the object of the Commission's inquiry as a singular, as opposed to an ongoing, phenomenon. The mayor also argued that the abuses for which other truth commissions

---

[11]During the GTRC's operation, commissioners distanced themselves from the GTCRP in other ways as well. For example, they requested that the GTCRP change its name, to prevent confusion and allow residents of Greensboro to distinguish more easily between the two groups (Magarrell & Wesley, 2008, pp. 80, 150). The Project ultimately decided to keep its name. For more on the Commission's attempts to establish their independence, see Magarrell & Wesley, 2008, pp. 69–80.

were instituted were dissimilar to the events of November 3, 1979: "To pattern the project," he said, "from the model of what happened in South Africa, over many years of abuse and inhumane treatment, to the November 3rd, 1979 event here in Greensboro is almost like comparing apples to oranges." Councilperson Florence Gatten reinforced the point:

> I disagree respectfully with basic assumptions that are being put forward [by those in favor of the truth and reconciliation commission]…[T]he recent visit and comparison of the truth and reconciliation process in Peru, where they are discussing, quote, "Twenty years of murders, tortures, and rapes," end quote, is a specious one….[W]hatever Greensboro you envision, it is not one characterized by twenty years of murders, tortures, and rapes. Nor is a single incident in 1979 emblematic of racial divisions in our community that would justify the South African model.

According to Gatten, what happened in Peru took place over two decades, while what happened in Greensboro was described as a one-time "event" and "a single incident in 1979."[12]

In the *Final Report*, commissioners framed their object of inquiry differently, writing about it in more expansive terms. They described it in terms of multiple "local events" within a "timeframe"—a timeframe that spanned "the lifetime of most of those involved in the confrontation on Nov. 3, 1979" (GTRC, 2006, p. 23). They then continued, "But because historical events at larger scales often figure prominently in community consciousness, we have also examined key events that loom large in collective memory such as the importance of the United States' history of Constitutional rights, slavery, white supremacy, key labor or civil rights organizing efforts and geopolitical conflicts" (p. 23). They also noted that they augmented this historical context by investigating "26 years" of "rumors and misinformation," as well as "hundreds of newspaper articles, films and other media portrayals" (p. 23). Thus, although the commissioners never described their object of inquiry as a "pattern of abuses," they did make significant rhetorical gestures in that direction.

The commissioners also addressed the council members' claims that November 3 should not be compared to events in South Africa and Peru. They did so by transforming what council members framed as a difference of order into a difference of degree. As rhetoricians Chaim Perelman and Lucie Olbrechts-Tyteca (1969) noted, differences of order involve qualitative distinctions, in which the things being compared are of two separate classes; differences in degree are quantitative, in which both things belong to a single class (pp. 345–49; Jasinski, 2001, p. 11). To accomplish the transformation, commissioners began by reintroducing Holliday and Gatten's objections to the truth commission process. They wrote, "Many have said that comparing the killings in Greensboro in 1979 to apartheid South Africa is a forced parallel and that the two have nothing in common" (GTRC, 2006, pp. 13–14).

---

[12] Magarrell and Wesley (2008) summarized perspectives like those expressed by Holliday and Gatten here as follows: "For some in Greensboro, any comparison of the Klan-Nazi killing in their city with the notorious system of apartheid in South Africa was offensive. So, in their eyes, turning to a truth commission inspired by the South African experience was ill-conceived, out of place, and misleading" (p. 229).

The difference expressed here is a difference of order. In response to this objection, commissioners acknowledged that there is, indeed, a difference between the Greensboro context and the South African context; however, they framed the difference as a matter of "scale," not a categorical difference. That is, they described the difference between the Greensboro killings and the atrocities in South Africa in quantitative not qualitative terms: they mentioned the "massive and widespread human rights abuses," the "thousands of state-sponsored disappearances and killings," the "massive displacement, enslavement, starvation, torture and rape of women," the "shocking" numbers, and the horrific statistics (pp. 13–14). What commissioners preserved in framing the difference in this way was the qualitative similarities between the Greensboro event and the crimes in other countries. No less than three times in the space of three paragraphs, commissioners shifted their discussion from the quantitative differences to the qualitative similarities.[13] Take, for instance, the following excerpt: "While there is a difference in scale, much of what the GTRC has had to review is similar to incidents experienced on the local level in South Africa, where, like members of the Ku Klux Klan and Nazi party, individuals used race as a reason to treat others as less than human" (p. 14). "Greensboro's 1979 killings," commissioners continued, "shared with international tragedies the pain felt by survivors, the impact on others directly involved in violence, and the unresolved nature of the legacy of these events" (p. 14). To strengthen the comparison, commissioners went on to note that, when examined at the "local level," the atrocities committed elsewhere in the world look much like the events of November 3rd, 1979 (p. 14).[14]

Quantifying Change to Construct Transition

A final, related problem for commissioners had to do with the political context in which their inquiry took place. Truth commissions, as Hayner's (2001) and the commissioners' (2006) definitions suggest, (typically) operate during periods of

---

[13] Similarly, Magarrell and Wesley (2008) transformed a difference of order to difference of degree in *Learning from Greensboro*: they noted that, in one sense, the experiences in South Africa and Peru "have nothing in common [with Greensboro] and that each exists in its own world of difference" (p. 230); however, they then wrote that, in another sense, "many of the elements of human rights violations that occur anywhere in the world outside of the United States describe a paradigm in which Greensboro's narrative, while certainly more modest in scale, is actually quite at home" (p. 231).

[14] Commissioners made the same moves in a subsequent paragraph of the report: they began by highlighting the quantitative differences between the GTRC's and SATRC's objects of inquiry, but then they noted the following: "[W]hile the numbers are shocking, they are insufficient: they do not explain the inequities, the responsibility for what happened or the ways in which horror was inflicted…nor do statistics illustrate the suffering of victims" (p. 14). Then they continued, "It is this human picture at the local level that in many ways can be likened to the GTRC's exploration of restraints on labor organizing, anti-communism and deep-seated racism that were, in part, responsible for what happened here on Nov. 3, 1979" (p. 14).

political upheaval or transition. However, dissenting council members rejected the notion that Greensboro qualified as a place of political upheaval or political transition. Moreover, dissenters framed members of both the GTCRP and the Commission as incapable of bringing about a positive transition. Councilperson Gatten said in her remarks that those associated with the GTCRP and Commission were "locked in the 70s, locked in the past, looking back when we need to be looking forward" (Truth and reconciliation: Listen for yourself, 2005). She described the Commission's object of inquiry as "the wrong focal point" because "it does not address where we are now." For Gatten, the inquiry not only failed to address the needs of the present, but it also compromised the work that was already being done, by taking resources away from more positive initiatives that might yet bring about constructive change. "The Commission," she said, "will further polarize our community. It is not constructive. It is negative energy that our city does not need. It is living in the past. And it is using the past as a barrier to keep us from moving forward into the promise of our future" (Truth and reconciliation: Listen for yourself, 2005). In other words, the GTRC was hampering, not promoting, positive transition. Similar sentiments were expressed by Councilperson Robbie Perkins. Perkins contrasted his own forward-looking perspective with that of those who chose to spend their time "focusing on one event that happened on one day that we all regret happened" (Truth and reconciliation: Listen for yourself, 2005).

Commissioners addressed these critiques by attempting to frame the Greensboro context as a transition:

> We have been asked why a mechanism like a truth commission should apply in the United States, where no evident political transition is underway, and where there is a functioning court system and a vibrant media. We believe that, while some transitions are dramatic, like countries emerging from a civil war or a period of repressive rule, others are more subtle. In Greensboro, we believe that this effort arises out of a willingness to honestly move from a less respectful and less tolerant city to one that is more democratic and more inclusive. As Lisa Magarrell from the ICTJ has observed, "Any turn towards greater respect for all citizens of a community should be seen as a transition that can be aided by the truth." (GTRC, 2006, p. 14)[15]

Here the commissioners claimed that their goal was to help create a more democratic city—a move that situated the work of the GTRC squarely within the larger field of transitional justice, which has focused largely on democratic transitions. Furthermore, to support their claim that Greensboro was in a period of transition, the authors made use of a rhetorical strategy discussed in the previous section: they transformed a difference of order into a difference of degree. Whereas those opposing the truth and reconciliation process took the line that the Greensboro context— a city in a democratic country, with a "functioning court system and vibrant media" (Truth and reconciliation: Listen for yourself, 2005)—was qualitatively different than the transitional contexts in which other truth commissions had operated,

---

[15] In *Learning from Greensboro*, Magarrell and Wesley (2008) reinforced and expanded on the GTRC's argument: "First," they wrote, "any 'transition,' even in clear-cut cases, can be viewed with a long or short lens…The U.S. transition out of slavery, white supremacy, and denigration of the rights of minority populations is one that is far from concluded" (p. 234).

commissioners claimed that both the Greensboro context and the contexts in which other truth commissions operated could be classified as "transitional." They did so by suggesting that the differences in the "transitions" were quantitative not qualitative: "We believe that, while some transitions are dramatic, like countries emerging from a civil war or a period of repressive rule, others are more subtle" (p. 14).

Redefining Greensboro

At issue in this definitional dispute over the GTRC's status as a truth commission was the legitimacy of different conceptions of Greensboro.[16] During their meeting, the Greensboro City Council members described the city as progressive and evolving: the view of the city that they put forward was one that emphasized continuous, positive improvement with regard to issues of race and class.[17] The commissioners, on the other hand, challenged this vision of Greensboro in their *Final Report*, constructing an image of a city in which there were systemic problems, especially with regard to race, that had not been adequately addressed (Magarrell & Wesley, 2008, pp. 94–97).

The presentation of Greensboro as a progressive and evolving city came up throughout the mayor's remarks, as well as those of the other dissenting councilpersons. At the beginning of his statement, the mayor described Greensboro as a progressive city explicitly: "[P]rior to three years ago," he said, "I do not believe that there was more than a few dozen people who constantly talked about, contemplated, and considered the events of November 3rd, 1979 as holding us back from being a progressive city. Greensboro was a progressive city in 1979 and is even more progressive today" (Truth and reconciliation: Listen for yourself, 2005). Like the mayor, Councilperson Tom Phillips attempted to disassociate the city of Greensboro from November 3, 1979, by claiming that the event had not, as he put it, "divided our community over all these years." He, too, described the city as progressive and claimed that the Commission was the recent agenda of a select group of individuals, not a systemic concern in the city. Councilperson Gatten viewed the implications of the GTCRP and GTRC as a personal affront, asserting, "We're an evolving city, not the same city we were in 1979, and to suggest otherwise is a slap in the face to all of us, myself included, who have worked so hard to make changes."

Mayor Holliday also disassociated the events of November 3 from the city of Greensboro (Truth and reconciliation: Listen for yourself, 2005). He emphasized that the confrontations precipitating the event occurred "in other areas of the state"

---

[16] According to Magarrell and Wesley (2008), Signe Waller, one of the CWP survivors, composed a document for the commissioners entitled, "A City of Two Tales" (p. 159). Although Waller's document's title was not referring specifically to the different conceptions of Greensboro put forward by the City Council and the Commission, it is, arguably, an apt way to understand the arguments presented at the council meeting and in the *Final Report*. That is, at the heart of the arguments there are two competing narratives about Greensboro and its history.

[17] The views of the Greensboro City Council expressed here were not inconsistent with Chafe's (1980) claims about Greensboro's "progressive mystique" (p. 7).

and described the participants as "outside groups coming to Greensboro." To the extent that the mayor did attribute the events to more systemic problems in Greensboro, he claimed that race was not a major factor, nor, he said, did it further exacerbate Greensboro's "racial issues and areas of distrust." The polarity of the mayor's claims regarding race was striking. It probably would have been more persuasive for him to admit that racism was one of many causes of November 3, 1979. Instead, he made declarative statements that race did not play a major role in causing the event.

It was in response to these views about Greensboro that the GTRC presented its findings in the *Final Report*. One significant factor that allowed them to do so—in addition to the rhetorical moves that I have elaborated upon in prior chapters of this book—was the definition argument in their report, in which they laid claim to the title of "truth commission." In positioning the Greensboro inquiry as a truth commission, commissioners tapped into a tradition that had, in and through the operations of dozens of past truth commissions, constructed a measure of political and moral authority to act in the world. The commissioners themselves spoke to this point: "[W]e joined a world," they wrote (GTRC, 2006, p. 12). Then, in a remark that was consistent with my book's central argument, they added, "By adapting the truth commission idea to our own conditions we were able to draw inspiration and some comfort that what seemed to be an impossible task might actually be something we could accomplish" (pp. 12–13). Speaking from this seat of authority, the commissioners presented a different view about Greensboro: they contended that racism was a systemic problem in the city in 1979 and still was in 2006.

Commissioners rejected the mayor's claims about November 3, 1979. They asserted, unequivocally, that racism was one of the primary causes of the Greensboro killings. To make their case, commissioners provided the following evidence, in the form of a bulleted list:

- A group of demonstrators aiming to empower laborers in a poor black neighborhood were holding a "Death to the Klan" rally.
- The leading organizer of the rally was a local black activist who was outspoken on issues of racial inequality. This leader was widely demonized for his role in the city's traumatic 1969 incident of mass racial unrest prompted by the "Dudley/A&T Revolt."
- The "Death to the Klan" marchers were shot down by Klan and Nazis who were twice acquitted by all-white juries.
- The city acted to try to prevent subsequent citizen protest against the Klan and white supremacist violence. (p. 380)

What was perhaps most compelling about this list (and what followed it) was its trajectory, which, as the text unfolded from one bullet point to the next, implicated the city of Greensboro and Greensboro citizens more and more directly. The first two bullet points implicated the individuals and groups present on November 3, 1979; the third implicated the juries; and the fourth, the city. Through this organizational scheme, then, commissioners called attention to the fact that racism was not simply an individual matter but was also a systemic problem in the community in

1979. But they did not stop there. Commissioners went on, in the next paragraph of their report, to implicate the readers of the report by prompting them to imagine November 3, 1979 in "racial reverse":

> Imagine for a moment that these elements were racially reversed, viewed as a photographic negative. Imagine a group of demonstrators is holding a demonstration against black terrorism in the affluent white community of Irving Park. A caravan of armed black terrorists are allowed to drive unobstructed to the parade starting point, and photos are taken by the police as a fight breaks out and demonstrators are shot dead. Most of the cars are then allowed to flee the scene, un-pursued, even as they threaten neighborhood pedestrians by pointing shotguns through the windows. The defendants are tried and acquitted by an all-black jury. The first shots—fired by the black terrorists screaming "Shoot the Crackers!" and "Show me a Cracker with guts and I'll show you a black man with a gun!"—are described by defense attorneys and accepted by jurors as "calming" or "non-hostile" shots. Meanwhile, the city government takes steps to block citizen protest of further black terrorist violence including a curfew in the white neighborhood. The scenario is so unlikely as to be preposterous. Yet, in racial reverse, it is exactly what happened. (pp. 380–381)

The narrative here was intended, in part, to highlight the extent to which race was a factor in the events and aftermath of November 3, 1979. One of the things rhetorically significant about this passage was that, insofar as the report's readers accepted the claim that the scenario was "so unlikely as to be preposterous" and agreed with the commissioners that it went against common sense, they were forced to acknowledge that even their own notions of common sense had been shaped by racism.

At this point in the report, commissioners contended that racism was still a problem in the city. Writing now in the present tense, they noted, "Racism, it goes without saying, divides our community and suppresses dialogue. It also routinely acts through institutions to disadvantage entire groups of people. This is often so in the justice system, which was created by white leaders to protect the interests of the majority power structure" (p. 381). Contemporary instances of racism were presented here as a matter-of-fact: it still "routinely" disadvantaged many people and, according to the commissioners, the fact that it continued to divide the Greensboro community went "without saying" (p. 381). Once again, commissioners used a bulleted list to provide evidence to support their claim:

- [The] City Council voted 6–3, with the three black members dissenting, to oppose the truth and reconciliation process;
- Council members promoted rumors about the GTRC intimidating opponents and sowed confusion about our funding and our relationship to the GTCRP;
- Information known only to the GTRC, police and city officials was leaked to the media, jeopardizing the public hearing testimony;
- Police officials met with representatives of Mount Zion Baptist Church without GTRC staff about a GTRC event planned there;
- Prospective statement givers and community dialogue participants indicated being discouraged to participate. (p. 382)

The fact that commissioners used the same format—a bulleted list—to support *both* their claim that November 3, 1979 was "woven through with issues of race and class" *and* their claim that a pattern of resisting change continued in Greensboro presented an implicit argument that Greensboro was not as progressive as some council members would have led citizens to believe. Furthermore, both here and in the text surrounding these bullet points, commissioners described the city as maintaining the "status quo," "protecting... stability," "resisting change," and "suppressing efforts" (p. 382). They also use terms like "indifference," "discomfort," and "distaste" in reference to their critics (p. 382).

Thus, throughout the report, commissioners clearly positioned themselves in opposition to city leaders. It is worth noting, however, that they did not do so primarily by aligning themselves with the history of civil rights activism in Greensboro or with the members of the GTCRP. Instead they primarily drew upon their status as a truth commission to position themselves in opposition to the city leaders. They referred explicitly to their process as one of "truth and reconciliation" and mentioned their public hearings, a genre that identified them with other truth commissions. They also reiterated the goals of their endeavor—goals that identified them with other truth commissions. That is, they claimed, in this same section of the report, that their primary aims were to foster dialogue and accountability, seek and speak the truth, honestly examine the past, and bring about justice—which, they said, was a prerequisite "to restore trust and to heal" (p. 382). In short, it was primarily the commissioners' identification with other truth commissions that gave them a place from which to stand—an *ethos*—to challenge views about Greensboro presented by some of the city leaders.

They again made use of their *ethos* as a truth commission when critiquing the United States justice system (pp. 307–309). They claimed that the justice system was imperfect, but not "randomly" so. "It tends," they wrote, "to be disproportionately imperfect against people of color and poor people" (p. 377). To speak against the inherent injustices in the justice system, commissioners made use of an act of dissociation that Desmond Tutu and others frequently employed during the operation of the SATRC. They distinguished "retributive justice" from "transformative justice," and privileged the latter:

> The "retributive justice" model of the U.S. legal system confines judicial inquiries to the proof of a defendant's guilt (criminal cases) or liability (civil cases), under a narrowly defined set of laws and rules of procedure. As a result, the examination of the role of individuals and institutions, outside of the particular defendants on trial, is limited solely to their relevance to those particular proceedings. Similarly, the scope for defining and addressing other types of harm and other stakeholders in the incident is also very narrow. The courtroom is the realm of technical knowledge and expertise, with little leeway for richness of context or consequences that surround wrongs...The promise of "transformative justice" is in drawing the community to the table to discuss what wrongs were done and to whom and by whom. Transformative justice also facilitates exchange of diverse perspectives on why these wrongs occurred and what should be done. In this way, transformative justice works in concert with retributive justice, not as a repeat or replacement of it. (p. 259)

Having positioned the GTRC as a truth commission earlier in the report, here the commissioners laid claim to one of the characteristic argumentative devices of the rhetorical tradition of transitional justice. On the one hand, using the retributive/transformative distinction provided commissioners with a critical framework, giving them a place to stand from which "to take a fresh and more dispassionate look at the procedural and substantive issues involved in these trials" and from which to expose how the process "inevitably reflects and also is influenced by the prevailing social and political contexts, and how in this particular case the system failed some expectations for justice" (p. 377)—especially the expectations of those who hoped the courts would address racial inequities. On the other hand, the distinction allowed the commissioners to avoid completely rejecting the United States legal system. That is, they were able to validate the importance of the retributive justice of the legal system, even as they were able to speak to the ways that the courts have repro-duced racial and economic inequities. "By looking at the issues more holistically," they wrote, "truth commissions can better diagnose the underlying causes and consequences, which may not be relevant to particular legal proceedings" (p. 259).

Reactions and Responses

The Commission's definition arguments mattered because they provided a place for the commissioners to stand—grounds, constructed in part by prior truth commis-sions, from where they were able to speak against the status quo and offer different views about Greensboro than those of the mayor, the dissenting city council mem-bers, and others. Establishing this authority allowed the commissioners to speak of injustice in the United States legal system, attribute blame to city officials and the Greensboro police for their actions and inactions on November 3, 1979, and bring into relief the systemic racism and economic inequalities in the city (GTRC, 2006). It also helped ensure that their recommendations were heard (GTRC, 2006, p. 383–390). These recommendations included, but were not limited to, formal apologies from those involved in November 3, 1979 (p. 384); the construction of memorials and historical exhibits to commemorate the tragedy (p. 384); the formation of dis-cussion forums for the community and "a healing workshop or retreat for children of CWP members, shooters and others directly involved in the events of Nov. 3, 1979" (p. 384); the institution of anti-racism training for city and county employees (p. 385); the institution of a living wage for city and county workers (p. 385); the city's issuing of "annual reports on race relations and racial disparities" (p. 386); the development of a curriculum "based on the events of Nov. 3, 1979," for primary and secondary students (p. 387); and the formation of a community justice center in Greensboro (p. 387). Commissioners believed that such recommendations, if acted upon, would have significant consequences for the people of Greensboro.

The release of the *Final Report* resulted in a substantial amount of commentary and debate in the opinion pages of Greensboro's local newspaper—the *News & Record*.[18] As a few headlines attested, some editorials claimed that the report merely

---

[18] As a means of ensuring that their recommendations were discussed by community members, commissioners invited various groups from the Greensboro community to pledge to serve as des-ignated "Report Receivers." Over 45 groups pledged to do so, including the Greensboro Police Department and the Griffin Knights of the Ku Klux Klan.

confirmed suspicions that the Commission was biased toward the Communist Workers Party: "Commission proposes political agenda," "Truth Commission shows obvious bias," and "We hold these truths to be self-serving" (Clark, 2006, p. A11; Vickers, 2006, p. A6; Millar, 2006, p. A8). Others claimed that the report was a major achievement and that the Commission had done a good job maintaining a balanced and objective stance. Signe Waller, one of the survivors of November 3, 1979, described the report as a "milestone" (2006, p. A15); Dean Driver, a citizen of Greensboro, wrote, "Contrary to the expectations of those who claimed the commission was biased toward the victims [i.e., the CWP], the report actually distributes blame among nearly everyone involved" (2006, p. A10); and Z. N. Holler, one of the members of the Task Force that helped establish the GTRC, noted, "The Truth and Reconciliation Commission did its best—an excellent best, in my opinion—to try to seek out, sort through, understand and present fairly the complexities of what happened [on November 3rd, 1979] and why" (2006, p. A7). Still others, like Edward Cone, took a more nuanced perspective, noting that the report was flawed and, in some places, inconsistent—particularly regarding its stance toward the Communist Workers Party—but nonetheless was of extreme value to the community (2006, p. H1). Additionally, several articles urged members of the community to read and debate the findings (Ahearn, 2006a, p. B1; 2006b, p. B1).

The Greensboro City Council's response to the report was, not surprisingly, lackluster. The council did eventually agree to meet on July 18, 2006 to discuss the Commission's findings (Banks, 2006b, p. A1),[19] and, at that meeting, after debating the Commission's report and recommendations for seventy-five minutes, they agreed to discuss the report further and planned to instruct Greensboro's Human Relations Commission to do so as well ("City council advances," 2006, p. A8; Banks, 2006c, p. A1). Many of the Commission's supporters viewed this meeting as a positive step toward healing: the *News & Record* reported that, while some council members "registered skepticism" and "criticized much of the TRC's work," "no one opposed contentions by [Yvonne] Johnson, Goldie Wells, and Dianne Bellamy-Small [the council's three black members] that Greensboro has problems of class and race relations that its leaders should address" ("City council advances," 2006, p. A8). But the promised discussions were not quick in coming. On December 12, 2006, an article appeared in the paper lamenting the fact that "[it has] been almost seven months since the Greensboro Truth and Reconciliation Commission issued its report examining the events of Nov. 3, 1979, and their consequences, and the docu-

---

[19]Not all the council members initially agreed to do this. Shortly after the report was released, councilperson Mike Barber claimed that he did not want to get involved "in a dialogue about something that happened 26 years ago" ("Full council," 2006, p. H2). Similarly, councilperson Tom Phillips said he would only read the report if something piqued his interest, noting, "I've got better things to do with my time" (Banks, 2006a, p. A1). Phillips also claimed that the council had "more important things to do" than discuss the report. Later, when the council scheduled a meeting to discuss the report, Phillips claimed he would not attend, stating, "We don't need this kind of continuing discussion about everything" (Banks, 2006b, p. A1). But, after making these comments, Barber and Phillips received at least some pressure to attend such a meeting ("Full council").

ment hasn't shown up on the City Council's radar since July" ("City needs," 2006, p. A8). In March of 2007, the council voted down a resolution to "seriously consider" the recommendations of the GTRC (Banks, 2007, p. A7).[20]

However, in spite of the city's initial response, the GTRC's *Final Report* did have some effects—in addition to generating this commentary and debate in the pages of the *News & Record*—that suggest that it was at least somewhat successful. It prompted several apologies from members of the community. One resident of Greensboro, Julie Shelburne, submitted her apology as a letter to the editor: "I don't understand why it is so hard for many of our city's leaders to accept the results of the report made by the Truth and Reconciliation Commission....I was here in 1979 and was quite ignorant of the wrongdoing. I would like to apologize to [Nelson] Johnson, Jackie Clapp, Signe Waller and so many others who suffered. I hope others will join me in this" (2006, p. A10). In addition to such apologies, the report prompted a number of forums and discussions in Greensboro about November 3, 1979 and race relations in the city. Over the past several years, Greensboro residents have gathered at City Hall, at the Greensboro Public Library, and in a number churches to consider the Commission's findings and strategize about ways to implement the Commission's recommendations (Alexander, 2007a, p. B2; 2007b, p. B3; "Calendar," 2007, p. GR29). Many of Greensboro's colleges and universities have also incorporated the study of November 3, 1979 into their curricula (Alexander, 2006e, B1). Of these educational initiatives, one of the most successful has been a communications course at the University of North Carolina at Greensboro, which, in the spring of 2007, organized a seminar for community members. The seminar explored "issues raised by the killings and their aftermath" through a series of spoken-word presentations, documentary films, art and drama, and academic papers (Alexander, 2007c, p. B1).

Moreover, following the release of the report, an international forum was held at Bennett College for Women in Greensboro to compare the work of the GTRC with the work of other truth commissions and "to help people from other U.S. communities that have begun similar projects, or are considering them, to consider options and avenues for their work" (Alexander, 2006a, p. A1). Representatives of other truth-seeking initiatives from Northern Ireland, Sri Lanka, South Africa, Sierra Leone, Peru, as well as other U.S. communities met for a series of round-table discussions (Alexander, 2006b, p. A1; 2006c, p. B4; Jarboe, 2006, p. A1). The forum served to further legitimate the positioning work that the commissioners had been attempting to do in the *Final Report*: the event suggested that the GTRC was in fact a legitimate truth commission, and the group of international delegates reaccentrated the rhetorical tradition that the Commission had attempted, throughout its operation, to remake in Greensboro.

---

[20] Mayor Holliday also rejected the Commission's recommendation that Greensboro's public bodies should issue an apology to the survivors and members of the Greensboro community. He said, "If that's the standard, then 'we would issue an apology for every crime in Greensboro that occurred when we weren't there to protect the citizens'" (Banks, 2006a, p. A1). "The problem with an apology," the mayor continued, "is it makes it look like all the police department is at fault" (p. A1).

Participants in the forum met in private for two days, but at the end of each of their sessions, they shared their discussions with the news media. On the next day, they spoke to the Greensboro public. According to the *News & Record*, many of the forum's participants in attendance were surprised to learn that truth commissions "appear to be a growth industry" in the United States (Alexander, 2006c, p. B4). For example, Eduardo Gonzalez, who served on the Peruvian TRC, remarked, "I'm impressed that there is an emerging trend in this country to recover memory that has been repressed for decades...This is going to be important if the U.S. is going to strengthen itself as a nation" (p. B4). Rich Rusk—a representative of a Georgian organization working to construct a memorial to honor four African Americans who were murdered in 1946 by an unknown assassin—expressed encouragement that initiatives like his were occurring elsewhere in the United States (p. B4). At one point, he said, "It's a very spooky feeling to be doing this...We thought we were all by ourselves" (p. B4). The forum, in other words, functioned to build solidarity between participants, helping them to assemble the grounds for their subsequent speech and action in their own communities.

The gathering was especially important for the members of the GTRC, whose stance toward the Greensboro City Council was, at least according to the following commentary, amplified by the forum's other participants:

> The city's truth and reconciliation project was opposed at the outset three years ago in part because opponents, such as Mayor Keith Holliday, feared it would only reinforce a negative image of Greensboro...But participants from other communities and countries in a two-day convention of truth and reconciliation projects at Bennett College said Friday that Greensboro's effort has burnished the city's image. The only damage, they said, has been to opponents' reputations. (Alexander, 2006d, p. B1)

The article continued by citing forum participants, each of whom praised the commissioners for their achievements and roundly critiqued the council members who opposed the process. Mark McGovern, who attended the forum on behalf of a truth group in Northern Ireland, claimed that the Commission's work was "a remarkable set of best practices" and "an extraordinary achievement" (p. B1). "The problem," he continued, "is city officials" (p. B1). Similarly, Eduardo Gonzalez described the *Final Report* as "a towering achievement," and he went on to say that the Commission's recommendations offered "a golden opportunity for Greensboro to... reverse its imprudent decision to oppose the project" (p. B1). Doria Johnson—the head of committee in South Carolina to memorialize lynching victims—said that the Greensboro City Council's "refusal to wrap their arms around the truth-and-reconciliation process simply exposes them for who they are" (p. B1). These individuals certainly reinforced the viewpoints that commissioners offered in their *Final Report*. But more than this, these practitioners of transitional justice identified themselves with commissioners through their remarks, thereby reinforcing the commissioners' definition arguments and serving to legitimate the commissioners' claims to their title.

Redefining the Rhetorical Tradition of Transitional Justice

As this chapter has demonstrated, commissioners reaccentuated the widely accepted definition of "truth commissions" to identify with other truth commissions, garner authority for their version of reality, and bring about change in the community. Complicating this rhetorical reaccentuation, however, was the fact that the commissioners did not issue their report in a rhetorical vacuum; they issued their report in a context in which opposing definitional arguments circulated. There was, in other words, a definitional dispute over the status of the GTRC (Schiappa, 2003). While this definitional dispute rarely surfaced explicitly in the statements of the council members or in the writings of the commissioners, it had a great impact on the Commission's ability to garner authority.

The way in which commissioners reaccentuated Hayner's (2001) definition of "truth commissions" helped them lay claim to their title. But their arguments in the *Final Report* aside, even their *repeated use* of the title had power: the Commission's title—spoken thousands of times, and printed in newspapers and ceremony programs, on websites and weblogs, and on banners and fliers—reinforced that the Greensboro inquiry was a legitimate truth commission.[21] Titles are, after all, constitutive. To borrow from Kenneth Burke's (1966) oft-cited discussion of "terministic screens," the title "Truth and Reconciliation Commission" is not only "a reflection of reality, [but] by its very nature as a terminology it must be a selection of reality; and to this extent it must function as a deflection of reality" (p. 45). "Nomenclature," Burke continued, "necessarily directs the attention into some channels rather than others" (p. 45). In other words, titles shape how we perceive and understand the world. They are more than mere labels; they give things "a particular status" (Schiappa, 2003, p. 114). I take it to be highly significant, then, that, though the mayor and dissenting Greensboro City Council members repeatedly attacked the Commission on definitional grounds, and did so in ways that suggested the inquiry was not a truth commission, they continued to refer to it as such. To my knowledge, at no point did any of the Commission's critics call for a name change.

While it is difficult to say, less than decade after the Commission's operation, how (and how extensively) the commissioners' claims to the title of truth commission will shape the rhetorical tradition of the field of transitional justice, there is evidence to suggest that they will indeed shape the tradition to at least some extent. One indication of this fact was Pricilla Hayner's own reconceptualization of the term truth commission. At the time the Commission was being formed, Hayner worked as the research program director for the ICTJ. In a telephone interview with Sally Bermanzohn, one of the survivors of November 3, 1979, Hayner reportedly said the following:

> Many countries are holding truth commissions organized by governments or nongovernmental organizations…[these] many truth-seeking projects reflect a global realization that

---

[21] Similarly, Magarrell and Wesley (2008) have noted the importance of the GTRC's "self-identification" as a key consideration in determining its status as a truth commission (p. 239).

something is missing in the process of addressing human rights abuses, even when the victims have successes in courts. A nation, or a community within a nation, needs to reflect, to
come to terms with specific incidents or patterns of injustice. (Bermanzohn, 2003, p. 370)

Note, in the space of a few lines, Hayner's definitional maneuvering around her
own definition of "truth commissions": here, unlike in *Unspeakable Truths*, she did
not distinguish between "truth commissions" and "truth-seeking projects"; she
implied that nongovernmental organizations may be the organizing force behind
truth commissions; she suggested that truth commissions can operate at a national or
community level; and she expanded the object of inquiry of truth commissions to
include "specific incidents" as well as "patterns of injustice."[22] Both Hayner
(Bermanzohn, 2003, p. 370) and the commissioners (GTRC, 2006) used definition
arguments to meet the contingent demands of a particular context. They both seemed
to acknowledge, even if only implicitly, that definitions are best conceptualized prag-
matically, as rhetorical tools with which to act in communities and in the world.

Definitional work—e.g., naming and labeling, classifying and categorizing,
describing and designating—has been and will continue to be of great importance
to the field of transitional justice. Making lists about mechanisms of transitional
justice and describing their elements has been a means of finding a foothold in a
shifting landscape, of developing a framework in which to situate new knowledge.
However, while such lists have been necessary, there is an associated risk. As these
lists become more and more commonplace, the boundaries of the field may become
reified, making it more difficult to see the full potential of novel approaches. As
such lists gain rhetorical force through repetition, stakeholders may be less likely to
try new approaches and may ignore potentially transformative ideas. There is, therefore, an ongoing need to analyze and critique such rhetorical activity, attempting to
uncover what definitions have masked and to explore the gaps in our discourse.
When we do this work, we allow ourselves to be confronted by new questions, and
we create opportunities for creative insights and—one would hope—novel and
more effective approaches.

References

Ahearn, L. (2006a, May 26). City hall seeks escape clause for human relations. *News & Record*,
    p. B1.
Ahearn, L. (2006b, May 28). Bellwether city: A book for the train ride home. *News & Record*,
    p. B1.
Alexander, L. (2006a, July 1). Overseas truth groups to come here. *News & Record*, p. A1.
Alexander, L. (2006b, July 6). International truth groups to gather today at Bennett. *News &
    Record*, p. A1.

---

[22]Hayner was even more explicit in an interview with Chelsea Marshall, the Commission's public
hearings coordinator: "[T]he difference in definition is much, much less important than the bigger
picture of what [the GTRC] was supposed to do" (Marshall, 2006, p. 85).

Alexander, L. (2006c, July 7). Studying the past can provide lessons. *News & Record,* p. B4.

Alexander, L. (2006d, July 8). TRC's effects on city praised. *News & Record,* p. B1.

Alexander, L. (2006e, August 20). This term's homework: truth report. *News & Record,* p. B1.

Alexander, L. (2007a, March 6). Church to discuss '79 killings. *News & Record,* p. B2.

Alexander, L. (2007b, March 8). Public will get its say on report of '79 killings. *News & Record,* p. B3.

Alexander, L. (2007c, April 13). Seminar to address topics of race, class. *News & Record,* p. B1.

Banks, M. M. (2006a, June 1). Holliday: No apology necessary. *News & Record,* p. A1.

Banks, M. M. (2006b, June 8). Council heatedly agrees to review. *News & Record,* p. A1.

Banks, M. M. (2006c, July 19). City finally joins 'truth' dialogue. *News & Record,* p. A1.

Banks, M. M. (2007, March 7). Council votes down resolution on TRC. *News & Record,* p. A7.

Bermanzohn, S. A. (2003). *Through survivors' eyes: From the sixties to the Greensboro massacre.* Nashville, TN: Vanderbilt University Press.

Bickford, L. (2007). Unofficial truth projects. *Human Rights Quarterly, 29*(4), 994–1035.

Boraine, A. (2001). *A country unmasked: Inside South Africa's Truth and Reconciliation Commission.* Oxford: Oxford University Press.

Burke, K. (1966). *Language as symbolic action: Essays on life, literature, and method.* Berkeley, CA: University of California Press.

Calendar. (2007, October 28). *News & Record,* p. GR29.

Chafe, W. H. (1980). *Civilities and civil rights: Greensboro, North Carolina, and the black struggle for freedom.* New York, NY: Oxford University Press.

City council advances truth, reconciliation. (2006, July 19). *News & Record,* p. A8.

City needs fresh ideas to build race relations. (2006, December 12). *News & Record,* p. A8.

Clark, D. (2006, May 31). Commission proposes political agenda. *News & Record,* p. A11.

Cone, E. (2006, June 4). TRC delivers a flawed but useful report. *News & Record,* p. H1.

Driver, D. (2006, June 21). TRC report presents historic opportunity. *News & Record,* p. A10.

Full council should discuss truth report. (2006, June 11). *News & Record,* p. H2.

Greensboro Truth and Reconciliation Commission. (2006). *The Greensboro Truth and Reconciliation Commission final report: An examination of the context, causes, sequence and consequence of the events of November 3, 1979.* Retrieved March 1, 2012, from http://www.greensborotrc.org/

Hayner, P. B. (2001). *Unspeakable truths: Confronting state terror and atrocity.* New York, NY: Routledge.

Holler, Z. N. (2006, July 5). TRC did well to seek, report truth. *News & Record,* p. A7.

Jarboe, M. (2006, July 9). Truth project's report called means to change. *News & Record,* p. A1.

Jasinski, J. (2001). *Sourcebook on rhetoric: Key concepts in contemporary rhetorical studies.* Thousand Oaks, CA: Sage.

Magarrell, L., & Wesley, J. (2008). *Learning from Greensboro: Truth and reconciliation in the United States.* Philadelphia, PA: University of Pennsylvania Press.

Marshall, C. (2006). Transitional justice in 'non-transitioning' societies: Evaluating the success of the Greensboro Truth and Reconciliation Commission (Thesis). Available March 1, 2012, at http://www.worldcat.org/title/transitional-justice-in-non-transitioning-societies-evaluating-the-success-of-the-greensboro-truth-and-reconciliation-commission/oclc/71782529?referer=list_view

Martin, J. R., Matthiessen, C. M. I. M., & Painter, C. (1987). *Working with functional grammar.* London: Arnold.

Martin, J. R., & Rose, D. (2003). *Working with discourse: Meaning beyond the clause.* New York, NY: Continuum.

Millar, I.A. (2006, June 22). We hold these truths to be self-serving. *News & Record,* p. A8.

Perelman, C., & Olbrechts-Tyteca, L. (1969). *The new rhetoric: A treatise on argumentation.* Notre Dame, IN: University of Notre Dame Press.

Schiappa, E. (2003). *Defining reality: Definitions and the politics of meaning.* Carbondale, IL: Southern Illinois University Press.

Shelburne, J. (2006, June 5). Resident apologizes; city should do so, too. *News & Record*, p. A10.

Truth and reconciliation: Listen for yourself. (2005, April 20). *News & Record* [Audio file]. Retrieved April 20, 2008, from http://blog.news-record.com/staff/scoopblog/2005/04/truth_ and_recon_1.shtml

Vickers, C. (2006, June 10). Truth commission shows obvious bias. *News & Record,* p. A6.

Waller, S. (2006, May 29). It's been said. *News & Record*, p. A15.

Chapter 6
"Inescapable Networks of Mutuality": The Development of Transitional Justice in the United States

Abstract Having demonstrated in Chaps. 3–5 how the Greensboro Truth and Reconciliation Commission used the rhetorical mechanisms of transitional justice in an attempt to establish its authority, this chapter looks more broadly at the development of the field of transitional justice in the United States. It surveys several US-based initiatives to explore how the rhetorical tradition of transitional justice is being reaccentuated elsewhere in the country. Through this examination, it considers the place of transitional justice in liberal democracies, and it discusses the ramifications of the book's central arguments for scholars and practitioners working in the field of transitional justice.

J.E. Beitler III, *Remaking Transitional Justice in the United States*,
Springer Series in Transitional Justice, DOI 10.1007/978-1-4614-5295-9_6,
© Springer Science+Business Media New York 2013

"I love it that in my home state of North Carolina we are taking leadership from the ANC [African National Congress], from people in South Africa, and of course making it our own as we will. I believe that the death of hope is an act of violence. I hope that we re-establish a level of hope. And I think it can begin in Greensboro, I think it can spread to other places."

Si Kahn, executive director of Grassroots Leadership in Greensboro ("Testimony,"
2005, p. H1)

Introduction

Advocates of the Greensboro Truth and Reconciliation Commission often championed it as "the first of its kind" in the United States (GTCRP, 2004). However, while the Commission may have been the first of its kind *in* the United States, it was not solely *of* the United States. This book has explored how the GTRC drew upon the rhetorical tradition of transitional justice—a tradition with roots outside of the United States—to garner the authority to bring about change in Greensboro. In making this claim, I do not mean to suggest that the Commission did not rely on other rhetorical traditions in its bids for authority; it certainly did.[1] However, the GTRC's authorization was bound up, in significant ways, with the discursive practices of the SATRC and the ICTJ—organizations whose members included Desmond Tutu, Bongani Finca, Lisa Magarrell, Peter Storey, Louis Bickford, and Pricilla Hayner.

Chapter 1 of this book provided an overview of these arguments and contextualized them historically, socio-politically, and theoretically. Chapter 2 made the case that the field has, in fact, given rise to a rhetorical tradition, and it surveyed the work of other scholars to highlight some of the prominent features of that tradition at the level of word, argument, and genre: the ideograph of reconciliation (and its relationship to other important terms, such as *ubuntu*), the *ethos* of representivity and unrepresentivity, and the genre of the final report. Chapters 3–5 then demonstrated how the GTRC and its advocates reaccentuated those features in Greensboro. More specifically, Chap. 3 explored Bongani Finca's performance of *ubuntu* in his speech

---

[1] This book has focused primarily on the ways in which the GTCRP and GTRC reaccentuated the rhetorical resources of past truth commissions—and, in particular, of the SATRC. There were, however, other rhetorical traditions circulating in Greensboro during the operation of the GTRC, not all of which were consistent with those of the rhetorical tradition of transitional justice. As Murphy (1997) noted of rhetorical traditions more generally, "[T]here are layered and dissonant voices within and between traditions. Traditions 'speak' to each other and to pressing problems of the day. No one tradition can finalize the world or itself" (p. 73). Thus, one possible avenue for future research would be to consider the interplay between various traditions and how the GTCRP and GTRC orchestrated them (p. 74). Such work would benefit from a sustained exploration of the ways in which the GTCRP and GTRC drew upon the rhetorical traditions surrounding the civil rights movement, the practices of civil religion in the United States, and the research practices of the academy. It might also consider whether or not the reaccentuation of these traditions amplified or attenuated the effects of the rhetorical tradition of transitional justice.

at the GTRC's Swearing In and Seating Ceremony, which functioned to endorse the commissioners and position them as authorities in the community. Chapter 4 showed that the GTRC, like the SATRC before it, constructed its organizational *ethos* in two, seemingly incongruous ways throughout its operation: as both representative and unrepresentative of the Greensboro community. This *ethos* allowed commissioners to seek widespread public support even as it suggested that the Commission was a model for community members to follow. As Chap. 5 demonstrated, not all members of the community were receptive to the Commission. In the introduction of their *Final Report*, commissioners used Pricilla Hayner's widely accepted definition of "truth commissions" to position themselves alongside past truth commissions and lend credibility to their narrative about systemic racism in Greensboro.

In the present chapter, I begin by considering what my findings suggest about the development of transitional justice in the United States and in other liberal democracies. To illustrate how the field is developing in these contexts, I survey several US-based initiatives. Following this survey, I discuss the ramifications of the book's central arguments for scholars and practitioners working in the field of transitional justice, and I suggest how these stakeholders might use rhetorical knowledge to promote transitional justice more effectively elsewhere.

The Shape of the Rhetorical Tradition in the United States

To date, most of the world's TRCs have operated in emerging democracies and have enjoyed state-sponsored support. Because the TRC model has relied on a centralized authority structure, the rhetorical tradition of transitional justice has been propagated, in large part, by state spokespersons and tied, unsurprisingly, to the state interests of the emerging democracies.[2] However, in the United States and other countries where democracies are already in place, TRCs have not gained nearly as much traction at the national level. One plausible reason for this is that the goals of political reconciliation offered by TRCs are, as Daniel Philpott (2006) has pointed out, often seen as incompatible with the values of liberalism (pp. 11–44).

Philpott (2006) listed several reasons why the two are often seen as incompatible. For one thing, many view political reconciliation as inconsistent with the notion that criminals should be punished for their crimes. Mechanisms of political reconciliation, such as TRCs, typically do not provide accountability in the form of punishment, or they suggest that criminals should be punished in ways that vary from the punishment practices of the liberal tradition (p. 26). Another reason political reconciliation and liberalism are often seen as incompatible is because the former—and all it entails, including forgiveness, repentance, etc.—is viewed as an "improper concern of the state" (p. 27). The tradition of liberalism demarcates "spheres of activity in

---

[2] As Salazar (2002) illustrated with respect to the SATRC, the work of TRCs is often implicated in projects of nation building and democratization.

which the state is not to interfere"; and reconciliation, with its ties to personal belief, is one of those spheres (p. 27). A third, more practical reason that Philpott mentioned is that calls for political reconciliation do not guarantee social unity: if the public views attempts at political reconciliation as unsuccessful or as "depriving victims of their due," then "it will regard political reconciliation as a drain on the legitimacy of the new regime" (p. 34).

Despite these reasons, some scholars have claimed that political reconciliation and liberalism could be made more compatible, although, as Jonathan VanAntwerpen (2010) highlighted, there are different perspectives about how best to do so (pp. 41–45). One perspective surveyed by VanAntwerpen—which was put forward by Amy Gutmann and Dennis Thompson (2000)—is that the answer lies in rejecting conceptions of reconciliation that understand it to mean "comprehensive social harmony" and that expect "an entire society to subscribe to a single comprehensive moral perspective"—which Gutmann and Thompson described as "an illiberal aim" and "deeply undemocratic" (as cited in VanAntwerpen, 2010, p. 41). The other perspective VanAntwerpen surveyed—which was advanced by Daniel Philpott (2006)—is that what is required for greater compatibility is not a thinner account of reconciliation but "a reconfiguration of widely held liberal understandings of democratic deliberation and public reason, a rethinking of liberal theory prompted by both the promise and the challenge associated with political theologies of reconciliation" (as cited in VanAntwerpen, 2010, p. 45).

Given the challenges facing both of these approaches, a national truth and reconciliation in the United States seems to me somewhat unlikely. However, as the work of the Greensboro Truth and Reconciliation Commission illustrated, the apparent incompatibility between liberalism and political reconciliation has not closed off all possibilities for the development of the field of transitional justice in the country. I would argue, moreover, that the case of the GTRC provides an indication of how the field might continue to develop, both in the United States and in other liberal democracies. Some of the GTRC's defining features included the following: it operated independently of government authority; it developed through grassroots means and community-based partnerships; it received support from NGOs (such as the ICTJ) and philanthropic organizations (such as the Andrus Family Fund); and it drew upon the rich rhetorical resources of past truth commissions. These features of the Greensboro initiative suggest that, in the United States and other liberal democracies, the field of transitional justice will be much more decentralized. Rather than looking solely to the government for support, future truth-seeking initiatives will likely find their support in a developing transnational network of local stakeholders, non-governmental organizations, and those affiliated with past transitional justice initiatives. This network will likely take the place of the nation-state as the primary means of TRC authorization, and—to the extent that new TRC initiatives gain traction—it will foster the proliferation and development of the rhetorical tradition of transitional justice in these contexts and beyond.

Recent truth-seeking initiatives in the United States help to substantiate these claims about the development of the field. In what follows, I provide brief sketches of several of these initiatives, some of which are ongoing: the Mississippi

Truth Project (MTP), the Maine Tribal-State Child Welfare Truth and Reconciliation Commission (METRC), the Metropolitan Detroit Truth and Reconciliation Commission on Racial Inequality (DTRC), the Liberian Truth and Reconciliation Commission Diaspora Project (LTRC), and two short-term truth commissions that addressed poverty-related issues. While these examples are not, of course, sufficient to provide a comprehensive picture of the field of transitional justice in the United States, they do offer an indication of the ways that the field is developing, particularly in relation to the authorization of the TRC mechanism.[3]

The Mississippi Truth Project

The Mississippi Truth Project has stated that its origins are a 2005 open letter from Rita Bender—the widow of murdered civil rights worker Michael Schwerner—to Mississippi Governor Haley Barbour, challenging him on his belief that the recent conviction of her husband's killer "closed the books on the crimes of the civil rights years, and that we all should now have 'closure'" ("Timeline of the MTP," n.d., para. 2). In response to Bender's letter, a diverse group of individuals formed the Mississippi Coalition for Racial Justice, aimed at promoting statewide conversations about race. Two years later, the Coalition began to consider the prospects of a statewide truth and reconciliation commission, and eventually created the MTP—the goal of which would be to establish the Mississippi Truth and Reconciliation Commission (para. 9). Since that time, the MTP has written, revised, and circulated a Declaration of Intent for the Commission (para. 12–15); applied for and received funding; hired and trained part-time staff members (para. 13); and begun collecting oral histories from individuals around the state (para. 27, 29, 31–32). It is hoped that the yet-to-be-formed Commission, along with the ongoing work of the project, will "create a culture of truth telling that will bring to light racially motivated crimes and injustices committed in Mississippi between 1945 and 1975" ("What is the MTP," n.d., para. 1).

Like the Greensboro initiative, the MTP began as a grassroots operation. It is telling that, instead of receiving a charge and support from the State of Mississippi, the initiative was born in response to the governor's claims. As a grassroots operation, the MTP has been garnering authority through local engagement: its statewide oral

---

[3] Given the scope and focus of this book, I have chosen to limit my survey to initiatives that include the words "truth project," "truth commission," or "truth and reconciliation commission" in their titles. There have, of course, been other types of transitional justice initiatives as well. For example, in "A Sampling of Truth-seeking Projects in the United States," Magarrell (n.d.) compiled a list that included—but was not limited to—national inquiries (e.g., the Commission on Wartime Relocation and Internment of Civilians and the Tuskegee Syphilis Study Ad Hoc Advisory Panel to the Assistant Secretary for Health and Scientific Affairs), state inquiries (e.g., the Oklahoma Commission to Study the Tulsa Race Riot of 1921 and the 1898 Wilmington Race Riot Commission), and academic inquiries (e.g., the Brown University Steering Committee on Slavery and Justice). Such initiatives are a fertile ground for future study.

history project and Welcome Table initiative—which aims to promote dialogue about race among members of diverse communities ("Welcome Table," n.d.)—serve as a means of raising awareness and support for its work, in addition to fostering its long-term goals. The MTP has also garnered authority by identifying itself with the civil rights movement. In July 2007, for example, the initiative received endorsements from "[c]ivil rights veterans and scholars of the civil rights movement" to establish a truth and reconciliation commission ("Timeline of the MTP," n.d., para. 8).

More importantly for my purposes, the initiative has been connected with the network of support that helped authorize—and now includes—the GTRC. The MTP's website, for example, includes a video endorsement from Archbishop Emeritus Desmond Tutu ("MTP Partners," n.d.), as well as many resources from the International Center for Transitional Justice ("Basic Information," n.d.). The website also includes links to a documentary about the GTRC by filmmaker Adam Zucker, along with a guide—produced in partnership with both the ICTJ and the Andrus Family Fund—for facilitating discussion about the film ("MTP Partners," n.d.). In April of 2008, representatives from the GTRC attended a meeting of the MTP ("Timeline of the MTP," n.d., para. 11), and, in late 2009, the Reverend Peter Storey—who served as Nelson Mandela's prison chaplain and was involved in the Greensboro initiative—met with MTP stakeholders to discuss the project (para. 23). Through these individuals, documents, and media, the rhetorical tradition of transitional justice has again been reaccentuated. To give just one example, it is clear that the MTP has worked to establish an *ethos* of representivity. The project's members have noted that they are "composed of leadership from diverse faith and social communities and organizations" (para. 3). At one point during their operation, they even sought to reinforce their claim to representivity by becoming more inclusive in terms of youth participation. In one of the entries on their timeline, they wrote, "Aware of an absence of youth participation, the Coalition reaches out to the Jim Hill Civil Rights/Civil Liberties Club (CRCL)—consisting of students from Jim Hill High School, Murrah High School, and St. Andrew's Episcopal School" (para. 5).

Maine Tribal-State Child Welfare Truth and Reconciliation Commission

In addition to the MTP, there is currently an initiative underway in the State of Maine to establish a TRC to address injustices committed against people indigenous to the region: members of the Wabanaki tribes. Leaders and supporters of the Maine initiative have traced the origin of the injustices against the tribes to the arrival of Europeans in the fifteenth century ("History & Background," n.d., para. 1). Since that time, 16 of 20 Wabanaki tribes have been destroyed (para. 1), resulting in "a 90-percent population depletion since first contact with Europeans" (Attean & Williams, 2011, para. 8). More recently, in the 1950s and 1960s, the Indian Adoption

Project relocated children from their families by placing them in the foster care system (para. 10). Esther Attean and Jill Williams (2011)—who are both involved in the initiative—have noted, "In Maine, Wabanaki children were removed from their homes and communities at a per-capita rate 19 times higher than that of non-Native children. Agencies in charge of child protection often removed children first and asked questions later, if they asked questions at all. Many tribal members lived in fear of losing their children" (para. 10). While the initiative's leaders have admitted that there has been some progress to address these issues—such as the 1978 Indian Child Welfare Act—they have also observed that "Maine's child welfare history continues to impact Wabanaki children and families today" ("History & Background," n.d., para. 3).

Like the MTP, the Maine initiative is a grassroots operation—a point which Attean and Williams (2011) emphasized by contrasting it with other TRCs; they wrote, "[U]nlike other official truth commission projects in the Americas that were conceived of and instituted by high-level politicians, this one is being initiated and planned by a group of Indigenous women working in and around the child welfare system, some of whom were taken from our families by the state as children" (para. 3). Support for the project has been garnered, in part, from the existing Wabanaki tribes and from the Maine Indian Tribal-State Commission. Once again, however, support has also come from the transnational network of those working in the field of transitional justice. Like the GTRC and MTP, the Maine initiative received funding from the Andrus Family Fund, and Jill Williams—who works with the fund and is assisting those in Maine—was the executive director of the GTRC. The initiative's website also mentioned the "guidance and support" that it has received from the ICTJ ("TRC Partners & Supporters," n.d., para. 9–10).

The Maine initiative's distance from the state—and its reliance on the field of transitional justice for support—may be more directly tied to its ultimate goals than was the case for the GTRC or the MTP. For those currently working on the project, some of the key goals include "developing a new type of relationship between the state and the tribes, as well as deepening a sense of autonomy and self-determination within the Native communities" (Attean & Williams, 2011, para. 21). To begin to achieve these goals, stakeholders have been reaccentuating the rhetorical tradition of transitional justice—particularly through the use of the ideograph reconciliation. For instance, Williams and Attean wrote, "While the reconciliation-related goals of other truth commissions have largely been about finding ways for Indigenous and non-Indigenous people to live together on the same land without violence, the reconciliation goals in Maine run deeper" (para. 21). In this passage, Williams and Attean invoked the term "reconciliation"; however, they chose not to define the term as "peaceful co-existence." Instead, they reaccentuated the term to advance the goal of decolonization: "[W]hile we use the term 'reconciliation' to describe the effort, we see the commission as a piece of a larger effort towards decolonization, undoing the centuries of harms inflicted upon the Wabanaki people" (para. 7). In other words, the ideograph reconciliation, for the Maine initiative, has been used in an attempt to bring about the restoration of national autonomy.

Metropolitan Detroit Truth and Reconciliation Commission on Racial Inequality

The Metropolitan Detroit Truth and Reconciliation Commission on Racial Inequality was impaneled in November of 2011 to investigate "racial oppression of people of color by individuals, structures and institutions" in Detroit and Southeast Michigan (Michigan Roundtable for Diversity & Inclusion [MRDI], 2011a, p. 1). As the DTRC's charter has highlighted, this oppression has caused economic and wage disparities, fewer employment opportunities, higher poverty rates, more restricted access to education and health care, higher incidences of illness, and lower life expectancies (p. 2). To seek the truth about racial oppression and begin to address the many associated problems, the nine-member DTRC will engage both individuals and institutions, inviting them to bear witness to the injustices and to address "their own individual histories of conscious or unconscious perpetuation of patterns of racial privilege and oppression" (p. 3). Like other TRCs, the DTRC will conclude its work by issuing findings and making recommendations about ways to address the past and to create a better future (p. 3).

There are several ways in which the DTRC initiative has already reaccentuated the rhetorical tradition of transitional justice. The initiative's website, for example, notes, "This model of a Truth and Reconciliation Commission is based upon similar efforts around the world, most notably in South Africa, and Greensboro, North Carolina" (MRDI, 2011b, para. 5). Additionally, the organization's charter begins with the motto "Without Truth, no Healing; without Forgiveness, no Future" (MRDI, 2011a, p. 1)—drawing upon the common sayings of past truth commissions and, more specifically, upon the title of Desmond Tutu's (1999) book *No Future without Forgiveness*. Furthermore, Desmond Tutu's daughter Naomi Tutu gave the keynote address at the Commission's impaneling ceremony.

The Detroit initiative also reaccentuated the rhetorical tradition of transitional justice in and through its mandate—which drew upon much of the language of GTRC's mandate. The GTRC's mandate began as follows:

> There comes a time in the life of every community when it must look humbly and seriously into its past in order to provide the best possible foundation for moving into a future based on healing and hope. Many residents of Greensboro believe that for this city, the time is now. (GTCRP, 2003, p. 1)

The Detroit initiative's mandate echoed much of this language:

> There comes a time in the life of every community when it must look honestly and seriously into its past in order to provide the best possible foundation for moving into a future based on healing and hope; a future that is consistent with the United States of America's founding promise of equality and opportunity for all. (MRDI, 2011a, p. 1)

The GTRC's mandate, which began and ended with references to the Commission's timeliness, helped establish an opening, an opportunity, for the initiative and suggested its necessity. Beginning with the phrase "There comes a time" and ending with "opportunity for all," the Detroit initiative's mandate utilized language from the Greensboro mandate to establish a similar opening; however, it marshaled this opportunity for a slightly different goal—namely, to promote equality. The mandate endings shared much as well. The GTRC mandate read:

> The passage of time alone cannot bring closure, nor resolve feelings of guilt and lingering trauma, for those impacted by the events of November 3, 1979. Nor can there be any genuine healing for the city of Greensboro unless the truth surrounding these events is honestly confronted, the suffering fully acknowledged, accountability established, and forgiveness and reconciliation facilitated. (GTCRP, 2003, p. 2)

The DTRC's mandate made similar claims:

> Truth and Reconciliation will begin when individuals and institutions come together in a spirit of honest reflection to promote racial justice and equality. The passage of time alone cannot cure these ills. There can only be genuine healing for the residents of Detroit and Southeast Michigan when the truth surrounding the structural causes and consequences of racial privilege and oppression are honestly confronted and understood, the suffering caused by such inequality fully acknowledged and forgiveness and reconciliation facilitated. (MRDI, 2011a, p. 6)

In these passages, there was an emphasis on the ways that healing does and does not come about. Both mandates suggested that what is necessary to bring about change is a *kairotic* moment—a moment of opportunity or crisis. To temper the force of what was a potentially threatening notion for some audience members, both mandates employed the passive voice to make these claims.

There were, moreover, less explicit examples of reaccentuation, of which I will only mention one. During the Commission's impaneling ceremony, members of the Detroit initiative constructed the *ethos* of the DTRC in ways that reaccentuated the *ethos* established for the GTRC. In their oath, the commissioners were asked to pledge to do their work without bias or prejudice—thereby establishing their objectivity (Michiganroundtable, 2011). But they were also positioned in terms of representivity. Peter Hammer, the director for the Damon J. Keith Center for Civil Rights, introduced the commissioners as follows:

> I think you are already getting the sense of how powerful they are, and the hope throughout this entire process is that each one of you can see parts of yourselves in each one of them, and that—conversely—each one of them represents a different part of our communities, and—collectively—I think you can see the power and the wisdom that this commission is going to bring in terms of their life experience. (Michiganroundtable, 2011)

In these remarks, Hammer began by calling attention to the issue of authority, claiming that the commissioners were "powerful." According to Hammer, this power was grounded in a two-fold representivity: the commissioners represented individual residents of Detroit and Southeast Michigan, and they represented different parts of the region. Like the *ethos* constructed for the GTRC, the *ethos* constructed for the DTRC both distanced commissioners from the community and aligned them with the community, setting them up to accomplish different facets of a complex mandate.

Liberian Truth and Reconciliation Commission Diaspora Project

One of the most striking examples of a truth commission that has operated in the United States is the Liberian Truth and Reconciliation Commission. Liberia formed a Truth and Reconciliation Commission in 2005; and, while Liberia's political history is too complex to adequately recount here, a few remarks about this history are necessary to understand what the LTRC has to do with the development of transitional justice in the United States. Liberia was originally established in the 1820s by the American Colonization Society as a colony for freed African-American slaves. These Americo-Liberians settlers, as they came to be called, established their country's independence in 1847. However, like most colonial narratives, this one involved conflict and marginalization of peoples: the West-African region that would become Liberia was not unoccupied when it was settled by the Americo-Liberians, and the history of Liberia from the middle of the nineteenth century to the end of the twentieth century involved a series of conflicts between the indigenous Liberians (who made up the vast majority of the Liberian population) and the Americo-Liberians. The latter controlled Liberia for much of the twentieth century, and they often imposed their cultural beliefs on the former. However, in 1980, a military coup, led by indigenous Liberians, gave way to a shift in political power. The new leadership took a more authoritarian approach to governing than the previous regime, and two civil wars followed, lasting from 1989 to 1996 and from 1999 to 2003 (Dunn-Marcos, Kollehlon, Ngovo, & Russ, 2005, p. 4). It has been estimated that, during these wars, over two hundred thousand people were killed and hundreds of thousands were displaced from their homes (p. 2). In response to these forced displacements, the United States developed a resettlement program for Liberian refugees. More than 24,000 Liberians have traveled to the United States since 1989 (p. 1).

The authoritarian government was ousted in 2003, and a transitional government was formed in the country, leading to peaceful, democratic elections in 2005. Following the elections, President Ellen Johnson-Sirleaf called for the establishment of a truth and reconciliation commission to address the mass atrocities committed in the country; and, on May 12, 2005, the Liberian National Transitional Legislative Assembly (NTLA) established the LTRC. Its aim was to investigate "gross human rights violations and violations of international humanitarian law as well as abuses that occurred, including massacres, sexual violations, murder, extrajudicial killings and economic crimes, such as the exploitation of natural or public resources to perpetuate armed conflicts, during the period January 1979 to October 14, 2003" (NTLA, 2005, sect. 4a).

What is important for my purposes is the fact that the truth-seeking process was not limited to those living within Liberia but was extended to include displaced Liberians. The non-governmental organization Minnesota Advocates for Human Rights (MAHR) partnered with the LTRC to collect statements from Liberians living in the United States and elsewhere (MAHR, n.d.).[4] Statement-taking began in

---

[4]The Minnesota Advocates for Human Rights also collected statements in the United Kingdom and in Ghana.

Minnesota in 2006, and statements were subsequently collected from Liberians living in other US cities, including Atlanta, Chicago, New York, Newark, Philadelphia, Providence, and Washington (Barry, 2007; MAHR, n.d.).

The case of the LTRC highlighted another way that the field of transitional justice may develop in the United States. In this case, the US-based non-governmental organization gathering testimony had even stronger international ties than the GTRC did; its authority was warranted, in large measure, by the Liberian government. Despite this difference with the GTRC, the case of the LTRC confirmed the importance of transnational affiliations in the authorization of transitional justice endeavors in the United States. If political reconciliation proves to be incompatible with liberalism in the country, the US may see a growing number of TRCs that operate inside its borders but are authorized from without.

Poverty Truth Commissions

Two additional, short-term truth commissions were formed to address questions of poverty in the United States, and these truth commissions, too, speak to the importance of transnational affiliations as a means of authorization. From July 15 to 17, 2006, the Poor People's Economic Human Rights Campaign (PPEHRC) held a 3-day truth commission in Cleveland, Ohio, attended by over 500 people. The Commission's website noted that it was "modeled after similar commissions in Africa and Latin America" and that it "brought people from all across the USA and the world to bring to light the actual suffering and economic human rights violations that many Americans endure on a daily basis" (PPEHRC, 2006). The Commission was comprised of both domestic and international commissioners—one of which was South African Winnie Mandela. In addition to the PPEHRC's truth commission, a smaller poverty truth commission was organized by Union Theological Seminary in New York City on April 13, 2007. The day-long truth commission was, according to its website, "inspired by the Truth and Reconciliation work done in places such as South Africa and Peru" and "based on the United Nations' Universal Declaration of Human Rights" (Poverty Initiative, 2007). As the truth commissions' websites highlighted, both of the initiatives drew upon the resources of the field of transitional justice. In fact, one of the commissioners at Union Theological Seminary's Poverty Truth Commission was Nelson Johnson, who helped organized the November 3, 1979 rally in Greensboro and was later instrumental in forming the GTRC.

Implications for Scholars and Practitioners of Transitional Justice

The findings in this book—and, more specifically, the claims about the development of the field of transitional justice in the United States—have implications for scholars and practitioners of transitional justice. This penultimate section of the book highlights some of these implications, with the hope that those working in the field of transitional justice might be able to draw upon my work in their future endeavors. The implications sketched in the next section attest to the value of attending, with care, to the rhetorical activity surrounding truth commissions and other mechanisms of transitional justice.

Implications for Scholars Studying Transitional Justice

There has been a tendency, in the study of truth commissions, to conceptualize these institutions as national projects that operate, largely, in and through the civil society of a given country. For example, Hayner (2001) surveyed twenty-one truth commissions in *Unspeakable Truths*, and she arranged her descriptions of these truth commissions by the country in which they were instituted. Given that most truth commissions are instituted by national governments, such divisions are not surprising. However, what these divisions elide, and what my study has brought into relief is the importance of transnational forces in the development and authorization of truth commissions. While I do not mean to suggest that all past truth commissions relied on international affiliations to the extent that the GTRC did (although many certainly may have), I think there is a need among scholars studying truth commissions—including those studying national commissions—to pay greater attention to the transnational forces that have given rise to and sustained these institutions. Such a research agenda may be generative in furthering our understanding about how truth commissions work (or don't work) as political and social tools to bring about change.

The need for a more thorough account of the ways that transnational forces have given rise to and sustained truth commissions is predicated, in part, on the emergence of a global civil society. Civil society has typically been defined as the sector of society comprised of voluntary groups and organizations—which include, but are not limited to, religious institutions, trade unions, mass media, and political parties—that are not controlled by the government. It has been understood to provide some protections against the interests of the state even as it frequently serves state interests. In recent years, however, expanded and enhanced networks of communication have developed, which have given rise to "an interweaving and strengthening of ties between multiple civil societies" (DeChaine, 2005, p. 5). The result has been the development of what some are calling global civil society—the societal sphere comprised of multiple civil societies that are interconnected by common values and interests, often across geographical spaces and nationally defined territories. As D. Robert DeChaine's (2005) work on humanitarian NGOs has highlighted, global civil society offers a viable source of political authority for non-governmental actors (like those who founded the GTRC as well as the commissioners themselves), and the political authority garnered through global civil society may serve to further attenuate the authority of the nation-state. DeChaine has written, "'Through its circumnavigation of political boundaries, the transnational social forces that make up global civil society 'undermine states' monopoly of legitimate authority over a territorially defined populace, which is one of the central ideas of sovereignty'" (p. 6).[5] This undermining of the "legitimate authority"—the sovereignty—of the nation-state means that, for some members of the state, "global identifications begin to displace, and sometimes override, national ones" (p. 30).[6] Authority is thereby redistributed so that "national governments are increasingly sharing traditionally sovereign powers with nonstate actors, signifying a weakening of state powers in relation to national autonomy" (p. 50). (Take, as just one example from my study, Bongani Finca's attempts at the Swearing In and Seating Ceremony to establish global identifications between the people of Greensboro and the people of South Africa. While it is unlikely that Finca's remarks alone overrode the audience's national identifications, they, together with the many other global identifications established through the truth commission process, may have attenuated some individuals' alignments with the city and strengthened alignments with the Commission.) To avoid looking at international forces in the study of the development of truth commissions is to risk missing important ways in which these institutions act in their communities and nations.

We should, then, focus on truth commissions not simply as national projects operating in civil society but also as transnational phenomena that operate in and through global civil society. DeChaine's (2005) conceptualization of NGOs has provided an excellent model for how we might begin to think about truth commissions, at least as they are emerging in the United States context. For DeChaine, the emphasis on NGOs as "monolithic organizational 'structures'" has been problematic, insofar as it has presupposed that such organizations are isolated from one another and has obscured the "ever-shifting currents, nonlinear interconnections and interimbrications, and often less than tangible imaginative energies" between them (p. 155). To address this problem, DeChaine, referencing Arjun Appadurai's notion of "new neighborliness," recommended reconceptualizing NGOs as "shifting flows of people, ideas, resources, and most of all, power"—an act of definition that DeChaine claimed would allow scholars to better attend to the ways in which resources, both material and non-material, travel in and among organizations (p. 155). Studying truth commissions not as monolithic organizational structures but as shifting flows of resources may help us better understand how they function as social tools—and, perhaps more importantly, how they might function as *more effective* social tools—to redress inequalities. Moreover, to the extent that the interconnections that DeChaine mentioned are discursively constructed (as many of them are), there is an ongoing need to attend to the rhetorical activity surrounding transitional justice initiatives.

The bulk of *Remaking Transitional Justice in the United States* has focused on *ethos*, the subject position constructed by and for the GTRC through discourse. Future research might unpack other aspects of the rhetorical tradition surrounding truth commissions, including its characteristic commonplaces, appeals to *pathos*

---

[5]DeChaine quoted Deibert (1998, p. 35) here.
[6]DeChaine quoted Hall (1992, p. 302) here.

and *logos*, genres, and figures of speech and thought. In describing the rhetorical tradition surrounding truth commissions in more detail, such research promises to offer communities a much more robust model for action, both at and below the institutional level. Communities and countries looking to institute truth commissions would, I think, find it exceedingly valuable to have detailed descriptions not simply of typical committee structures and their functions but of the genre conventions of public hearings and final reports; the characteristic commonplaces employed by truth commissions (e.g., "bygones will not be bygones" or "the truth makes free"); the reoccurring ideographs (e.g., truth, reconciliation, *ubuntu*); the common appeals to *ethos, pathos,* and *logos*; and other distinctive rhetorical moves. Ultimately this research might enable communities to take up the rhetorical tradition of transitional justice in new ways.

Implications for Practitioners of Transitional Justice

To other communities and individuals looking to address past violence or injustices, this book highlights the importance of establishing affiliations outside of the community in order to garner the authority to act—i.e., the importance of working in and through global civil society to bring about change. A second, and no less significant, thing at stake here for practitioners of transitional justice is the way in which they conceptualize how truth commissions—and, by extension, other forms of transitional justice—function as models for other countries and communities.

There has been a tendency among those who advocate for (and those who study) truth commissions to describe them as models at the structural or institutional level. For example, Elizabeth Kiss (2000) noted that it is the "institutional repertoire of truth commissions [that] may be helpful in developing innovative approaches to a variety of moral and political challenges" (p. 92). Furthermore, to the extent that truth commissions have been conceptualized as models for action, there has been a tendency to focus on the large-scale, pragmatic policies implemented by truth commissions, such as amnesty, reparations, etc. While these tendencies have not been unproductive, they may have given short shrift to some of the other ways that truth commissions have functioned as models.

What has often been elided in the current model talk surrounding truth commissions are the patterned ways of using language, the figurative and argumentative devices, and the genres—all of which may be used as *rhetorical* models for subsequent rhetorical performances. In bringing into relief the ways in which the rhetorical tradition surrounding truth commissions has been reaccentuated in a new context, *Remaking Transitional Justice in the United States* has served to complement the emphasis on truth commissions as institutional models or models of large-scale policy: it has suggested that truth commissions also provide countries, communities, and individuals with models of rhetorical action at the level of discourse, clause, and even grammar. In making explicit the different ways that the GTRC and GTCRP constructed the tension between representivity and unrepresentivity, this study may better allow subsequent truth commissions to use these subject positions strategically as they work to establish broad community support. While I am not advocating that subsequent truth commissions make rhetorical moves identical to those of the GTRC, my findings suggest that members of future truth commissions may benefit from paying careful attention to the figurative and argumentative devices of past commissions.

Furthermore, in some cases it may actually be more effective to perform facets of the rhetorical tradition of transitional justice without establishing a truth commission at the institutional level. As Magarrell and Wesley (2008) have noted, implementing a truth commission is not easily accomplished, and it is not "always appropriate" given the context (p. 242). Truth commissions require considerable financial resources, as well as volunteers who are willing to give of their time and energies, often without compensation. Moreover, establishing these institutions to "dig up" the past is likely to engender resistance—and even open hostility—from various sectors of the community. Given these constraints, communities might choose to perform *one* of the many genres of truth commissions (e.g., they might hold a one-day discussion to address a particular concern). Or they might reaccentuate aspects of the rhetorical tradition in novel institutional configurations (e.g., they might facilitate a working group, comprised of representatives from different sectors of the community, to investigate racial or economic inequities and offer recommendations to the city government).

These suggestions are not inconsistent with recent calls for truth and reconciliation in the United States.[7] For instance, in her call for the use of truth and reconciliation processes to address the history of lynching in the United States, Sherrilyn Ifill (2007) spoke to the variety of institutional forms that truth and reconciliation processes may take:

> Without question, conversations within communities about racial violence will have to take many forms. Some discussions may take the form used by the Truth and Reconciliation Commission in South Africa, in which witnesses come forward to give written or oral statements to a group of commissioners. In other instances, a form of town hall meeting may be appropriate. But productive conversations on race must provide opportunities for community members—black and white—to…talk to one another. (p. 152)

In addition to the town hall, another form for performing the rhetorical tradition of transitional justice that Ifill proposed was community conferencing, which she described as "facilitated discussion that enables those who have been 'affected by behavior that has caused serious harm' to work together to find solutions and to repair harm" (p. 151). Similarly, Southern Truth and Reconciliation—an organization to which Ifill belonged and served on the advisory board—advocated for truth and reconciliation forums—one of "a 'menu of options' from which constituent communities might discover and develop their own ideas for community-building events, programs and activities to promote restorative justice, healing, and dialogue"

---

[7]Moreover, as Gready (2011) noted, instead of trying to negotiate multiple genres and methodologies, privileging "one genre tributary or form of truth" may help ensure that a truth commission's products are not "fragmentary and mutually undermining" (p. 56).

(Southern Truth & Reconciliation, 2007). Kiss (2000) proposed yet another alternative form: the short-term public hearing. Such a hearing would incorporate "some of the institutional aspects of a truth commission" and could offer members of broken communities the opportunity "to air grievances, educate the public, offer reparations, and create opportunities to move forward in a spirit of reconciliation" (p. 93). Each of these options—town halls, community conferencing, truth and reconciliation forums, and short-term public hearings—may be viable alternatives to formal truth commissions. While developing these alternatives may be difficult, making the resources of the rhetorical tradition of transitional justice transparent is, I think, a productive first step.

There are, of course, potential risks to such work. Even as the rhetorical tradition of transitional justice provided resources for the GTRC, it also created constraints that may have limited the GTRC's effectiveness. For example, adopting the language of reconciliation and forgiveness may have created unrealistic expectations about what counted as success for the Commission. When Virgil Griffin refused to express any remorse about his actions on November 3, 1979 during his testimony to the Commission, some in the community wondered whether the GTRC was simply providing a platform to perpetuate the November 3rd confrontation and tarnish Greensboro's image. Moreover, in framing the endeavor in Greensboro as a "Truth and Reconciliation Commission," the initiative tied itself to an institutional model that, by definition, was to have an end date. Past truth commissions had operated for finite periods of time and concluded by releasing reports, so the Greensboro initiative did so as well. While the commissioners did invite groups to read and discuss their *Final Report* before disbanding, it may have been that the initiative, framed in different terms, could have better enabled *ongoing* dialogue.

Erik Doxtader (2004) has raised additional concerns about transposing reconciliation initiatives from South Africa to other contexts, such as Greensboro:

> Reconciliation appears to have come into its time. Talk of its potential is widespread, and calls for its practice are now heard as a serious alternative to realist doctrines that offer little solace to those caught in the grip of total violence…In all of this, there is little doubt that reconciliation's current cachet has much to do with its prominent role in the South African transition from apartheid to constitutional democracy. Over the last decade, South Africa's 'unique experiment' has been read by many as a precedent, the basis for a model that can be installed and employed productively in other situations. Among a number of larger efforts, the mandate for the recently created Truth and Reconciliation Commission (TRC) in Greensboro, North Carolina, shows a strong family resemblance to the charge that was handed to the South African TRC in 1995. Imitation may not be risk-free. While it is still [in its] early days, reconciliation's (over)claimed potential may harbor some significant costs. Backed by multimillion-dollar budgets, several international organizations currently devote themselves to advocating reconciliation and providing resources for its formal development, work that has led some to question whether reconciliation represents a new mode of colonial logic. (pp. 379–380)

The fact that calls for reconciliation—and, by extension, all aspects of the rhetorical tradition surrounding truth commissions—may represent a "new mode of colonial logic" is a legitimate risk. Truth commissions may impose particular ways of thinking, acting, and being on others, and they may serve as a means of exploiting—or maintaining power over—individuals, groups of people, or entire countries.[8] Note, however, that the fact that this risk exists does not in and of itself mean that countries and communities should simply eschew the truth commission approach: in a world increasingly characterized by deterritorialization and globalization, many strategies for addressing past human rights violations run the risk Doxtader articulates. What is necessary is to be actively engaged, throughout any truth-seeking process, in identifying and working to mitigate the ways that the process may be harmful, while attempting to meet the contingent demands of the new context and bring about positive change.

On Last Words

Did the Commission work? Was it successful? These are the questions that I am asked more than any others when talking to people about the GTRC, and they are some of the most difficult questions to answer. One of the reasons evaluating the success of the Commission proves difficult has to do with the nature of the Commission's mandated objectives, which tended to be abstract and subjective. How does one gauge the extent to which the Commission reconciled the community, clarified people's confusion, acknowledged people's feelings, or facilitated changes in social consciousness? Does it matter that people defined reconciliation and healing in different ways? And what is the extent of the Commission's impact that would count as success? If 500 people claim to have benefited from the process is that sufficient to count the Commission as a success? If two people claim to have been reconciled is that sufficient? And should we even evaluate the Commission based on its own objectives?

As these questions imply, the question of the Commission's success depends on the criteria one chooses to evaluate success. If one chooses to evaluate the success of the Commission based on the response of city government, the Commission would likely be deemed a failure: the Greensboro City Council voted "to oppose" the Commission's work, and many of the Commission's recommendations for the city have not been implemented. But if one chooses to evaluate the Commission based on its ability to prompt public engagement and community dialogue, the case could be made that the Commission was, at least somewhat, successful. The public events of the GTRC generated a modest, but not insignificant, audience turnout.

---

[8] Similarly, Gready (2011) highlighted that the diffusion of the practices of transitional justice may not always have positive effects. In *The Era of Transitional Justice*, for example, he noted that testimonies from truth commission hearings that circulate beyond their immediate contexts may get appropriated by human rights discourse in ways that "erase" and "decontextualize" the stories (p. 79). "The reification of victimhood," he continued, is "almost a condition of hearability," leading to further marginalization of those who have testified (p. 79). Given that the reception of testimony "can easily create new contexts of vulnerability and violation," Gready argued for "greater control for the testifier in the realms of representation, interpretation and dissemination" of his or her testimony (p. 82).

Attendance at both the Swearing In and Seating Ceremony and the Report Release Ceremony was over five hundred people, and there were several hundred individuals who attended the Commission's three public hearings. Moreover, as Magarrell and Wesley (2008) have noted, despite the fact that the council voted not to endorse the Commission, they were forced to publicly consider—and discuss—the events of November 3, 1979 (p. 174).[9] With regard to the *Final Report*, many organizations pledged to read and discuss it, and several have done so. Furthermore, a few of the Commission's recommendations have been or are being taken up by Greensboro citizens. For example, the Commission's recommendations prompted a minimum wage campaign in Greensboro, led the Department of Social Services in Guilford County to institute Undoing Racism workshops, and resulted in a number of college course offerings devoted to the events of November 3, 1979 and the work of the Commission.

Another measure by which one might deem the Commission successful was in its creation of a public forum for survivors of November 3, 1979 to tell their stories and be heard. Given that former CWP members' stories were not validated by the city or the judicial system, the creation of such a forum was not insignificant. In her book *Shattered Voices: Language, Violence, and the Work of Truth Commissions*, Phelps (2004) persuasively argued that the public testimonies prompted by truth commissions affect a kind of justice, balancing the destruction of language that results from physical violence. She wrote, "The processes by which truth commissions gather stories have great potential for creating a kind of justice that not only publicly exposes truth and vindicates people, but also a kind of justice that is dynamic and ongoing, not perfect of course, but a visible manifestation of an ethical and political commitment that honors truth, individual worth, dignity, and equality" (p. 72). In creating a space for survivors to speak and be heard, the GTRC may have helped to constitute the kind of justice Phelps mentioned here—a justice that involved the restoration of language to those who had been previously silenced.

One might also claim that the Commission was a success to the extent that its advocates, with the help of the AFF and the ICTJ, were able to build a transnational network of individuals and organizations. This network, which helped the GTRC establish its authority, may have positive implications for people beyond those living in Greensboro. I have already mentioned several initiatives that are drawing upon the work of the Greensboro initiative to garner authority for themselves. Moreover, as a result of the relationship forged with Bongani Finca, members of the GTCRP sent a 23 person delegation to South Africa for 10 days in November 2007, during which time "participants both shared the Greensboro Truth and Reconciliation process with their South African counterparts and learned from the rich struggle that has emerged out of apartheid" (GTCRP, 2007, para. 1).

---

[9]Magarrell & Wesley (2008) wrote, "[T]he fact that the 'official' city engaged at all, even in this negative way, was an important part of the process of revealing the truth about November 1979 and its aftermath in the community. The process was so present in the community that it *did* matter, it could *not* be ignored. And despite the discomfort of the city…they entered the dialogue about what the report and recommendations meant" (p. 174).

One might also evaluate the success of the GTRC with regard to its long-term impact; however, I believe there are reasons to resist doing so. For one thing, as Magarrell and Wesley (2008) have noted, it may be too early to say what the long-term impact of the Commission will be (p. 207). A second, perhaps more important, reason to resist doing so is that it could be perceived as a "last word" about the Commission. Setting aside the presumptuousness of a general pronouncement about the Commission's efficacy, I worry that such "last words" risk closing off future possibilities and serving to undermine, however slightly, the ways in which the work of the GTRC may yet shape the community. There is, in other words, a finality to "last words" that risks contributing to inaction: to the extent that the Commission is understood to be a failure, community members may choose not to engage its findings seriously; to the extent that it is deemed a success, community members may be tempted to view the Commission's work as sufficient.

What is the alternative to issuing a presumptuous "last word"? I believe that the appropriate critical stance in response to questions about the overall success of the Commission is the stance taken by the commissioners themselves—namely, hope. In her wonderful book *Tactics of Hope: The Public Turn in English Composition*, Paula Mathieu (2005) distinguished wishing from hoping, and, drawing upon the work of Ernst Bloch, she defined the latter as follows: "To hope," she wrote, "is to look critically at one's present condition, assess what is missing, and then long for and work for a not-yet reality, a future anticipated" (p. 19). For me, this definition exemplifies the stance taken and promoted by GTRC commissioners, who, through-out the entirety of their operation, attempted to critically assess their situation, to work actively for a better future through their speeches and writings, and to prompt others to do the same. Even at their last public event, the Report Release Ceremony, commissioners resisted dwelling on their successes and emphasized the work yet to be done by members of the community. Here I am reminded, in particular, of the words of Commissioner Muktha Jost, who, in describing the challenges faced by the Commission, made the following observation:

> Our work shows that there is much from the past about November three that needs to be redeemed. When we consider how this past can be redeemed, we realize the immensity of the work ahead for you. As we present our findings and conclusions, we want to remind you that this is the result of a modest but spirited and sincere approach for the truth around November three. We believe that it's important to recognize that we are not free from human rights abuses and injustice here in the United States, and we hope that the truth about the past will help us understand the present better and build a safer, more just, and inclusive future. It is in that spirit that we present to you our findings, conclusions, and recommenda-tions. (Seel, 2006)

It is this stance of hope, as defined by Mathieu and performed by Jost and the other commissioners, which I believe we would do well to emulate.

Such a stance does not mean withholding any and all judgments: we can and should critique the ways in which the Commission was problematic and validate the ways in which it was exemplary. Nor does such a stance mean that we cannot or should not speak of the particular successes and failures of the Commission. But it does mean that, in making these judgments, we should avoid issuing the last words on the matter. The question of the Commission's long-term success is best treated as an open question. It is, I think, in this spirit that commissioners concluded their *Final Report*:

> We believe the truth and reconciliation process in Greensboro opened up the debate around Nov. 3, 1979, in a positive way and has successfully engaged a broad spectrum of the community in an effort that offers hope for reconciliation. As a Commission that looks a bit like Greensboro in microcosm, we found that this process—and our own struggle to hear and understand each other—had a profound impact on our perceptions of the issues we explored. Our individual and collective commitment to the truth helped us persevere. And the human stories and emotions we encountered along the way moved us to do our best to leave behind a legacy we hope will serve Greensboro for years to come. We cannot say what the future will hold for this community or what the long-term impact of this process will look like, but we hope that this process also serves as a learning tool for others in this county who, like Greensboro, are burdened by a legacy of hurt and inspired by the possibility of honestly coming to terms with their own history. (GTRC, 2006)

In this excerpt—which serves as the commissioners' own last words—one can find evidence for many of the arguments made in the preceding pages of this book; that said, when reading this passage, I am moved most of all by the commissioners' hopefulness, which cuts through the text fiercely and confidently.

References

Attean, E., & Williams, J. (2011). Homemade justice. *Cultural Survival Quarterly. 35*(1). Retrieved March 1, 2012, from http://www.culturalsurvival.org/publications/cultural-survival-quarterly/united-states/homemade-justice

Barry, E. (2007, September 18). From Staten Island haven, Liberians reveal war's scars. *The New York Times*. Retrieved October 17, 2007, from http://www.nytimes.com/2007/09/18/nyregion/18liberians.html?_r=2&oref=slogin&oref=slogin

Basic information on truth commissions. (n.d.). Retrieved March 5, 2012, from http://www.mississippitruth.org/pages/truth-comms.htm

DeChaine, D. R. (2005). *Global humanitarianism: NGOs and the crafting of community*. Lanham, MD: Lexington.

Deibert, R. J. (1998). Altered worlds: Social forces in the hypermedia environment. In C. J. Alexander & L. A. Pal (Eds.), *Digital democracy: Policy and politics in the wired world* (pp. 23–43). Oxford: Oxford University Press.

Doxtader, E. (2004). The potential of reconciliation's beginning: A reply. *Rhetoric & Public Affairs, 7*(3), 378–390. doi:10.1353/rap. 2005.0005.

Dunn-Marcos, R., Kollehlon, K. T., Ngovo, B., & Russ, E. (2005). *Liberians: An introduction to their history and culture*. Washington, DC: Center for Applied Linguistics.

Gready, P. (2011). *The era of transitional justice: The aftermath of the truth and reconciliation commission in South Africa and beyond*. New York, NY: Routledge.

Greensboro Truth and Community Reconciliation Project. (2003). Mandate for the Greensboro Truth and Reconciliation Commission. Retrieved October 5, 2007, from http://www.greensborotrc.org/mandate.php

Greensboro Truth and Community Reconciliation Project. (2004, June 12). The swearing in and seating ceremony of the Greensboro Truth and Reconciliation Commission [Ceremony program]. Copy in possession of author.

Greensboro Truth and Community Reconciliation Project. (2007). Delegation to South Africa. Retrieved June 2, 2008, from http://www.gtcrp.org

Greensboro Truth and Reconciliation Commission. (2006). *The Greensboro Truth and Reconciliation Commission final report: An examination of the context, causes, sequence and consequence of the events of November 3, 1979.* Retrieved March 1, 2012, from http://www.greensborotrc.org/

Gutmann, A., & Thompson, D. (2000). The moral foundations of truth commissions. In R. I. Rotberg & D. Thompson (Eds.), *Truth v. justice: The morality of truth commissions* (pp. 22–44). Princeton, NJ: Princeton University Press.

Hall, S. (1992). The question of cultural identity. In S. Hall, D. Held, & T. McGrew (Eds.), *Modernity and its futures* (pp. 273–316). Cambridge: Polity.

Hayner, P. B. (2001). *Unspeakable truths: Confronting state terror and atrocity.* New York, NY: Routledge.

History & Background. (n.d.). Retrieved March 5, 2012, from http://www.mainetribaltrc.org/history.html

Ifill, S. A. (2007). *On the courthouse lawn: Confronting the legacy of lynching in the twenty-first century.* Boston, MA: Beacon.

Kiss, E. (2000). Moral ambition within and beyond political constraints: Reflections on restorative justice. In R. I. Rotberg & D. Thompson (Eds.), *Truth v. justice: The morality of truth commissions* (pp. 68–98). Princeton, NY: Princeton University Press.

Magarrell, L. (n.d.). A sampling of truth-seeking projects in the United States. Retrieved March 1, 2012, from http://www.mississippitruth.org/documents/sampling.pdf

Magarrell, L., & Wesley, J. (2008). *Learning from Greensboro: Truth and reconciliation in the United States.* Philadelphia, PA: University of Pennsylvania Press.

Mathieu, P. (2005). *Tactics of hope: The public turn in English composition.* Portsmouth, NH: Boynton/Cook.

Michigan Roundtable for Diversity & Inclusion. (2011a). Charter for the Metropolitan Detroit Truth and Reconciliation Commission on Racial Inequality. Retrieved March 1, 2012, from http://www.miroundtable.org/Roundtabledownloads/FinalMandate2011.pdf

Michigan Roundtable for Diversity & Inclusion. (2011b). Race, residence and regionalism. Retrieved March 1, 2012, from http://www.miroundtable.org/raceresidenceregionalism.htm

Michiganroundtable. (2011). Race2Equity conference. Retrieved March 1, 2012, from http://www.youtube.com/watch?v=l4BBcpegrRA&feature=player_embedded

Minnesota Advocates for Human Rights. (n.d.). Liberian Truth and Reconciliation Commission Diaspora Project. Retrieved October 17, 2007, from http://liberiatrc.mnadvocates.org/Home.html.

MTP Partners. (n.d.). Retrieved March 5, 2012, from http://www.mississippitruth.org/pages/partners.htm

Murphy, J. M. (1997). Inventing authority: Bill Clinton, Martin Luther King, Jr, and the orchestration of rhetorical traditions. *Quarterly Journal of Speech, 83*(1), 71–89. doi:10.1080/00335639709384172.

National Transitional Legislative Assembly. (2005). Truth and Reconciliation Commission of Liberia Mandate. Retrieved June 2, 2008, from https://www.trcofliberia.org/about/trc-mandate.

Phelps, T. G. (2004). *Shattered voices: Language, violence, and the work of truth commissions.* Philadelphia, PA: University of Pennsylvania Press.

Philpott, D. (2006). Beyond politics as usual: Is reconciliation compatible with liberalism? In D. Philpott (Ed.), *The politics of past evil: Religion, reconciliation, and the dilemmas of transitional justice* (pp. 11–44). Notre Dame, IN: University of Notre Dame Press.

Poor People's Economic Human Rights Campaign. (2006). National truth campaign: Shining a light on poverty in the U.S.A. Retrieved October 17, 2007, from http://www.economichumanrights.org/ntc_report1.shtml

Poverty Initiative. (2007). Poverty truth commission. Retrieved October 17, 2007, from http://www.povertyinitiative.org/events/event_pages/4-13-07_truth_commission/4-13-07_truth_commission_main.html

Salazar, P. J. (2002). *An African Athens: Rhetoric and the shaping of democracy in South Africa*. Mahwah, NJ: L. Erlbaum.

Seel, Laura (Producer). (2006). *Greensboro Truth and Reconciliation Commission report release ceremony* [DVD]. Greensboro, NC. (Obtained from Laura Seel.)

Southern Truth and Reconciliation. (2007). About us. Retrieved October 17, 2007, from http:// www.southerntruth.org/index.htm

Testimony in search of truth. (2005, October 30). *News & Record*. p. H1.

Timeline of the Mississippi Truth Project. (n.d.). Retrieved on March 5, 2012, from http://www. mississippitruth.org/pages/timeline.htm

TRC Partners & Supporters (n.d.). Retrieved on March 5, 2012, from http://www.mainetribaltrc. org/links.html

Tutu, D. (1999). *No future without forgiveness*. New York, NY: Doubleday.

VanAntwerpen, J. (2010). Reconciliation reconceived: Religion, secularism, and the language of transition. In W. Kymlicka & B. Bashir (Eds.), *The politics of reconciliation in multicultural societies* (pp. 25–47). New York, NY: Oxford University Press.

Welcome Table. (n.d.). Retrieved on March 5, 2012, from http://www.welcometable.net/index. htm

What is the Mississippi Truth Project? (n.d.). Retrieved on March 5, 2012, from http://www.mississippitruth.org/

Appendix

Reverend Bongani Finca's Keynote Address at the Greensboro Truth and Reconciliation Commission's Swearing In and Seating Ceremony, June 12, 2004[1]

Rev. Bongani Finca: I bring you all greetings, very warm greetings. I also bring you a lot of respect and admiration and a message of congratulations, solidarity, and encouragement from South Africa. And I bring it to this occasion which is unique, an occasion which is indeed the first of its kind in the history of our struggle to build reconciliation based on truth. As South Africans we believe that this occasion perhaps better deserves to be referred to as one small step for man and one giant leap for mankind.

To the commissioners about to be inaugurated into office, I bring a special message of support of love and solidarity from the members of the Truth and Reconciliation Commission of South Africa, from our esteemed chairperson, his grace the Archbishop Desmond Tutu, who writes in his personal letter to yourselves as commissioners, and I quote, "The task of a Commission such as this is to bring to life the truth in order to promote reconciliation." He continues to say, "You have the additional burden of initiating the first TRC in the U.S. Many will be looking to you to assess whether similar commissions might be helpful in other communities also."

Let me begin my own remarks with the words I wrote in December 1995, when I stood, as these commissioners will stand today, and took my oath to be a commissioner in the South African Truth and Reconciliation Commission. I called my thoughts that day "When Hope Decays":

> When hope decays there is a particular stench in the air, of bitterness, of strife, of holding on for dear life to things that neither heal nor help. When hope decays there is anger that pulls down what others try to build. There is frustration with those who build, with those who dream, and with those who think, for how dare they dream and hope and think, because

[1] Copyright 2004 by Reverend Bongani Finca. Reprinted with permission.

J.E. Beitler III, *Remaking Transitional Justice in the United States*,
Springer Series in Transitional Justice, DOI 10.1007/978-1-4614-5295-9,
© Springer Science+Business Media New York 2013

our hope has decayed. But when hope is reborn, we dream the dreams which others scorn.
We sing the songs of birds that fly. We embrace our past with all its shame, and say to it you,
too, belong to us. We hope, we dream, we think, because our hope is reborn.

We, as the South African Truth and Reconciliation Commission, are humbled
and honored that the Greensboro Truth and Reconciliation Commission has been
established using the model of South Africa. As we think of that model, we pay
tribute to Nelson Mandela, who became the author and the pioneer of that model.
As you will remember, he emerged out of prison, having spent twenty-seven past
years of his life, crushing stones and confined in cells. But he emerged with a message which was later adopted as a preamble to our constitution, and I quote from
that preamble: "We need to find understanding, but not vengeance. We need to find
reparation, but not retaliation. We need to find ubuntu, but not victimization."

These are the pillars of the route you have chosen to deal with the shame of
November three, 1979, eleven hours twenty-three, at the corner of Carver and Everitt
Street. You have awakened, as we did, to the truth that bygones will not be bygones
until they are confronted honestly, truthfully, and responsibly addressed. You have
realized, as we did, that the tears on the eyes of those who were victimized will not
be dry. No amount of ignoring those tears will make them dry. They will only be dry
when we stop and face them and confront our shame and dry them. You have found,
as we did, that the truth must be told, that the record must be set straight, that forgiveness must be asked for and pardon must be given, before we can move together
as communities and as nations. You have learned, as we did, that our past will continue to haunt our present, until we agree to face that past with all its shame and
address it.

So people of Greensboro, we as South Africans, we salute you. We do not wish you
success, because you have already succeeded. The installation today of this Commission
in the U.S. soil, the first of its kind, is a victory beyond words. Truth has won over lies.
Memory has won over amnesia. Understanding has won over revenge.

But as you take this step today, and as you travel together on this road for the next
eighteen months, we assure you that it will be a long walk for your commissioners.
We urge you, be gentle with them. Be firm in your demand for the truth, but be kind
to one another.

In our language we have a saying that a person is a person because of other persons. In that saying we recognize that a person is not complete until she embraces
other persons and struggles to make them complete also. We recognize that a person
cannot be fulfilled until she finds fulfillment for others also. We recognize that we
cannot have real peace until we move in isolation and find peace for those on our
side and for those who live on the other side. But ubuntu goes further than that. It
says if you appear a bit taller than others who stand with you, it is not because you
are really taller than them, but it is because others are carrying you in their shoulders. For this Commission to fulfill its mandate, and to do the task that you have set
for it to do, we urge you as the community of Greensboro, to carry the commissioners on your shoulders, to support them, to encourage them, to be with them, and to
pray fervently for them.

It is the first of its kind in the U.S. It must set a model that must succeed. If it does succeed, it will give us all hope that one day there will be truth commissions on Iraq, that there will be truth commissions on Ireland, that there will be truth commissions on the Middle East. If it succeed, as it must, it will give us hope that one day we will know the truth of Rwanda and know the truth of Burundi and know the truth of Angola. If it succeed, as it must, it will give us all hope that one day we will know the truth on neighborhoods and ghettos, on villages and towns and cities, where the blood of the innocent has been spilt, and the cloud of silence has hovered over the national shame.

Today I am proud to be South African, but today I am also proud to be a little tiny part of Greensboro. We salute you. We praise you. We thank you. We will travel with you, until the dream of realizing the truth is realized, because there is no alternative to truth for us to be healed. We need it. So let truth reign.

I do thank you.

Index

J.E. Beitler III, *Remaking Transitional Justice in the United States*,
Springer Series in Transitional Justice, DOI 10.1007/978-1-4614-5295-9,
© Springer Science+Business Media New York 2013

Printed by Publishers' Graphics LLC